Battle for Burma

Battle for Burma

E. D. Smith

HOLMES & MEIER PUBLISHERS, INC.
New York

First published in the United States of America 1979 by
HOLMES & MEIER PUBLISHERS, INC.
30 Irving Place, New York, N.Y. 10003

Copyright © 1979 E. D. Smith

Library of Congress Cataloging in Publication Data
Smith, E. D.
  Battle for Burma
  Bibliography: p.
  1. World War, 1939–1945—Campaigns—Burma.
  2. World War, 1939–1945—Personal narratives, English.
  3. Smith, E. D. 4. Burma—History—Japanese occupation,
  1942–1945. 5. Soldiers—Great Britain—Biography.
  I. Title.
  D767.S6   1979   940.54′25   78–25679
ISBN 0–8419–0468–5

PRINTED IN GREAT BRITAIN

Contents

Illustrations

Maps

ACKNOWLEDGEMENT

The Author and Publishers thank the Imperial War Museum for all the illustrations in this book, and Alan R. Gunston, LSIA, who drew the maps.

Foreword

We left England in the first week of January 1942 in a large convoy bound for India, with the news from the Far East far from encouraging. The Pearl Harbor disaster had clipped American power at sea in a dramatic fashion; the Japanese were gobbling up the colonial possessions of Holland and Britain; there was an air of shocked disbelief in the country we were leaving behind.

It was some time before we learnt, over the ship's radio, that the Japanese had launched yet another attack, this time into Burma. As we were going out as officer cadets, hoping to join the Indian army after six months at an OTS, that item of news had greater significance for us than for others on the ship – and by the time the *Stratheden* had docked in Bombay, the Japanese had sent the Allied army reeling back towards the border with India. Thereafter, the war in Burma continued to influence our lives, even though eventually I went to the Middle East – a reprieve for which I was extremely grateful and have remained so to this day!

There was a strange, almost unreal, atmosphere in India. British colonial rule, based on the invincibility of European arms, had been stripped bare in a few weeks by the soldiers of Nippon. The whole continent seethed with unrest, which was being fanned into open agitation by Gandhi and his fellow Congress leaders. However, our world as cadets was to be a narrow one with our only real contact being the British instructors, officers, and senior NCOs, who were given the unenviable task of transforming us from callow schoolboys into inexperienced subalterns within the space of six short months. Their reaction to the débâcle in Burma was of stunned disbelief and open incredulity. The majority of the instructors had spent several years in India and without being deliberately racialist, genuinely believed that one white soldier was more than capable of seeing off two or three coloured ones. How then, they asked, could those little yellow men with prominent teeth, peering myopically through thick glasses, thrash British soldiers in battle after battle, culminating in the ignominious scuttle from Burma?

Those caricatures that poked fun at the Japanese to illustrate training lessons – which had abounded before Burma fell – now seemed to jeer back at us. Everything had happened so swiftly that no one really knew what lessons to teach us or what might be relevant in the future. Jungle warfare was beyond the ken of the pre-war Indian Army: with few exceptions, the instructors at Bangalore had years of experience only in fighting the Pathans on the North West Frontier, and after a few half-hearted attempts at teaching us the obvious about operating in 'thick country', they turned with relief and unbounded confidence to the world of picquets, sangars, and tribesmen. Their attitude to the Pathans, who engaged in bouts of belligerency, bound by a code of unwritten rules rather like a dangerous kind of wrestling, was one of admiration and respect – and it appeared as if those feelings were reciprocated by the tough inhabitants of the North West Frontier.

Now there was a new enemy: strong, cruel, and ruthless. There were no rules except survival because surrender or capture offered no guarantee whatever that death would not follow, often after a wide variety of tortures.

I mention such matters only to show how deeply the psychological effects of the 1942 Burma campaign bit into us, from senior officers down to British privates and Indian sepoys. It was to take a considerable time before we ceased to think of the Japanese soldier as a superman, ten feet tall, as opposed to his more likely height of five-and-a-half feet. Burma cast a shadow over our lives, over the training we carried out, and the lectures we tried to absorb in the drowsy heat of the afternoon. Some officers and soldiers did go to the Middle East, it is true, but they were the lucky ones: gloomily we sensed that, inevitably, our future lay in the jungles of Burma and our nightmares contained grinning Japanese, ready to open fire at us from cunningly concealed ambush positions.

From the lowly level of a newly commissioned subaltern, morale in India did not seem to improve until dramatic newspaper headlines in 1943 told the world about Wingate and the Chindits. Whatever the military pundits have said or written about them subsequently, the news that British and Gurkha soldiers had penetrated behind the Japanese forward positions, cocking a snoot at the dreaded foe, had a most remarkable effect on our spirits. Naturally, we were in no position to evaluate results or know whether any long term military gains were achieved – only later came the whispered stories about heavy casualties, declaring that the survivors were in a sorry mental and physical state, with allegations of mismanagement, even by our new god, Orde Wingate. There were ripples of criticism, yes, but the tonic of aggressive action was like a strong medicine that surged through British and Indian units. We *could* beat the Japs.

After basic recruit training had been completed at the regimental centre, the emphasis was switched to the jungle warfare techniques required for Burma. British defeats in the Arakan during early 1943 only served to reinforce early lessons that the Japanese were tough opponents. The key to a change in our fortunes lay in imaginative and thorough training for war. To this end, many junior officers were sent on courses run by ex-Chindits. We came back to the centre astonished that our bodies had been capable of surviving such taxing experiences. Burma continued to rule our young lives; we waited for a call to go there as reinforcements. The officers and men who had survived the Sittang Bridge disaster during the first campaign delighted in regaling us with stories designed to increase our foreboding. After the bridge had been blown, two of our battalions had been so reduced that next day, a single, sadly truncated unit continued to fall back with the remnants of Burma Corps towards Assam. Death by drowning or at the hands of the Japanese had decimated two fine battalions of the 7 Gurkha Rifles.

As far as we were concerned, it was a military struggle between British and Indian units on the one hand and the Japanese on the other, then in full occupation of Burma. Only after going to Calcutta on local leave did I realize that there were Americans in India. There they swaggered around the bars and cafés on Chowringee, looking positively affluent and well-dressed, especially when compared with the British in their drab, badly tailored uniforms. No one could really explain to me what they were doing in India, except spending money in an open-handed manner and picking up the most attractive of the girls in that noisiest and dirtiest of cities, Calcutta.

After the war, there was to be another reminder about the American presence in South East Asia, when an Errol Flynn film showed that romantic hero of the screen winning the war in Burma. I can recall the strong feelings of shocked disbelief when British audiences saw the gallant Flynn at the head of an intrepid band of Americans, recapturing Burma without a single reference to the 14 Army. It was treated as a joke by most people but there were many bitter complaints by ex-servicemen from the 'Forgotten Army', angrily expressing their feelings about the part played by the Americans in Burma as depicted in the film.

Inevitably the fuss died down, but the publication of *The Stilwell*

Papers reopened the controversy. Now we heard about the Chinese and their part in the struggle as well as being angered by the fiercely anti-British sentiments expressed by Stilwell. We were tempted to ask important questions: *Was* American participation in Burma of any great significance? What role *did* the Chinese play? Why did it take the Allied forces more than three years to defeat the numerically inferior Japanese army, especially when, during the last year, the ground forces fought without any real support from their airmen? Those questions prompted me to begin writing this short account of *The Battle for Burma*.

I was aware that the Burma campaign had been well-charted by historians and chroniclers of recent events. Moreover, the original brief invited me to concentrate on the battles rather than on the background; but the deeper I burrowed, the more I realized that the major questions could not be answered by recounting military actions only – quite the reverse, in fact. Compared with other theatres of war, the number of fighting men at the sharp end on both sides were remarkably few. Dwarfing the battalions and brigades were multitudinous problems of administration that were magnified by primitive communications, forbidding terrain, and the cruel vagaries of a tropical climate. Such factors had to be carefully considered before any assessment could be made about even the most famous of the Burma battles – Kohima, Imphal, Meiktila, and Myitkyina.

Although the fighting men in the front lines were comparatively few, the ferocity of the conflict was often inhuman and invariably exacting. Unlike the campaigns in Italy and Normandy, where the bulk of the casualties were inflicted by long-range weapons, the very nature of the country in Burma dictated that brutal hand-to-hand clashes decided the outcome of countless encounters. For such a reason it is not surprising that more Victoria Crosses were won during the Burma campaign than in Italy or Normandy. The tempo of the fighting rarely slackened even when the Japanese faced final defeat, for they refused to recognize the inevitable. No quarter was ever sought or granted by either side. It was not a campaign of mass movement; local actions tended to influence the way formations reacted to events.

Some 30 years ago, the extent of the participation by the Americans and Chinese was unknown to those not directly involved in Burma: we knew little about the strategic and political factors that dictated how the campaign was to be fought. Divided counsel; Roosevelt's championing of Generalissimo Chiang Kai-shek; Churchill's burning obsession with the speedy recapture of Singapore, the pride of British power in Asia; the Anglo-American decision to defeat Nazi Germany before concentrating the bulk of their resources against Japan: these were the main threads in the fabric that transformed a campaign which could have been won quickly, into a dog-fight stretching over three years until the Japanese surrendered to the atom bomb. The Japanese had conquered Burma at a time when their army was fully committed elsewhere in the Pacific, as well as fighting a campaign on the mainland of China. Thereafter those fronts would not allow the dispatch of large-scale reinforcements to Burma. The comparatively puny Burma Area Army would have been hard pressed to hold the outer perimeter against concerted Anglo-American thrusts from India, especially if those had been made in conjunction with a full-blooded offensive by Chinese divisions from Yunnan. To elaborate on such a hypothetical theme would be pointless, however, because the military aspects of any campaign will always be dictated by national policies and strategic aims of the combatants, be they allies or foes.

An early outline of this book had been fashioned to cover the main battles in as much detail as was possible. Later, further study, research, and thought imperceptibly influenced me into taking a more general look at the whole campaign – even to the extent of omitting detailed descriptions of the major encounters. It is not the book I intended to write, but I hope that it accurately reflects a campaign that won few headlines during World War II, even though the ferocity of the fighting rarely diminished from start to finish. The soldiers of many races who fought for the possession of Burma had to struggle with the fickle hazards of nature as well as against a human foe. Bill Slim wrote 'The war in Burma was a soldiers' war'. So it was, even though the decisions and divisions of the Allied leaders in council, and disagreements between senior commanders, invariably dictated how the campaign was fought in the jungles and plains of Burma, Assam, and around Imphal.

It is not the critic who counts, and moreover, I was not in the arena with face marred by dust, sweat, and blood. By deliberate intent, I have not pointed fingers of scorn at, or directed words of criticism against those who led armies, corps, and divisions on both banks of the Chindwin. I have tried to highlight the important points without denigrating those who had heavy responsibilities on their shoulders, who had to make vital decisions in the heat of battle, without accurate information about the enemy's intentions, dispositions, or morale. Only historians have the leisure of hindsight, ample time to deliberate, and access to evidence handed down to posterity.

This book could not have been written without generous help and advice from many friends. The list is too long to enumerate, but I thank them all with sincerity. I must mention John·Andrews of the Ministry of Defence (Central) Library for his patience and co-operation over the last two years. To Pat Luxton for typing the final draft, against the clock, goes my sincere gratitude. Finally this book would not have been completed without my wife's resolution in trying to decipher illegible writing, before being asked to type rough drafts over and over again. As a soldier's daughter, and a soldier's wife, she has had the training and temperament to grin and bear it. In return, she has my love and devotion – for always.

Sidmouth/Westbury
1975 – 1977

CHAPTER 1

In the beginning – defeat and despair

What counts is not necessarily the size of the dog in the fight – it's the size of the fight in the dog – Dwight D. Eisenhower

Prior to December 1941, few could have foreseen that the peaceful British colony of Burma would become a bloody battle ground for nearly four years and that the first half of 1942 would witness a horrifying mass exodus of starving, terrified refugees, struggling to reach safety over the mountain tracks into India. No one will ever know the exact death toll but it was to be measured in tens of thousands. Men too weak to speak crawled in the dirt, dying of hunger and thirst, of malaria and other tropical diseases. It was a sorry end to British rule in Burma, for nothing was ever to be the same again in that country – the clock could not be put back by a Great Britain weakened by the war. The final military victory in 1945 was to open the door to complete independence and a final farewell to the British.

The story of Japan's entry into World War II began not in 1941 but much earlier when she clashed with, and then invaded, China, seeking opportunities to expand outside her over-populated islands. Thereafter the possibility of a direct confrontation with the United States was ever-present, although the strong isolationist feelings of most Americans gave the Japanese leaders some hope that their plans for expansion in Southern Asia would not end in open warfare.

When Germany overran Europe in 1940, the temptation for the Imperial Conference in Tokyo to advise entry into the war alongside their Axis partners must have been strong indeed. There were, however, moderates who counselled caution, and their arguments were supported by the admirals who were only too aware of the combined strengths of the United States and British navies. Japan wanted to take her pick of the Dutch and British colonies without military confrontation with America, to seize the Dutch East Indies, Malaya, Siam, and Burma, and thereafter to establish a strong defensive perimeter around her newly acquired possessions. Thus ensconced, with oil, tin, and the other invaluable commodities she so badly needed within her sphere of influence, Japan hoped that the United States and war-weary Britain would accept her new gains as a *fait accompli*. The artistic people of Japan decided to follow Bushido, the way of the warrior, an audacious resolution that was to earn them the hatred of most of the world instead of the popularity that they, like the Germans, have so constantly sought in recent times.

Japan made a disastrous choice which was to lead to untold calamity and horror, but in 1941 such a decision did not appear to be eccentric or irresponsible. She had seen how Britain, Holland, and France had used naked force to seize colonies in the Far East without being ostracized by their neighbouring states: now she intended to snatch away those rich possessions at a time when their European rulers seemed powerless to stop her. Her liberating expansion in the East was to be called 'The Greater East Asia Co-Prosperity Sphere'. The Japanese wanted to win co-operation by force and establish a new era, governing according to their ideas of Eastern civilization. Western imperialism was to be put to death and meanwhile the people of Japan, in all sincerity, felt that the other countries of Asia would welcome being saved by their liberating armies. It was possible that, initially, a few misguided souls might oppose them but dissidents could be removed without too much trouble.

Hitler's sudden attack on Russia on 22 June 1941 could have radically changed the situation, especially when German diplomats pressed Japan hard to take up arms and strike the Russians in the back at a time when they were in desperate straits. But Germany's humiliating and casual disregard of formal consultation with her Eastern Axis partner meant that the Japanese leaders were more inclined to wait and see before taking any such decision. The Asian Co-Prosperity Sphere appeared to offer more attractive rewards than did a stab in Russia's eastern flank. When Japanese statesmen began to take a more belligerent attitude in South East Asia, the alarmed American government reacted by imposing a trade embargo on all war materials – strict economic sanctions that President Roosevelt hoped would cause the Japanese government to think carefully before translating their sabre-rattling into open aggression. It was also an attempt to hold up and blunt Japan's military drive against China, whose cause had long been espoused by the United States.

The American government's action, much tougher than had been anticipated even by her allies, meant in effect that a complete embargo existed on Japan's trade in oil and steel. She was left in no doubt that her plans for an extension of political control within French Indo-China were to cease. Such a declaration had some immediate, obvious effects: Japan's reserves of oil would dwindle month by month unless she reversed the measure by diplomatic means. Failing this, she could put into operation her grand design to seize the unprotected colonial possessions of the European powers, now subjugated by Germany – except for Britain, grimly fighting for survival. To make matters more critical for Japan, the British and Dutch followed the United States lead, in spite of the efforts of Japanese diplomats to drive a wedge between the three governments.

And yet the Japanese had reasonable grounds for thinking that peaceful means might persuade the United States to soften or even lift the embargo. In spite of President Roosevelt's careful and resolute steering of the nation towards war, the vast majority of the American people were isolationist, still wanting peace, preferring to watch the European war from afar, without seeking open conflict with Japan. The House of Representatives confirmed this feeling when the bill to introduce compulsory military service was passed by a single vote. Against such a background the Japanese sought not only to reverse the embargo but also to allay American suspicions so that an alternative sudden pre-emptive strike would catch their adversary unawares. But what the Japanese did not know was that the Americans were already aware of their intentions, and knew about preparations for war. For the United States had broken their opponents' code system and as a result were able to read all communications between the Japanese ambassador and his masters in Tokyo. In retrospect, it seems that Roosevelt and the two or three men who were privileged to participate in this eavesdropping, must have appreciated that the harsh trade embargo was bound to force Japan into war – which it did on 20 December 1941.

Winston Churchill commented that the Japanese were not 'injured innocents', citing their long and bloody war in China: he maintained that their decision to strike 'was madness to gain surprise'. Up to the very end he had asserted that the Japanese would pull back at the last moment. Although he had been kept informed by President Roosevelt, the British Prime Minister did not know how his American friends were obtaining such red-hot information, nor had he any prior knowledge about the fatal decision made by the Japanese Imperial Conference on 1 December.

On 7 December the Japanese sent a note to the American government which acknowledged that negotiations had failed. Its delivery was so timed that it arrived after bombs had already begun to fall on Pearl Harbor. Up to that moment President Roosevelt and General Marshall had been convinced that war in South East Asia was inevitable but that Japan would strike at British and Dutch territory, deliberately avoiding American interests and possessions. To the very end, and in spite of the broken code, the American preoccupation with remaining neutral was the blind spot that encouraged the Japanese. There was genuine shock and amazement throughout the United States when Japan took the final irrevocable step.

The story thereafter was summed up by Churchill on 12 December when he assessed Japanese superiority to be such that they could take 'almost any point they wish, apart from, it is hoped, Singapore. They can go round with a circus force' – which is just what they did. The Japanese High Command estimated that Malaya and Singapore would fall in about 100 days: in the event, they needed only 70 days. Nevertheless, they had no systematic overall time-table, although at the time it certainly appeared as if there were one. Evidence now available shows that the campaign was a daring venture, conducted by a series of improvisations, often brilliantly executed. It was a leap into the unknown, accepted as inevitable by many of Japan's leaders, although some of the more far-seeing had grave doubts. These were recorded at the time, not after the war with the benefit of hindsight.

*　　*　　*

Burma, one of the smaller and less significant countries ruled by Britain, had spent a comparatively uneventful history during its 50 years as part of the British Empire. Now its story became lurid in the extreme. No longer was it to be an oriental paradise inhabited by cheerful, picturesque people; through no fault of its own it became an ill-fated arena for some of the most horrible fighting of the war. It was to remain a contested land until the end of World War II.

After being annexed by Britain as the result of three wars in the 19th century, Burma had been attached to India. Its major race, the Burmese themselves, had a clear, national consciousness. The linking of their economy with that of India was an artificial arrangement because their culture, language, and religion (a form of Buddhism) meant that there were never any true ties between the two countries. It was an unnatural union and it was resented by the Burmese. Belatedly, in 1935 Burma had been allowed to set up its own legislature, with a constitution which, to some extent, met the growing demand for national freedom and the desire to shed the unpopular links with India. It is important to realize that the Burmese desire for freedom was deep-rooted, because this was to colour their attitude to the British and Indians when the Japanese began to overrun their country.

Although there had been an artificial political union between India

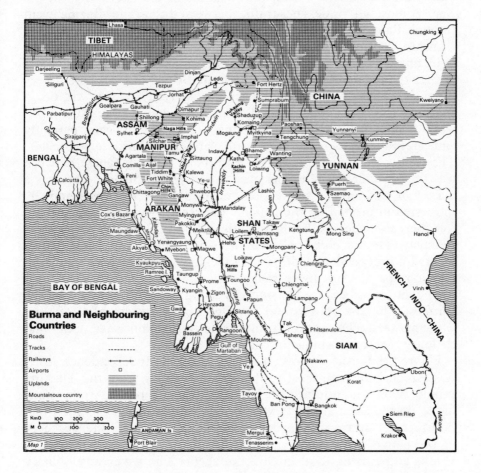

Map 1

Burma and Neighbouring Countries

Roads
Tracks
Railways
Airports
Uplands
Mountainous country

and Burma, the British had never built up communications between the two countries. There was no railway link, the few roads were no more than tracks, usually impassable during the monsoon season. The isolation of Burma from India was to have a powerful influence not only during the 1942 retreat but also on the subsequent battles to win back Burmese territory from the Japanese in the later stages of the war. Almost all trade and traffic between India and Burma went through Rangoon. As a result, the importance of this town was more than just that of a capital city.

In many respects the desire for independence within Burma was greater than it was in India, although the British did not take it very seriously. There were revolutionary parties ready to seek aid or do anything to bring about the end of British colonial rule. And Japan was not slow in assessing these feelings. Over several years, patiently and carefully, contacts had been made with many Burmese politicians. The results were surprisingly successful and a pro-Japanese network was set up, chiefly under the agency of Colonel Suzuki who was a master of all kinds of subversion and espionage. He was genuinely interested in promoting the national desires of Asian peoples seeking freedom, and it seems that he took the claims of Japanese propaganda seriously. He sincerely believed that his country supported movements for independence rather than seeking to impose long term subjugation and slavery under military rule. Such a man of ideals was most influential because his sincerity could never be doubted by the Burmese plotters who wished to bring about the downfall of their white masters. The cause of revolution in Burma flourished under that curiously naïve but colourful character, Suzuki.

Before the Japanese invasion started, a Burma Independence Army was established, with most of the recruits coming from the Thakimi people, 30 of whom joined the two divisions of Japanese troops waiting to invade Burma. During the British retreat, when the army met disaster after disaster, the troops complained bitterly of the treachery of the native population, citing fifth-column activities by Burmese monks and cursing local intelligence agents who gave away military locations to their enemy. The Burmese Independence Army no doubt helped the Japanese by its very presence: its activities lowered the British troops' morale as they began the retreat.

On 20 January 1942 the Japanese 15 Army invaded Burma, using 33 and 55 Divisions to strike southward, with Rangoon as their main objective. They had everything in their favour because by that time the Allies were in complete disarray in South East Asia. Singapore, Malaya, Hong Kong, the Philippines, and the Dutch East Indies had fallen. The list was long, the reverses sudden and complete. In Malaya, the British had placed undue confidence in the many natural obstacles that existed, anticipating that the Japanese would be forced to confine their movement along the few roads that led south, that the larger rivers would halt progress and prove difficult to cross. Such also were their hopes in Burma, although the task of the defenders was made more difficult by other factors, too. Burma had been tossed from one military command to another – from being under India to General Wavell's short-lived South West Pacific Command and then back to Delhi once more, when it was too late to rectify a hopeless situation. There was no master plan to defend the country, too few troops and, as became increasingly apparent during the final stages of the retreat, the few available Allied planes had to operate from civil airfields that were not strategically sited. As a result, the RAF was in no position to save the ground troops and their links to the west from constant, accurate harassment.

At a later date General Wavell admitted that he had under-estimated the danger to Burma and had not appreciated the weakness of his own troops. Chiang Kai-shek did offer to send a Chinese army into Burma to assist in the defence. There was much, indeed fatal, hesitation before the offer was accepted. The Generalissimo claimed that initially his offer was brusquely rejected by Wavell. Whether there was a peremptory refusal or not, Wavell's initial reluctance stemmed from the fear that Chinese troops would overstretch his administrative facilities. Such a refusal puzzled the Chinese because they tended to live off the land like hungry locusts.

The original disagreement between Chiang Kai-shek and Wavell also reflected British reluctance, in Delhi and Whitehall, to allow Chinese soldiers into Upper Burma, because it was feared that they might remain there permanently. Early disasters soon changed these attitudes, but by then it was too late. The 1st Burma Division was a scratch formation containing a high proportion of Burmese units untried in war and quite unfitted to do battle with seasoned Japanese troops who repeated the tactics successfully employed during the Malayan campaign. The other division, 17 Indian, arrived only in mid-January. It was equipped and trained to operate in the Middle East – although its units were to fight with gallantry in the new, bewildering jungle conditions. Their defended positions and road blocks were bypassed, outflanked, and cut off; troops trained for skirmishes with Pathans on the North West Frontier and the open warfare of the Western Desert were confused by the jungle, demoralized by strange enemy tactics, and continually strafed from the air;

intelligence about the enemy was non-existent and, inevitably, the roads selected for withdrawal were vulnerable. Further reinforcements came in the shape of 7 Armoured Brigade, which arrived on 20 February but by then the pattern of defeat had clearly evolved. Nevertheless, the disciplined, experienced brigade played a valuable part in the withdrawal by providing badly needed communications and acting as a rearguard on numerous occasions.

Before considering the part played by the Chinese, it must be remembered that one of their divisions was the equivalent numerically of a strong British brigade, a corps to a division and an army to a corps. This was one of the reasons – but not the only one – for the Generalissimo's insistence during the later stages of the campaign, that ideally three Chinese divisions were needed in defence to hold one enemy division and that five were needed when attacking a single Japanese division.

Early in January, the Chinese 6 Army took over the Mekong River sector from 1 Burma Division in the Yunnan province. Their 5 Army did not play an active part in the campaign until the middle of March, after moving into the Sittang valley front. 66 Army remained on the sidelines, apart from 38 Division under the redoubtable General Sun Li-jen, whose troops fought with commendable gallantry and distinction on more than one occasion. British military historians tend to denigrate the part played by the Chinese during the first campaign but American sources, including General Joseph Stilwell, his staff, and war correspondents, have portrayed their efforts in more generous terms. A major snag was that it took a considerable time for the Generalissimo to even agree to his troops serving under British control. Not surprisingly, therefore, there was little co-operation; British headquarters tended to be unsympathetic towards their newly arrived allies with their inefficient and paltry staff system. To complicate matters further, Chiang Kai-shek in Chungking continued to send confusing orders that bore little relation to the tactical situation facing his subordinate commanders. When the leadership was good, the Chinese fought bravely. General Sun's division maintained an admirable fighting spirit even in adversity and its morale was higher than that of certain units in Burma Corps composed of British or Indian soldiers.

The strange personality of Generalissimo Chiang Kai-shek cast a turbulent shadow over the final stages of the retreat from Burma; thereafter he disturbed numerous Anglo-American councils of war that took place during the following years. He never completely trusted the British. Chiang and his attractive wife used every means possible to persuade Roosevelt's diplomatic and military representatives, accredited to the wartime capital of Chungking, that Japan could best be defeated on the Chinese mainland. For Chiang was fighting two enemies – the Japanese invaders and the waiting, watching, ever-patient communists under Mao Tse-tung. In the short term he needed American aid, in the form of air support and money, to keep his mercenary Chinese war lords actively engaged in the struggle against the Japanese; while his long-term aim was to emerge from the war strong enough to crush the communists within China. It became increasingly difficult for the allied leaders to ascertain which of these two aims was uppermost in the Generalissimo's mind, but in 1942 his unreliability had not become apparent.

One man arrived in Burma on 11 March who knew more about the Generalissimo's China than did his President, back in Washington. His name was General Joseph Stilwell and he came without any GIs to command. His personality caused irritation, occasionally aroused affection, and frequently produced open hostility between this sarcastic-tongued general and his British partners in India and Burma.

It was not the lightning advance of the Japanese invaders into southern Burma that alarmed the American government so much as the ever-increasing danger of losing the means of resupplying China by air, and by land over the Burma Road. The retention of Upper Burma and after it was lost, its recapture, became a matter of paramount importance to the United States. It was the linchpin of a strategy that was often at variance with British priorities in Asia. As a result General Stilwell arrived in Burma with a tiny band of American advisers but without any executive command, in an attempt to shore up the Chinese effort and to make it clear to all that the United States had firm interests in the struggle for Upper Burma. Stilwell's knowledge of China had been gained when he had served there in various capacities over a period of 15 years. He spoke Chinese fluently and was accepted by Chiang Kai-shek although, for his part, the tough, fiery American had little respect for the man he nicknamed 'Peanut'. It was late in March before the Chinese leader agreed to let his troops come under General Alexander's control, and by that time the campaign had been lost: the retreat was on, with the British dogged but dispirited and tired, the Chinese uncertain and frightened, the Japanese determined, merciless, and cruel.

A change of commanders could do little to save such a situation. The decision to cancel the dispatch of the Australian division to Rangoon was a wise one because the Aussies would have arrived too late to save the city and might have met a fate similar to the one suffered by their countrymen when Singapore fell earlier that year. As it was, 63 Brigade from the Indian Army, straight off the ship was thrown into battle, forced to face the victorious Japanese with nothing in their favour except courage.

Rangoon was doomed when the fateful and controversial decision was taken on 23 February to blow up the Sittang Bridge, leaving hundreds of British, Indian, and Gurkha troops stranded on the far side, with the stark choice of trying to cross the wide, swift-flowing river by swimming, by improvised means of flotation, fighting to the death, or risking surrender into Japanese hands when their captors had already achieved a notorious reputation for cruelty and ruthless treatment of prisoners. It is not known how many men died, drowned, or just disappeared for ever, after being trapped on the wrong side of the river. With the confused reports at the time and the garbled information that was being passed to him when the terrible decision had to be taken, Major-General Jackie Smythe, commanding 17 Indian Division, had no alternative but to give the order to blow the bridge. The alternative was to allow the Japanese to seize the bridge intact. It was a ghastly dilemma for any commander because it was one that not only condemned hundreds of his men to death but earned him censure in the eyes of his superiors. General Smythe was not given any active field command again during World War II. His final comment summed up the tragic quandary that faced him: 'But hard as the decision was, neither Punch Cowan (Chief of Staff) nor I had any doubt that I must give this permission. Nor indeed, despite the controversy which subsequently surrounded this operation, have we ever doubted the necessity.' (*The Valiant*).

Rangoon fell on 8 March with the newly arrived General Alexander and his HQ narrowly escaping the clutches of the Japanese. Without the port, there was no means of supplying the retreating armies except along two roads that ran from Rangoon to Mandalay, routes that were constantly strafed and bombed by the Japanese air force. Along those vulnerable routes, the retreating armies had to withdraw, tied to the roads because the troops were not equipped or trained to move far from the tenuous supply lines.

Was there an overall Allied directive for the first Burma campaign? After the war General Alexander maintained that he was sent out to try and save Rangoon but once it was lost he never received any further directive. By that time it had become clear to him that a fighting withdrawal to India was inevitable. Nevertheless, Alexander could not, and did not, make public such intentions to the Chinese at too early a stage, fearing that they might disintegrate or be withdrawn

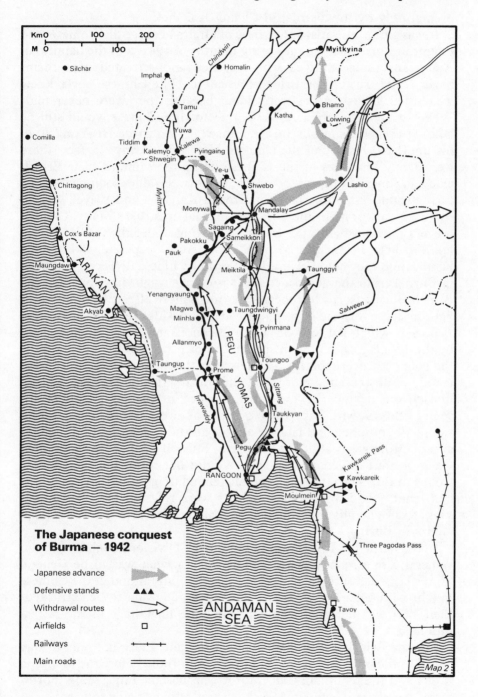

Km 0   100   200
M 0   100

Silchar

Imphal

Chindwin

Homalin

Myitkyina

Tamu

Bhamo

Katha

Loiwing

Yuwa

Comilla

Tiddim

Kalemyo   Kalewa

Pyingaing

Shwegin

Ye-u

Shwebo

Lashio

Chittagong

Myittha

Monywa

Mandalay

Sagaing

Cox's Bazar

Pakokku   Sameikkon

Pauk

Maungdaw

Meiktila

Taunggyi

ARAKAN

Akyab

Yenangyaung

Magwe   Taungdwingyi

Salween

Minhla

Pyinmana

Allanmyo

PEGU

Taungup

Prome

YOMAS

Toungoo

Sittang

Irrawaddy

Taukkyan

Pegu

Kawkareik Pass

RANGOON

Kawkareik

Moulmein

**The Japanese conquest
of Burma — 1942**

Three Pagodas Pass

Japanese advance

Defensive stands

Withdrawal routes

ANDAMAN
SEA

Tavoy

Airfields

Railways

Main roads

Map 2

prematurely by the distrustful Chiang Kai-shek.

It was a most unsatisfactory state of affairs because the Chinese who fought in Burma during the spring months of 1942, and the handful of Americans under Stilwell who marched and retreated with them, never really trusted the British thereafter. 'The Chinese never knew what their British Allies were doing because they were never told. When the British retreated in their sector the Chinese would still be holding their lines in blissful ignorance . . . ' So wrote Ho-Yungchi in his unofficial history of the Chinese New First Army. In fact, there were many instances of the Chinese doing the same to their British allies: in times of disaster, co-operation between allies soon melts. The early misunderstanding between Chiang Kai-shek and Wavell was, to some extent, responsible for this mutual mistrust. Many Chinese officers were hostile to the British, smarting under the insult of their offer to help being refused until times were desperate. With some justification they could claim that if the 11 Chinese divisions had been in Burma from the very start, their presence might have enabled the British Burma Corps to concentrate into a more effective, tightly knit fighting force, instead of being spread over a wide area with ineffective radio sets which led to poor communications generally. Such a claim by the Chinese cannot be dismissed out of hand. On the other side of the coin, however, the British view that the Chinese were unreliable could be substantiated more than once during the long retreat. Chiang himself was devious, always liable to cancel or change his orders; his senior officers, with one or two exceptions, were unpredictable, their troops ill-equipped and lacking almost all the necessities of a modern army. Moreover, although General Stilwell had been appointed Chief-of-Staff to Chiang Kai-shek, he did not command the Chinese troops in Burma so that the generals tended to ignore his instructions, and lengthy and unnecessary queries were referred back to Chung-king, to a Generalissimo who had no real knowledge of the true state of affairs in Burma.

In the battle for Yenangyaung the Burma Division sought help from General Sun Li-jen and his 38 Division in what was to be General Slim's last chance to try to save the oilfields but, although the Chinese fought with gallantry, enabling the Burma Division to be extricated, their best was not good enough – and the final stage of the retreat unfolded.

For the British and Indian troops it became a race not only to stay ahead of the pursuing Japanese but to reach India before the monsoon broke and the mountain trails into Assam became impassable. Fortunately for them, Generals Alexander and Slim remained unshaken in spite of repeated reverses. Alexander carried out the role of theatre commander, taking on the political negotiations and correspondence with Delhi, London, Washington, and Chungking. His tenure of command was short-lived but the part he played, particularly in relation to General Slim, was an invaluable one. He realized that Slim was the man to handle the tactical situation facing Burma Corps, so he left it to him and did not interfere.

Slim's name, little known outside the Indian Army, was heard more and more as the struggle for Burma continued. Much has been written about the exploits of the man who later became a field marshal, but nobody has covered the first campaign as lucidly and honestly as Bill Slim himself did in *Defeat into Victory*. His analysis has never been bettered but the words written about his own generalship were far too unkind, distorted by the bitterness of defeat. 'For myself, I had little to be proud of, I could not rate my generalship high. The only test of generalship is success and I had succeeded in nothing I had attempted ... I ought, in spite of everything and at all risks, to have collected the whole strength of my Corps before I attempted any counter-offensive... I might have risked disaster but I was more likely to have achieved success.'

Slim, in his own eyes was a failure but to those who served with and alongside him, he was the one commander who emerged with considerable credit from the gruelling, disastrous campaign. He was never in a position to collect sufficient forces for an effective counter-offensive, in spite of the self-condemnatory remarks quoted above. At no stage did he crack.

Anglophobe 'Vinegar' Joe Stilwell was to comment, 'He was not afraid of anything and looked it.' In the face of disaster, Slim's leadership was calmly impressive, his confident air had a steadying effect on his subordinates, while physical and mental robustness enabled him to withstand the constant strain imposed on his constitution. The last few weeks of the retreat and evacuation from Burma found events overtaking plans so that directives received from Wavell in Delhi, and Chiang Kai-shek in Chungking, were often irrelevant by the time they reached the retreating British and Chinese units. A Japanese thrust towards Lashio and the Burma/China Road was enough to cause the Chinese Fifth and Sixth Armies to withdraw in disordered haste towards the frontiers of China itself. At such a critical time the Generalissimo relayed a message instructing that the bodies of Chinese soldiers killed in battle were to be back-loaded to their homeland in pinewood coffins. Needless to say his edict was disregarded!

At one stage, there had been talk about a token British force also withdrawing into China but events did not allow this unrealistic proposal to be effected. As it was, most of the men of the Chinese 22 and 38 Divisions had to cross over the mountain passes from Upper Burma into Assam where they were to form the nucleus of the force that operated under Stilwell in 1943. Once again 38 Division came out of the ordeal in good order and with creditable morale. For the first time in history, Chinese soldiers set foot on Indian soil, not as conquerors, but as friends.

On 25 April Alexander ordered all his troops to make a general retirement south of the Irrawaddy and cross the famous Ava Bridge near Mandalay. That phase was carefully co-ordinated and controlled by Slim: there was to be no repeat of the Sittang Bridge disaster. By the evening of 30 April, the last sub unit and vehicle of Burma Corps had crossed the bridge, which was demolished just before midnight. Only the Chindwin remained, before India and safety was reached. The evacuation went as fast as possible under the circumstances, with rearguards being found from 1 Burma Division, 17 Indian Division, and 7 Armoured Brigade, in turn. There were moments of extreme danger when it appeared as if the Japanese had cut the line of withdrawal but the retreating army remained reasonably intact, although the mass of refugees made the task of the administrative services virtually impossible. For hundreds, indeed thousands, the long trek through the jungle seemed unending. As the tempo of the retreat increased, any semblance of control by the civil government collapsed. Officials disappeared seeking safety in flight to India, leaving behind anarchy and chaos. Gangs of dacoits roamed like packs of jackals, harrying stragglers and terrorizing and robbing the Indian refugees. No one will ever know how many thousands died on those precipitous, jungle-covered malarial tracks leading to Assam. The morale of the defeated soldiers was not helped by the helpless plight of those refugees.

By now everyone realized that within the first few days of the monsoon, the road to Assam would disintegrate and become an impassable morass. The question was, would the weather hold?

The history of 17 Indian Division states: 'It was a race against the weather because, if the rain broke, the road would become an impassable quagmire. It was a race against starvation because, if the withdrawal took too long, the reported meagre stocks along the road would become exhausted. It was a race against the enemy because he could make the journey to Kalewa by river in twenty-four hours ... and finally cut off the Army of Burma'.

The weather held until the main column had passed the boundary between Burma and India. After that it was a question of following the track down into the Imphal plain. Slim is reported to have said as the last of the rearguard passed him on the road: 'They might look like scarecrows, but they look like soldiers, too'. He was biased but justifiably proud of his men. It is equally comforting to find an American reporter, who had little respect for British strategy in South East Asia, writing: 'The British Tommy was a real and wondrous guy ... it wasn't his fault that he lost the war in Burma. He did what he was told to do. He grumbled and groused about it, but he did it. He never cracked, even during those horrible, searing, waterless days when he was trapped at Yenangyaung and everything was surely lost. Tommy was the symbol, perhaps, of all that is good in Britain. He was vulgar and crude. He was a quiet fellow with tremendous emotional reserve'.

The history of Burma Corps ended on 20 May when on Indian soil, General Slim handed over his responsibilities to 4 Corps under Lieutenant-General Irwin.

For a few days it was rumoured that Stilwell had been captured or killed by the Japanese. After a long, dangerous, and arduous march, 150 miles over terrible terrain and in unbearable heat, Stilwell eventually led his tiny command to safety. He was not a popular man with the members of his group; he sneered at them and lashed them on and on with his tongue, but they owed him their lives. At the age of 60 it was a remarkable feat by a man whose will to survive and determination to hit back at the Japanese drove him on – and back to an uneasy relationship with British, Chinese, and more often than not, his American superiors. His part in the struggle for Burma was only just beginning and an oft-quoted remark sums up his tenacity and pugnacious attitude: 'We got the hell licked out of us. It was humiliating as well. We ought to have found out why it happened and return.'

It was certainly a more realistic approach than the official communiqués read out at a press conference by Generals Wavell and Alexander when the evacuation was called a 'voluntary withdrawal and a glorious retreat'. It was time for all concerned to analyse the reasons for the failure, the overwhelming defeat in the first campaign for Burma. For defeat it was, at the hands of two Japanese divisions with a third, 18 Division, playing a role near the end. Some of the reasons have already been mentioned and need not be repeated. Burma was in no way ready for the onslaught – there were grave military, political, and psychological weaknesses. No one in authority wanted to take any unpleasant steps before the Japanese invasion began and after that it was too late to organize anything properly. If the Chinese had been in position before the invasion got under way, then the Japanese might well have met with severe setbacks to their ambitious timetable. The list of imponderables was, and is, a long one; what was certain was that the task of recapturing Burma would be slow and arduous. The varied aims and aspirations of the British, American, and Chinese governments were not to help the Allied commanders work in easy relationship with each other, except for the one common goal, the defeat of Japan.

The retreat had cost more than 13,000 British and Indian casualties against the comparatively light 4,500 losses of the Japanese. It had been the British Army's largest-ever retreat, more than 900 miles in four months. It was the end of one more tragedy in the long list of Allied disasters after Pearl Harbor.

With one difference, the remnants of the Burma Army did survive to fight another day. And although military commentators at the time did not appreciate the crucial part played by the tanks of 7 Armoured Brigade, as they shepherded the retreating units to safety in India, Slim and one or two other officers did not forget that there were areas of Burma where armour could play a vital role. But it was to be many months before such opportunities were to be granted, months of mixed fortunes, frustration at delays, and anguish when early hopes remained unfulfilled.

CHAPTER 2

Consolidation amid divided counsel

The mightiest rivers lose their force when split into several streams — Ovid

By the middle of 1942, there were no longer any Allied troops left on Burmese soil, apart from a comparatively small corner in the north which was inhabited by Chinese. The Japanese soon found out that the country they now owned was a disturbed one, with the various races which had learnt to live together in mellow amity under the British, quickly reverting to tribal differences, organizing themselves for self-protection as anarchy spread. Much of this was due to the rapid growth of the Burma Independence Army.

After the fall of Rangoon the appeal of the army was strong but its members' recruiting methods were deplorable. The Burmese tend to resort to violence rapidly and for many, enlistment in the Burma Independence Army meant a licence to rob, kill, and pillage. A reign of terror spread behind the Japanese advance and it was not long before the law-abiding part of the population looked towards their conquerors for security and a measure of law and order. It was not, therefore, Japanese atrocities alone that started a terrified mass migration to India, soon to receive more than half a million refugees in the midst of war: it was the roaming bands of thugs vehemently claiming to be members of the new National Army. Japan was presented with an awkward situation. It was not willing to proclaim Burmese independence because, in spite of intensive propaganda advocating freedom from European colonial ties, Japan only fostered revolution in Asia when it suited its purpose. The explosive situation in Burma had to be dealt with quickly. A provisional government was set up: Burmese civil servants were promoted to fill the vacuum created by the sudden disappearance of their old British masters; the Burma Independence Army was suppressed and under a different guise, more regular in structure, was firmly placed under the new government's control.

All these steps were logical and prudent but the apparent and open repudiation of Burmese revolutionary nationalism by Japan was questioned throughout Asia as being contrary to Nippon's propaganda claims. Of greater significance, it was the start of a long conflict between Burmese and Japanese nationalism which was to play an ever-increasing part in the Allies' efforts to drive out the army of occupation.

The great flood of Japan's victories in South East Asia lifted the reputation of the Japanese soldier to extraordinary heights. Suddenly he was regarded as a superman, invincible, a being who could exist and march prodigious distances on a few grains of rice, who could outthink and outfight the previously all-conquering white soldiers from Europe. The strength of such feeling must not be underestimated because the stories taken back to India by the British, Indian, Gurkha, and Chinese soldiers gained in strength with time and repetition. The bitter, humiliating defeats suffered by her British masters meant that the war, with all its consequences, was at the gates of Mother India. No longer could India view events from afar: they were close at hand, along the borders with Assam, on the Indian Ocean, and in the skies over Eastern India.

The war gradually speeded up the tempo of Indian nationalism although, initially, Gandhi and Nehru were reluctant to take advantage of Britain's predicament, especially during the dark days of 1940. The political lull was short-lived, however, and 1941 saw the government of India proscribing thousands of Congress leaders accused of making anti-war speeches. By August 1941, 20,000 had been arrested, with 13,000 of them in jail or behind barbed wire. This trend continued until 4 December 1941 when the government dramatically released all the political prisoners. Three days later when the Japanese struck at Pearl Harbor to begin their 100 days of victories, the unsettled atmosphere in India did not pass unnoticed by statesmen and propagandists in Tokyo. Soon, Tokyo Radio was promising that, 'The armies of Nippon were coming to free India from a British tyranny'.

The Congress leaders were faced with a difficult situation which they approached in their own individual ways. Some felt that it would be madness to antagonize the winning Japanese just when they appeared to be in a position to take over India from the demoralized British. The only important figure in Congress who called for whole-hearted resistance to the Japanese, if they ever decided to invade, was C. R. Rajagopalachari, later destined to be the first Indian governor-general after independence. Gandhi, typically, preached a variation of his hymn of passive resistance, advocating loving non-co-operation as a means of defeating Japanese military might. No longer could the

British hide behind the oft-repeated promise of, 'Let us all wait until the war is over'. With some reluctance, Winston Churchill sent Sir Stafford Cripps on a fact-finding mission to India, with the authority to promise 'Complete and absolute self-determination and self-government for India as a fully fledged member within the Dominions.'

Cripps's mission to India was primarily an attempt to rally the country to its own defence before it was too late. It was also a gesture to the United States which viewed the unsettled state of affairs with genuine alarm and concern, coupled with traditional suspicions about British Imperialism. Few Americans really understood the complexity of Indian politics and problems, and had little sympathy for Britain in her attempts to guide the huge multi-racial country to peaceful independence. Overriding their distrust of British policy was the fear that the loss of India would bring their ally, China, to its knees. Cripps's mission gained American support but although he talked to all shades of political opinion in India – except the Japanese Army – nothing was achieved. Bombs on Indian towns only served to highlight Gandhi's realistic comment, 'Why accept a post-dated cheque on a bank that was obviously failing?' If the Japanese were coming, then there was little point in agreeing with the British proposals, which could only come to fruition in the event of victory – an Allied one – and that seemed utterly remote in 1942.

The increasingly angry bickering between Muslims and Hindus, and the pent-up distrust between British and Indians, did not make India the ideal springboard for a quick return to Burma. Moreover, eastern India was quite unprepared for the gigantic task of receiving military and civilian fugitives from Burma, especially as the proportion of sick among the returning troops and refugees was appallingly high. The few primitive hospitals were totally inadequate to meet such an emergency. In peacetime any exterior threat to India had been assessed as coming from and over the North West Frontier and hospitals, supply depots, and land communications had been established accordingly. In eastern India the opposite was true because after the Burmese Wars of the 19th century, there had been little military activity, apart from an occasional punitive foray against the Nagas and other Hill tribes. It was not surprising that the officers and men of the Burma Corps and the Chinese divisions, which withdrew to Ledo, were sore and angry about their reception, the poor accommodation given them, and the complete unpreparedness of the defences, with one single infantry brigade of raw troops in position to defend the threatened continent of India. For them, therefore, there was to be no rest, no official receptions or praise for their efforts to save Burma. Slim commented with pungency: 'They did not expect to be treated as heroes, but they did expect to be met as soldiers who, even if defeated, were by no means disgraced. Yet the attitude adopted towards them by certain commanders and their staffs was that they were only to be dragooned into some show of soldierly spirit by hectoring and sarcasm. Apart from its lack of comradely feeling this was profoundly bad psychology. How much wiser was the treatment of the troops who escaped from Dunkirk!'

The Chinese 22 and 38 Divisions had similar experiences at Ledo before being housed in prisoner-of-war camps in the little town of Ramgarh in Bihar. They found the British suspicious and the Indians seething with unrest because Gandhi's 'Quit India' campaign was in full swing. He had advised Congress to turn down the Cripps proposals, being obsessed with the idea that if the British left India then Japan would not invade the country. Thus, he promised, India would be spared the fate of Burma and Malaya.

Events within India added to the problems of preparing defences along the borders with Burma and, in the long term, plans for a return to that country. Gandhi openly proclaimed 'Direct Action' against the British, giving an ultimatum in late May before rousing the country to action and anger throughout June and July. Non-violent means were advocated in Gandhi's war of nerves: he hoped to drive the British into taking provocative steps that would make their position precarious at a time when the danger of an invasion appeared to be very real. It was a time for cool nerves and stout hearts. The Viceroy, Lord Linlithgow, a man who normally lacked imagination, rose to meet the biggest crisis during his tour of office. Linlithgow prevaricated while Gandhi played with fire until, unwisely, he called for open rebellion. Thereupon a series of well planned, secret swoops by the police in early August bundled Gandhi and his leading supporters back into captivity, to restore the self-respect of the Indian government. An open rising was averted and for the rest of the war, Congress remained inactive while most of its leaders languished in prison. Nevertheless, for six long anxious weeks in the late summer, the army and police were at full stretch as rioters cut communications, derailed trains, attacked and burnt more than 250 railway stations and destroyed so many post offices that few government employees in the provinces worst affected, Bengal and Orissa, ventured near their place of work while the storm of hate was at its height. At the time, the British felt that Congress had acted in direct collusion with the Japanese, but that suspicion has since been entirely disproved.

The equivalent of 37 battalions were deployed on internal security duties so that for a few vital weeks, planning for any future offensive action against the Japanese stopped, and previous ideas had to be radically changed. Of more importance, training was badly disrupted and few opportunities existed to study and practise the lessons learnt which had been recorded by senior commanders and their staffs during the retreat. The year 1942 was one of frustration, and for those away from India, and particularly the Allied leaders in London and Washington, the problems that beset Wavell and his subordinate commanders were not easy to appreciate.

For more than two years General Sir Archibald Wavell had been the unwilling recipient of a flood of telegrams and messages from Winston Churchill. In victory and defeat, in the Middle East and during the 1942 débâcle in the South West Pacific, he had been subjected to a barrage of praise, chiding scorn, and never-ceasing imaginative, and often impractical ideas from the Prime Minister. On 31 May Churchill surpassed himself by giving Wavell the aim of recapturing Rangoon by the end of September, even adding Bangkok as the next objective, for good measure. It was 'cigar-butt strategy' with a vengeance, divorced from the realities of India and the crippling defeat suffered by Burma Corps and the Chinese earlier that year. A tired, patient Wavell had already set in motion more practical and realistic plans, based on the few troops available, trained and ready for action. He fully recognized that no operations could be mounted while the logistical and supply arrangements were inadequate and paltry. The situation in eastern India, as already described, meant a further reappraisal of the original plans and eventually something far more modest was to emerge.

Early fears that the Japanese would advance on the eastern front gradually faded as it became clear that they were no more equipped to fight during the heavy rains of the monsoon season than were their opponents. At sea, the balance also changed when Admiral Somerville's victory in early spring led to the withdrawal of Japanese naval forces from the Indian Ocean. Unbeknown to the commanders in Delhi, this withdrawal would be permanent, as a result of the startlingly decisive American victory at Midway. Never again would the Japanese feel themselves capable of taking the offensive at sea except in local engagements. Midway was a strategic defeat for their navy and one that was to have great significance in the Far Eastern war.

The Japanese could not, or did not want to mount an offensive by sea or land against India although that fact was naturally not known to the Anglo-American Chiefs-of-Staff at the time. Even during the early months of 1943 the situation appeared to be more threatening than it

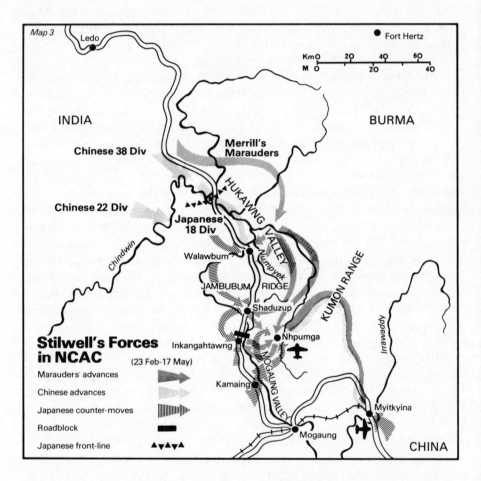

Map 3

Ledo

Fort Hertz

Km 0   20   40   60
M 0   20   40

INDIA

BURMA

Chinese 38 Div

Merrill's
Marauders

Chinese 22 Div

HUKAWNG VALLEY

Japanese
18 Div

Chindwin

Walawbum

Numpyek

JAMBUBUM   RIDGE

KUMON RANGE

Shaduzup

**Stilwell's Forces
in NCAC**

Inkangahtawng

Nhpumga

Irrawaddy

(23 Feb-17 May)

Marauders' advances

Chinese advances

MOGAUNG VALLEY

Japanese counter-moves

Kamaing

Roadblock

Myitkyina

Japanese front-line

Mogaung

CHINA

actually was. While spirits were still disturbed, much was done to restore morale in India. Even more was achieved by way of initiating far-sighted administrative plans, many of which had been conceived the year before. The construction of new airfields was rightly given a high priority: these were to radically change the balance of airpower over the whole Indo-Burmese front.

The new airfields guaranteed air superiority when and where it mattered, thus enabling the Chindits to operate in their deep penetration role in 1943/44, and the Americans to deliver by air to Chiang Kai-shek a healthy portion of the promised tonnage of equipment, weapons and supplies.

The two Allied generals who had emerged with credit from the 1942 retreat had been Stilwell and Slim. It was fortunate that those two dissimilar but strong personalities were in positions of authority during the difficult summer of that year. For Slim there would be no rest because he took over command of 15 Corps which was to bear the brunt of the riots as well as having to defend the Bengal coast, and mount an offensive into the Arakan. For Stilwell, the bitterness of defeat roused him to remarkable feats of energy, with ambitious plans to build up the remnants of the Chinese 22 and 38 Divisions to a force that could re-enter northern Burma and open up a road to China. This is what his president had directed but few Americans in Asia shared Stilwell's faith in the Chinese as soldiers. In addition, he had to persuade the Indian government to allow more Chinese troops to be flown from China to join his force at Ramgarh. The Delhi government reluctantly agreed: indeed, its British masters were persuaded to pay, accommodate, feed, and clothe the Chinese forces serving on their soil. Initially, Chiang Kai-shek was not enthusiastic about producing more men but when the Generalissimo heard that many of his divisions were about to be equipped with American arms, the opportunity was too good to miss. He had never lacked manpower; what he wanted was arms. The American Ferry Command subsequently flew 13,000 Chinese soldiers from Kunning over the Hump, the mountain range between Assam and China. Slim later wrote in *Defeat into Victory*: 'This was the first large-scale troop movement by air in the theatre and was an outstanding achievement. The young American pilots of the Hump should be remembered with admiration and gratitude by their countrymen and their Allies'.

Without Stilwell's driving force, the venture might never have come to pass – certainly it would have taken longer. When Wavell visited the Chinese at Ramgarh, he was visibly impressed, commenting, 'The men are good material and training keenly under their American staff'. Although Stilwell later recorded that Wavell looked aged and tired, the British Commander-in-Chief was well able to appreciate Stilwell's qualities, adding that 'Stilwell is pretty close and does not give much away but I like him'. The veteran American general's burning desire to avenge himself on the Japanese was wholly admirable but his failure to understand the situation in India and, in particular, the political unrest, led him to make tactless, impatient outbursts which did not make him the easiest of subordinates. His persistance broke down Wavell's reluctance to accept American-Chinese co-operation for the recapture of Upper Burma. 'Vinegar Joe's' faith in the Chinese soldiers gradually convinced his American compatriots that with training, equipment, and leadership, they would be capable of meeting, and defeating, the Japanese. But he never lost his suspicions about the British, publicly accusing them of dragging their feet. Typical of such thinking was his comment: 'If we can keep a fire lit under Wavell's butt, the job is in a fair way to get done'.

Stilwell's indomitable spirit prevailed. Within a short time his two Chinese divisions were reformed and making remarkable progress under picked American instructors. His repeated requests for American combat forces were turned down: he could be given tanks, rifles, mortars, and tommy-guns but he was not to get GIs in the theatre until a small group, later to be dubbed by the press as 'Merrill's Marauders', were drafted to India during the following year. The re-equipping of Chinese soldiers was acceptable, in accordance with Roosevelt's policy. The strategy of Pacific island-hopping from Australia had yet to be fully tested. Early victories showed it to be successful although rather costly, as the bloody battle for Tarawa showed. If Japan were to be defeated, the Americans still felt that it must be on the mainland of Asia – on Chinese soil. From their point of view this was the easiest, the cheapest road to Tokyo, and was to remain so until their amphibious strategy in the Pacific had been proven.

The opening of a road into blockaded Chungking meant a return to Upper Burma. With the American and Chinese governments fully supporting these proposals, the British Chiefs-of-Staff reluctantly had to accept them, although Churchill continued to have the deepest misgivings about a land campaign through Upper Burma into China. His views on Chiang Kai-shek were far less rosy and optimistic than Roosevelt's – and events were to show that he was nearer the mark than the American President.

A cure for the defeatist attitude in India had to be sought and it was tackled in different ways by the British, in the Arakan, and Stilwell champing at the bit to open the Burma Road. In the middle, playing a Machiavellian role, was Chiang Kai-shek, husbanding his strength while fighting the Japanese, and never reluctant to blackmail the Americans by hinting that he was seriously considering making peace offers to Tokyo. In time, the United States did realize that Chiang Kai-shek would neither surrender nor fight the Japanese to the death, but unfortunately for the Allied cause in Asia, the recognition of this fact was belated. In the meantime, Stilwell's plan for a road into China required all his sleeve-pulling tricks, playing off Wavell against Chiang Kai-shek and vice versa.

He originally sought permission to build a road from the plain of Imphal, along the trail which he and a small band of survivors had marched earlier that year; not surprisingly, the British were not prepared to give up the one and only major supply route on which their return to central and southern Burma depended.

The most feasible alternative was to open the old Burma Road, using Ledo as a jumping-off position. In conjunction with the projected road it was decided to train and equip Chinese divisions with American arms in the Yunnan, so that when the road neared the border, a large force would cross the Salween River and attack the Japanese in the rear. Thereafter the final stages of the road could be completed within China's territory. In American eyes this was the only reasonable, worthwhile strategy in Burma. The United States did not like the British proposals for a thrust into the Arakan, believing that the plan was of dubious importance, promising little in terms of strategic gains. They suspected that the British government intended to fight a cheap campaign and had decided not to risk any more defeats on the Indian-Burmese border at that stage in the war. It was unfortunate for the British that the results of their Arakan adventure only served to confirm American doubts.

Churchill's pipe dream of taking Rangoon by the end of September had been whittled away by many factors, which included the Indian riots of August, disruption to army training, lack of suitable craft for an amphibious assault, and a critical shortage of air power. The original plan for the Arakan had envisaged 14 Division advancing overland, supported by a seaborne assault by two brigades to seize the island of Akyab. Eventually all that was left of the earlier plan was a single division thrusting its way down the Arakan peninsula until it reached a point from where an attack could be made on Akyab, using the few landing craft that were still available in the Indian theatre.

The command arrangements for the Arakan offensive were extremely untidy and undoubtedly contributed to the eventual setback suffered by the British and Indian troops there. Major-General Lloyd's 14 Division began its advance in late 1942 with control exercised, not by Slim as 15 Corps Commander but by General Noel Irwin, commander of Eastern Army, with his headquarters installed at Barrackpore, on the outskirts of Calcutta. Slim's operational plan had been for 14 Division to exercise frontal pressure against the Japanese while a series of short amphibious hooks were made to outflank the enemy, with Wingate's Long Range Penetration brigade also playing a vital part in disrupting the defenders. Unfortunately General Wavell switched Wingate's LRP to another role elsewhere in the theatre. Lloyd's division set off in a slow methodical advance down the peninsula, pushing back the small groups of Japanese, stubbornly fighting a series of delaying actions. As the Americans had foretold, the Japanese, using only four battalions, never allowed Lloyd to gain overall freedom of movement, so that the campaign had dubious local tactical value only; no Japanese formations were moved to the south, until they switched to attack the British force. Stilwell's task of advancing from Ledo was not made any easier by the British probes towards Akyab.

Field Marshal Wavell's modest campaign, which always had limited objectives, including his wish to defeat a hitherto victorious enemy in order to boost the morale of the forces in India, was misrepresented with ill-fated timing by unwise and overgenerous publicity. Soon the American and British public were to be under the impression that the Allied march on Burma had begun, with a major offensive during the winter of 1942/43 to bring about the defeat of large Japanese forces. As a result, when the slow, almost tentative advance down the peninsula against an enemy who was vastly inferior in numbers was halted by the end of December 1942, a wave of cynicism and disillusionment spread through the armed forces in India. Anglo-American relations in New Delhi became strained, and needed vigorous action by Slim, Wingate, and other commanders, early in 1943, before the British and Indian soldiers ceased to think of their Japanese opponent as an invincible superman.

Defeats in the Arakan during the first few months of 1943 brought about a change of commanders. Mention has already been made that General Noel Irwin adopted an unusual chain of command for the Arakan operations, sending Slim and his Corps headquarters back to Ranchi, while he controlled Major General Lloyd. Lloyd, too, with a small headquarters, was required to handle no less than nine brigades, an impossible burden for a divisional commander. His forces were held up by the inland defences at Donbaik. There, camouflaged strongpoints and skilfully constructed bunkers, manned by a single Japanese company, inflicted heavy casualties whenever frontal attacks were launched against them. Irwin's remedy was to repeat a series of attacks on Donbaik throughout February. By the end of the month even Irwin had grave doubts about the validity of those barren tactics. Unfortunately a victim himself of the pre-campaign publicity, Churchill exhorted Wavell to carry on, and the Commander-in-Chief gave instructions that the attacks were to be pressed home, to succeed by sheer weight of fire power and overwhelming numbers. On 18 March 14 Division made one more attempt, but the result was the same, a complete disaster.

Even then, Irwin did not allow Slim to take over as operational commander. He sent Slim to the forward areas as an observer without any direct responsibility. Only after he had given a frank report to Irwin was Slim told to move to Chittagong and 'to be prepared to take over operational control in the Arakan'. The Japanese saw to it that Slim did not have to wait long before being given the unenviable task of saving an impossible situation. From the end of January, reinforcements from the Japanese 15 Division had been filtering their way into the Mayu peninsula, and on 5 April they struck. The headquarters of 6 Brigade was overrun, while 47 Brigade was reported to have disintegrated. The unfortunate Lloyd, after a final disagreement with Irwin, was replaced by Major-General Lomax. Slim found that Lomax had taken a cool look at the situation and in a competent manner had set in motion all the necessary steps to regroup the demoralized brigades. Belatedly Slim was ordered to take complete control of all troops in the Arakan. He and Lomax worked in harmony together, finally extricating the Arakan forces until they were back in the positions from where they had started a few months before with such high hopes.

The clash of personalities between Irwin and Slim led to the latter's shortlived dismissal and his wry remark, quoted by Ronald Lewin: 'I suppose that means I've got the sack. I shall join the Home Guard in England. I wonder if I shall find Irwin there?' Fortunately for the future 14 Army, another signal was winging its way from Delhi to Irwin, informing him that he had been replaced at Eastern Army by General Sir George Giffard. Irwin is reputed to have dispatched an immediate telegram to Slim: 'You're not sacked, I am.' And he then departed from the scene.

If 1942 was the year of defeats, the first seven or eight months of 1943 did not bring any dramatic victories or produce an agreed blueprint of Allied strategy in the Far East theatre either. The Americans looked up the Burma Road to China while their British allies gazed over the sea to Singapore, the fortress that had contained their hopes until one short dramatic campaign destroyed Britain's prestige in Asia. Churchill, restless as ever, dearly wanted to exact revenge by retaking Singapore, but the demands of the war in Europe meant that the Indo-Burma theatre of operations was at the thin end of an extremely long supply line. Roosevelt's faith in China continued to wax strong although there was open disagreement between his two commanders on the spot, Stilwell in India and Chennault, the picturesque ex-commander of the American Volunteer Group (the 'Flying Tigers'), who had come for a military adventure in China with his AVG crews. Chennault was well in favour with Madam Chiang and the powerful Soong family. He believed that the Japanese land forces in China could be contained by air power alone and accordingly sought the maximum share (nine-tenths) of the tonnage flown over the Hump. Such a demand meant that the 30 or so divisions in the Yunnan did not receive the equipment, weapons, and supplies so urgently required. Chennault's strategy was vigorously rejected by 'Vinegar Joe' Stilwell. In his view the notion of establishing numerous air bases without adequate Chinese ground forces to guard them was militarily unsound, but his objections were overruled. Chennault was directed to work with the Chinese government to construct yet more airfields in territory which could not be guaranteed to escape a major land offensive by the Japanese.

India's economy was under a considerable strain as a direct result of the war. To add to the problems of the outgoing Viceroy, Lord Linlithgow, and his advisers, an ungenerous monsoon resulted in a failure of the staple crops; panic set in, and excessive hoarding of grain and other commodities led to dangerously explosive situations in many parts of India. It was yet another reminder to the Americans that India was not a gigantic ready-made military base from where ambitious operations could be carried out without considerable forethought. And to ease the threatening famine, the military had to be used in some areas, both to enforce order and to help stamp out black market practices which threatened to spark off major riots. Fortunately for India, the newly appointed Viceroy, Wavell, did much to restore the situation by his energy, imagination, and improvisation – and for a time he enjoyed a real and, for him, unusual popularity.

The decision to establish an Allied South East Asia Command was taken at the Trident Conference, held in Washington in May 1943. It was agreed, in principle, to co-ordinate all land, sea, and air activities in the Far East although the selection of commanders to fill the appropriate posts was not finalized until the following conference, at Quebec in August. The appointment of Admiral Lord Louis Mountbatten as Supreme Commander heralded a new era, although the outlook when he took over in November 1943 was still bleak – but vastly better than had appeared likely earlier in the year.

The Indian political scene remained outwardly quiet but there were ominous signs beneath the surface that the days of the British Raj were drawing to an end. The requirements and demands of war superseded Indian demands for freedom – in British eyes anyway. India had to be transformed into a giant base, capable of supporting more than 30 divisions; of providing air support for Allied troops in the Arakan and in Central Burma, for Wingate's Long Penetration Group, and to continue flying the missions over the Hump into China. The vast distances involved, the hostile climate, the forbidding terrain, all served to highlight the importance of an ambitious construction programme of airfields, new roads, hospitals, and supply installations, as well as the improvement of existing dock facilities at the main port of Calcutta. Such a gigantic base demanded a military commander, and it was for this reason that Field Marshal Wavell was appointed Viceroy in October 1943. It was to be the fourth of his high posts during the war and in the end, it was to be the most difficult and taxing one. His successor as Commander-in-Chief was Field Marshal Sir Claude Auchinleck, an inspired choice because he had served a lifetime with the Indian Army, and was respected by British and Indian officers, as well as being a venerated father figure to the Indian sepoy and Gurkha riflemen.

The promotion of Giffard and Slim to 11 Army Group and Eastern Army respectively continued a happy partnership that brought much success. Although the Americans, and in particular Stilwell, did not find Giffard an inspiring commander or an easy person to work with, Slim paid him a generous tribute in *Defeat into Victory*. The two of them, working well together, knew what had to be done to restore the morale of the troops, which was at a low level after the setbacks in Arakan. They appreciated that the key to future success lay in tough, imaginative, vigorous training methods. And, soon to stir the imagination of all, from Winston Churchill down to the newest recruit, came the exploits of Wingate and his Chindits. Churchill's wrath at the failure of the Arakan enterprise was mollified, to some degree, by the new star that shone fitfully and for a tragically short period, in the Indo-Burmese theatre of operations.

Brigadier Orde Wingate's part in the campaign aroused bitter controversy at the time and the debate has continued to excite historians ever since. He arrived on the scene at a crucial period in the struggle for Burma. His departure was even more dramatic and unexpected, but by that time, his name was respected by friend and foe alike.

CHAPTER 3

Wingate and the Chindits

People with courage and character always seem sinister to the rest — Hermann Hesse

---

Although the United States continued to regard India and Burma as secondary theatres, the opening of secure land links with China remained high on their priority list. Any plan that would help Stilwell forward had American support providing it did not interfere with the promised airlift to China over the Hump. To Stilwell's annoyance and chagrin, the bulk of the monthly tonnage flown by the C-47s to China continued to be earmarked for Chennault, leaving little for the re-equipping of the American-sponsored Chinese divisions in Yunnan.

The pilots of the C-47s, operating over the Hump, soon became increasingly unhappy and disillusioned. The treacherous tropical storms that buffeted their aircraft while flying over wild, inhospitable terrain meant that many missions ended in disaster. Not for nothing were their aircraft dubbed the 'Flying Coffins'. Death for a worthy cause was one thing but the American air crews had abundant evidence to prove that numerous items of their precious loads were salted away after unloading in China, to be resold elsewhere: sophisticated equipment was found rusting and rotting because there was no one trained to use it. Corruption, too, was rife. President Roosevelt's idealistic championing of China was not viewed with favour by the majority of the American servicemen engaged on the Hump operation.

Stilwell's accusation that the British were sitting on their backsides after the Arakan reverse did not make as much impact as it might have done had his early probes into Upper Burma been more dramatic or opposed by more than a handful of Japanese. Moreover, a new hero had appeared in South East Asia and in a remarkable fashion captured the imagination of the British, and to a lesser degree, American public. At a time when the bitterness of defeat was real, and frustration at being at the narrow end of the longest supply line in modern war was seriously affecting the morale of the British and Indian soldiers, came the strange figure of Orde Wingate. It was not what he actually achieved in 1943 that mattered. Indeed, the few stings his

Long Range Penetration (LRP) columns inflicted on the Japanese were minuscule in effect and comparatively costly in lives. But the propaganda value to the Allied cause in South East Asia was of immense value, even if this fact was grudgingly admitted by the more orthodox of the senior officers. Fortunately for Wingate and his Chindits, Wavell and Slim were not among those who scoffed at and opposed his ideas.

Wingate was Wavell's man and came to India at his express bidding. The Commander-in-Chief hoped that the 40-year-old Royal Artillery officer could play as successful a role in guerrilla operations against the Japanese as he had done in Ethiopia when the Italians had been defeated by a comparatively small force of British and Indian troops. Wingate, therefore, was in a strong position for a junior officer and was quite ruthless in using his superior's name and influence whenever he felt the occasion demanded – which was to be more and more frequently after his 1943 'Loincloth' raids into Burma had become headline stories in the newspapers.

Between February and April 1943 Wingate's columns crossed over the Chindwin into Japanese-held territory. When the accounts were released to the Allied press it was not long before the LRP became the Chindits, taking their name and their namesake's emblem – half lion, half flying griffin – from the mythical Chinthe pagoda guardian. The public relations men had a field day, with much to regale their readers. Not only had British and Gurkha soldiers penetrated into and behind the Japanese forward positions, but there were countless stories of courage and drama, endurance, hardship, and even sacrifice to recount. As a result of the considerable hullabaloo, the eccentric and picturesque Wingate soon became a household name.

Two major questions must be posed and the evidence examined: on what pillars were Wingate's LRP raids based, and what did they achieve? The first part is easier to answer than the second, although even when Wingate had expounded his theories, he was liable to change his mind with startling impetuosity – a trend that became more noticeable during the few weeks before his death in the following year.

'Have no L of C on the jungle floor. Bring in the goods like Father Christmas down the chimney', proclaimed Wingate in colourful language. Such a doctrine implied absolute superiority in the air so that an army could strike at will, in the knowledge that it could call for supplies at the right place and the right time. And to do this, reliable communications by radio from ground to air and back to base were essential. But the calibre of the troops was never to be forgotten, Wingate reminded. If it was not possible to select the very best, then the volunteers had to be toughened and sharpened to withstand the mental and physical rigours which all would have to endure when living and fighting as guerrillas. Above all, they had to have absolute trust in the ability of the airforces to supply them with all they needed – weapons, ammunition, and supplies, for they would be in the heart of enemy territory and completely dependent on pilots and aircrews for their survival.

Several of the setbacks suffered by the columns engaged in Operation Loincloth were caused by lack of experience and faulty tactics, untested air resupply techniques, and indifferent communications. The uneven calibre of the British and Gurkha soldiers, selected as guineapigs for the ambitious experiment, made a difficult operation more hazardous. At the time, there was a widely held mistaken belief that Wingate deliberately chose mediocre troops, but such a theory ignored the ruthless pruning that took place during the weeks of hard training before the columns set off into Burma. Certainly the ordinary officers and soldiers who survived such rigorous training schedules were physically ready for their dramatic tasks. Nevertheless, Wingate made things more difficult by deliberately asking for inexperienced wartime units rather than those with a leavening of regulars who had some experience of active service. His theory was that green troops would be more malleable for his unorthodox mode of waging war 'in the guts of the enemy'.

The results achieved by the groups that crossed the Chindwin were not nearly as dramatic as the reports published at the time. The cost in lives was comparatively heavy, especially when the sick were added to the battle casualties. Mistakes were made, techniques devised during training had to be hurriedly changed, at every level a few commanders cracked, and many of the British and very young Gurkha soldiers were found wanting. Stilwell's comments were uncomplimentary. 'Wingate's forces were slogging heroically around the jungle, attempting little that couldn't have been done better by the Air Corps'.

Perhaps if Stilwell had lived to see the massive sledgehammer of the US Air Corps reduced to impotence and unable to control the jungle campaign in Vietnam, he might have revised his opinion and tempered his criticism to some degree. But he was not alone in doubting the validity of Wingate's concepts and doctrine – there were British officers who declared that after weeks of milling about in the jungle, the Chindits had failed to accomplish anything of real military value.

Lord Wavell's assessment was more generous: 'The enterprise had no strategic value and about one-third of the force which entered Burma was lost, but the experience gained was invaluable. The enemy was obviously surprised and at a loss ... in general Brigadier Wingate's theories of leadership were fully vindicated'.

The Japanese, too, took a realistic view, fearing that this was but a rehearsal, a precursor of what was to follow. It will be recalled that the Japanese plan was to establish a strong defensive perimeter around their recently acquired Asian territories, with the intention of destroying any Allied force attempting to penetrate the outer curtain. The first Chindit operations had shown that their defences, east of the Chindwin, could be pierced with ease – and this could happen again. The senior Japanese generals in Burma had different views and divided opinions on what should be done to rectify the situation. General Mutaguchi, commander of the 15 Army, advocated counter-offensive action rather than waiting for the British to infiltrate in even greater strength. He reported to his superiors that Imphal was being built up into a major base, the obvious linchpin of any future offensive launched by 14 Army under Slim. In June 1943, Burma Area Army under Lieutenant-General Kawabe was told to study the situation in detail and then prepare plans for an attack against the Imphal front. For planning purposes, Kawabe was told that, initially, seven divisions would be available – which meant that a defensive role would have to be adopted in the other sectors. If, however, the Allies struck first, then they were to be held, defeated and thrown back before the projected advance on Imphal began. By the end of December 1943 planning for Operation U-Go had reached a fairly advanced stage, but permission had to be obtained from imperial headquarters in Tokyo before final decisions could be taken. Japanese policy at the time was summed up by Prime Minister Tojo in these words: 'Now, on the threshold of a new year (1944), Japan will seek to consolidate her gains. She will go on doing so until ultimate victory is attained'. Although fear of a major British offensive was the prime reason for the counter-blow against Imphal, the initial revaluation of their strategy in Burma was undoubtedly caused by extreme apprehension, aroused by Wingate's exploits in early 1943.

During interrogation after the war, General Numato (Chief-of-Staff, Southern Army) said: 'It was found, as a result of the Wingate campaign in 1943, and the Japanese operations in opposition thereto, that the terrain in northern Burma was favourable for guerrilla warfare by small bodies of crack troops, but it was very difficult to defend ... therefore, it would be best to give up defensive tactics and resort to an offensive to destroy the enemy's bases for counter-operations such as Imphal, Kohima etc.'. (*The March on Delhi*).

Wingate's voice was heard for the first time in the high Allied councils of war when, at Churchill's bidding, he attended the Quebec Conference in July 1943. Once again, the United States propounded the same theme, that Japan could most effectively be defeated on the Chinese mainland, that India and Burma were of minor concern compared with the paramount importance of China's survival as an active ally. General Stilwell's mission of clearing up the north of Burma to enable a land route and petrol pipe-line to be driven through from Assam to China, was all-important in the American planners' eyes. They were prepared, however, to consider any project designed to help Stilwell fulfil his aim. This gave Wingate a wonderful opportunity. Vigorously supported by Churchill, Wingate expounded his theories, graphically describing how an enlarged Chindit force could cut off Stilwell's Japanese opponents from their supplies and reinforcements. Where the British senior commanders doubted, the Americans enthused. Not only did Wingate receive their unstinted support but General Arnold promised him 1 Air Commando, under Colonel Philip Cochrane, a mini-airforce to help Wingate put his exciting promises into practice. In addition 5307 Infantry Regiment was sent to India for training under Wingate although subsequently it operated with Stilwell. That small force had a special niche in the Burma campaign, being best remembered by the more striking title of Merrill's Marauders.

It was Wingate's chance and he took it. In September of 1943 he was promoted to major-general while plans were made for the LRP to be increased from six to twenty-five units, made up of seventeen British, five Gurkha and three West African battalions. The Commander-in-Chief in India, Field Marshal Sir Claude Auchinleck, had an uneasy relationship with Wingate although matters improved after the arrival of the Supreme Commander, Admiral Mountbatten, in November. Wingate had been allotted 70 Division but he soon complained that a large number of the infantry in the division did not measure up to the high physical standards he was seeking. Auchinleck disagreed with Wingate's assessment, pointing out that 70 Division would not be operating in a vacuum; its role had to be viewed against the background of the projected British offensive. In the end the argument was won by Wingate. India Command lost another complete British division, as well as eight other major units which, with the volunteer officers and specialists sent out from the United Kingdom, added up to the equivalent of two-and-a-half divisions being earmarked to produce the enlarged Special Force. The ill-assorted partnership of Auchinleck and Wingate rarely worked in harmony and much of the blame has to be put on Wingate's shoulders. His explosive remarks, often made in front of junior officers, frequently bordered on insubordination. As a consequence, he upset those whose co-operation Special Force so badly needed. To balance the ill will he engendered, Wingate's superhuman energy, uncompromising determination to excel, and dynamic drive, enabled Special Force to be trained and equipped in the short time available – but it was a close thing. Orde Wingate's questioning and audacious mind did not make him an easy colleague or even a loyal subordinate. Some of his scheming actions and methods were those of a man who distrusted others and, in turn, almost welcomed opposition from those who, initially, were prepared to help him.

The enlarged Special Force was not as powerful as an ordinary standard division would have been, with a normal quota of guns, tanks, and engineers. In addition, the number of aircraft needed to supply and support its columns was considerable and, once committed, the planes could not be made available to help other parts of the Burma front. Wingate's grand scheme was an expensive way of making war on the Japanese. Brigadier Joe Lentaigne, commander of 111 Brigade, commented with some truth: 'Well, if we are going to be part of Wingate's private army, let's relax and enjoy it. We're Chindits now and, by God, we had better all stick together because the rest of the army's going to be out for our blood'. (*The Road Past Mandalay*).

He was right. The Chindits became, and have remained, figures of controversy, with much of the heat rising from Wingate's unusual personality, and an unhappy relationship with the majority of his superiors in rank and appointment. In his world, there were and could be no neutrals, no shades of grey. But without him, the Burma campaign would have taken a different course – and no one can dispute the influence he exerted on events while he was at the zenith of his brief period of fame.

When Admiral Mountbatten arrived in Delhi to take over his appointment as Supreme Commander, he came with Churchill's full support and the good wishes of the US government. As far as Roosevelt was concerned, a leader who could further the American aim of opening up land links with China through Upper Burma was to be welcomed – and Mountbatten had already made a favourable impression on the Americans. General Stilwell became Mountbatten's deputy, which meant that his responsibility in this theatre was more complicated than before. He now wore three different command hats. As Deputy Commander Stilwell was under South East Asia Command; as Commander of all US forces in the China-Burma-India (CBI) theatre he had direct access to the Commander of the Armed

Forces, President Roosevelt; while Chief-of-Staff to the Generalissimo added yet another dimension to his role, involving direct political and military links with the erratic Chinese leader in Chungking.

For an officer who hated staff work and did not understand how the higher echelons of power operated, Stilwell found himself owing allegiance to separate headquarters in Delhi, Washington, and Chungking – as well as serving under the Supremo, Mountbatten, who received his instructions from the British Chief-of-Staff in London. It was a complex situation for any commander. Unfortunately Stilwell did not have the temperament and ability to work in harmony with those above him, even if he had been able to conquer his distrust of the British. Northern Combat Area Command (NCAC), where the US-trained Chinese Divisions began to probe forward with the aim of clearing the Japanese from Upper Burma, was under Stilwell's direct command. He, in turn, should have been under the overall command of 11 Army Group, but the prickly American refused to work under the Land Force Commander, General Sir George Giffard. As a result, an untidy compromise had to be sought whereby Stilwell accepted Slim's authority even though Giffard had Slim's 14 Army under his overall command. To throw in yet another bone of contention, Stilwell as Deputy SEAC outranked everyone in the theatre except Mountbatten.

Such a confused, complex command structure was not best suited to help the overall Anglo-American strategy, which was, 'to eliminate the Japanese from Northern Burma as the first step in developing, maintaining, and protecting air and land communications between India and China'. Although Churchill's eyes remained set on the shortest road to Singapore, including the early recapture of Rangoon in southern Burma, the British were junior partners in the Far East and as such had to accept that little American help would be forthcoming for operations they considered to be irrelevant. After receiving a bloodied nose in the Arakan, it was not surprising that the British were wary about risking another setback in Burma. Giffard and Slim hoped that the Japanese would come forward and take issue with them on ground of their own choosing, in an area where Allied superiority in armour, artillery, and airpower could be used to pound them to defeat. The Japanese, too, had been quick to recognize that Imphal, with its ever-growing base and stockpiling of stores, was the dagger pointing at the heart of Burma. If Imphal and Dimapur were to be snatched from 14 Army's possession then the imperial design of holding the perimeter of Burma with a small number of troops could be put into effect for some time to come.

Slim was content to wait for his opponents, certainly until the spring of 1944 when he believed that 14 Army have enough additional muscle, plus the necessary logistical backing, for a successful re-entry into Burma. But Allied plans had to be revised once again when Mountbatten was ordered to send back precious landing craft for the projected invasion of France. Modest advances by 15 Corps in the Arakan and 4 Corps up to the Chindwin, plus support for NCAC, chiefly in the shape of Wingate's Special Force, were planned to take place before the monsoon broke in 1944.

In Chungking the Generalissimo was so incensed by Mountbatten's inability to mount a major amphibious operation that he postponed the advance by the Chinese Expeditionary Force from Yunnan into Burma. Chiang Kai-shek's intransigence made it all the more important that Stilwell's immediate opponents, the veteran 18 Division, should be deprived of regular supplies and reinforcements. Wingate was given the mission of blocking the Bhamo-Myitkyina road as well as mounting something more ambitious against the railway/road focus in the Indaw-Mawli area. Of equal significance, Indaw had two airfields and in the original Operation Capital, a full-blooded airborne assault had been planned against those important targets. But Capital was discarded because once again, in American eyes, too many valuable resources were required for an operation they considered to be of minor importance.

For the projected Operation Thursday, Wingate had trained and equipped six small brigades, each consisting of four small battalions. In turn, each battalion was organized into two columns, both 400 strong, with British, Gurkha, and West African soldiers supported by their own organic mortars, engineers, and machine guns. Operation Thursday had been scheduled to begin during January 1944 but there were several changes to the plan, caused in the main by intelligence reports. These indicated that the Japanese had taken steps to guard the majority of the known crossing places along the Chindwin. Although the official purpose of Wingate's operation was to take the Japanese 18 Division from the rear and cut their lifeline, by the time 77 and 111 Chindit Brigades began their fly-in on 5 March, Wingate's horizons had widened until with lofty strategic vision, he looked beyond the mere cutting of supply lines. For a start he intended to seize and hold the Indaw-Bhamo line.

One of Wingate's weaknesses was an inability to trust subordinates, even those who had served him with proven loyalty from the very start of his enterprise. Not one of the brigadiers who led columns into Burma in 1944 or his principal staff officers really knew what Wingate's long-term aims were. He changed his mind with startling rapidity: he was moody and subject to sudden oscillations from heady euphoria to deep pessimism. For Wingate, propaganda was an all-important weapon: without skilful propaganda he would not have been able to persuade anyone to expand his Chindits, especially after the excessive casualties incurred in 1943 for mediocre results. Now he aimed high. If the Indaw-Bhamo area were seized quickly and victory complete, then he hoped to be in a position to hand over Special Force gains to conventional divisions following up behind. By repeating the process step by step, Wingate saw his private army being capable of leapfrogging a way right across South East Asia. Such an ambitious plan was not divulged at the time, but in correspondence with Mountbatten, Wingate showed that the ultimate aim was far removed from his original principle that LRP forces should operate, in a subsidiary role, to help the main forces achieve their mission. His obsession with Indaw and its airfield provides evidence of what was at the back of his mind, and certainly coloured directions he gave to Special Force after the operation had begun in March.

Prior to the start of the airborne invasion, the United States 1 Air Commando under Cochrane had been making vigorous efforts to destroy as many Japanese aircraft in the air, and on the ground, as possible. With the vulnerable WACO CG-44 gliders, towed by unarmed C47 Dakotas, having to stream their way over 150 miles of Japanese territory, it was vital to have absolute air superiority before the night of 5 March. Without this, Wingate and his men would not have been able to launch their offensive. Some British writers have been niggardly in acknowledging the tremendous, unselfish efforts made by 1 Air Commando, at a high cost to the pilots and their machines.

The concept of air commandos was dreamt up by Generals Arnold and Marshall as a tonic which they hoped would be able to revive flagging morale in the Burma theatre where, until 1944, British and Indian troops had suffered several defeats at the hands of numerically inferior Japanese. In command was Colonel Philip G. Cochrane who had already gained a distinguished reputation as an air ace in the skies over North Africa. It was not long before he and his men made their mark in South East Asia. After one of Cochrane's reconnaissance planes had reported seeing a large force of Japanese bombers on the Shewbo airfield, the Americans returned late in the afternoon and in a dramatic raid swooped down and strafed the Japanese bomber fleet. They caught the Japanese by surprise. Cochrane realized that the initial strike had to be exploited and sent twelve B25s (Mitchells) to hit the Japanese yet again. The Mitchells came in under 1,000 feet, and dropped a vast number of fragmentation bombs before leaving the burning base to a follow-up force of RAF Hurricanes. Next day a British reconnaissance aircraft was over the airfield and its photographs revealed that more than 100 aircraft had been destroyed.

This daring, well planned action was a catastrophic blow to Japanese air power in Burma. The potential air threat to the Second Chindit expedition had thus been removed. Cochrane's Air Commando was free to carry out an exhaustive programme of interdiction missions in conjunction with 221 Group RAF, to interrupt and destroy Japanese communications by attacking railways, road traffic, bridges and river crossings. Their joint efforts so disrupted Japanese communications that when the Chindit airborne invasion started, the reaction and build up against Wingate's strongholds was much slower and certainly more laboured than it would have been without the strenuous Anglo-American air offensive.

The devotion to duty of the American pilots, all of whom were volunteers, was tested to the maximum as the campaign continued and their numbers were gradually reduced. The support they gave to all the columns by bombing, reconnaissance, and strafing, played a big part in the success of the Chindits, whose reliance on the airforces was absolute. And the Air Commando and RAF rarely let them down. Another technique that was used for the first time to any great extent under operational conditions, was the evacuation of the wounded and the sick by air. A light plane force operated under Cochrane's overall command. The pilots, mostly sergeants and again volunteers, experienced their first action when 15 Corps in the Arakan sought urgent assistance when several units were surrounded and cut off by the Japanese. Lessons learnt there were invaluable when the pilots moved back to support the Chindits. It was a tremendous filip to morale for the British and Gurkha soldiers to know that, if they were hit they had a sporting chance of finding themselves back in a general hospital in India within hours of becoming a casualty.

No 1 Air Commando played a vital part in the Chindit operations. Moreover, their participation meant that American interest in Special Force was a real one, and one that was sustained to the very end. Wingate planned to establish strongholds, which were to be bases for rest and supply, sited in country 'so inaccessible that only lightly equipped enemy infantry can penetrate to it. . . . We can transport our defensive stores there by air; the enemy cannot'. Supported by artillery with their own protective garrison force, the concept was clear although as the plans for the three Brigades, 16, 77, and 111, unfolded, Wingate appeared to forget his original principle of establishing strongholds in difficult, close country.

With some 20 to 30 columns operating, forever changing their roles and continually regrouping, only the bare outline of operations can be given. Calvert's 77 Brigade was to be put down at three landing zones, to establish a base before dispatching a force to the Bhamo area; while another column was to intercept river traffic on the Irrawaddy as well as blocking road and rail movement northwards. In the final plan, 111 Brigade was also to fly in and land south of the Irrawaddy River, cross it and then strike towards Indaw, thereby disrupting Japanese troop movement towards the town from the south. The third force, 16 Brigade, under Bernard Fergusson, starting from far to the north near Ledo, had some 300 miles to cover on foot to capture Indaw and its airfields through country so appalling that the Japanese did not bother to patrol or guard it in any strength. Marching through terrible terrain, the timetable allotted to Fergusson was far too optimistic. Wingate's orders required Fergusson to co-ordinate his attack with that of the column from 77 Brigade. By extraordinary feats of endurance Fergusson, with most of his brigade, was lucky to arrive only a fortnight late. Wingate's overall aim was to dominate the area of Indaw and its airfields, astride the Japanese lines of communication to 18 Division – which was opposing Stilwell's efforts to capture the key towns of Myitkyina and Mogaung. After the Japanese made their intentions clear with the U-Go offensive towards the Imphal plateau and Kohima, fresh instructions were given and changes made in the roles of several columns.

After Operation Thursday had been launched, it seemed clear that Wingate had abandoned his original concept of operations. Previously he had maintained that Special Force had to operate in close proximity to 4 Corps but by selecting strongholds that lay in open country, he automatically accepted that there was little chance of his brigades linking up with Slim's main force, even if the Japanese had not launched their march against Imphal. The strongholds selected were conveniently near airstrips and dropping zones, but in country that was comparatively open and accessible.

During the last few weeks before Operation Thursday began, Mountbatten had to take the brunt of Wingate's tantrums and erratic temperament. Long, rambling letters were sent to the Supreme Commander, containing highly critical remarks about army and airforce authorities who, Wingate alleged, were doing their best to thwart him by earmarking aircraft and equipment for less important uses. These, and other provocative statements, Mountbatten took with admirable calmness.

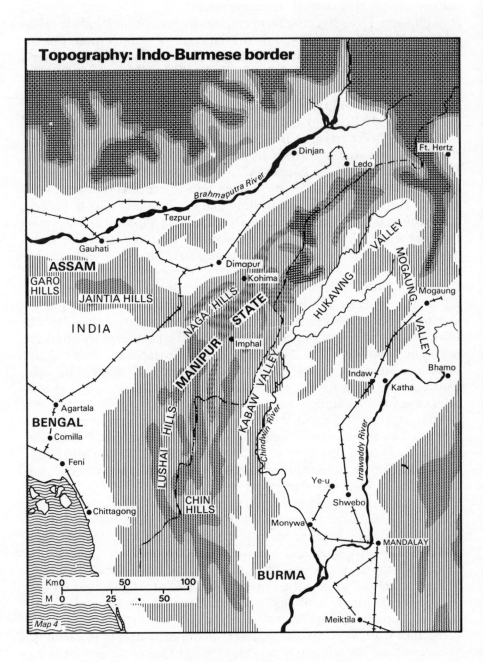

Topography: Indo-Burmese border

Ft. Hertz

Dinjan

Ledo

Brahmaputra River

Tezpur

Gauhati

ASSAM

GARO
HILLS

JAINTIA HILLS

Dimapur

Kohima

MOGAUNG VALLEY

HUKAWNG VALLEY

Mogaung

NAGA HILLS

STATE

INDIA

MANIPUR

Imphal

Indaw

Bhamo

Katha

KABAW VALLEY

Chindwin River

Irrawaddy River

Agartala

BENGAL

Comilla

LUSHAI HILLS

Ye-u

Feni

Shwebo

Chittagong

CHIN
HILLS

Monywa

MANDALAY

Km 0   50   100

M 0   25   50

BURMA

Meiktila

Map 4

When 16 Brigade began its long march into Burma under Brigadier Fergusson, progress was slow; it was extremely difficult country and the column was forced to move in single file, often faced with scrambles up and down gradients as steep as one-in-two. The Chindwin was reached ten days behind schedule and on 1 March Wingate flew in to meet Fergusson, urging him to move as fast as possible to the Indaw area. For some inexplicable reason he did not pass on to Fergusson recent reports indicating that Indaw had been reinforced by the Japanese. Fergusson was always under the impression that he was to set up a stronghold, named Aberdeen, and thereafter stop the movement of enemy reinforcements. Now it seems certain that Wingate had always intended to use 16 Brigade to seize the airfields, weary and depleted though Fergusson's troops were. It was yet another example of Wingate's inability to keep his subordinates fully in the picture.

Sunday 5 March dawned, the day when 77 Brigade under Brigadier Michael Calvert was poised to take off from the Lalaghat airfield in Assam. As the Chindits were operating under the overall command of Slim, the Army Commander and Wingate were both there to see the fly-in begin. About half an hour before take-off, a light reconnaissance aircraft from Cochrane's Air Commando arrived and photographs of the three landing strips, Piccadilly, Broadway, and Chowringhee, were produced for study. Those three strips were first to be used by 77 Brigade and then by 111 Brigade. The photographs showed Piccadilly to be covered with what appeared to be obstacles and subsequently proved to be felled tree trunks. Had the Japanese been forewarned with accurate information so that they were able to anticipate the exact landing spots? At Lalaghat an agonizing dilemma faced the commander, with three possible alternatives before him: to cancel the whole operation, to postpone it for a few days, or to carry on, using the alternative Broadway and Chowringhee airstrips only.

Reports handed down to posterity about Wingate's behaviour vary because of conflicting evidence. His detractors allege that he became highly emotional, claiming that the operation would now be a complete disaster. A factual account goes on to describe that Slim calmed him down and ordered the operation to go on, with troops destined for Piccadilly being diverted to the Broadway and Chowringhee strips. Calvert's account is very different. He maintains that Wingate asked him if he was prepared to go on. 'If we don't go on now I don't think we shall ever go as we shall have to wait for the moon and the season is already late. Slim and the airmen are willing to go on now that everything is ready; what do you think? I don't like ordering you to go if I'm not going myself'. (*Prisoners of Hope*).

Calvert maintains that after discussing the alternatives with his own second-in-command, he reported that he was prepared to take the whole brigade into Broadway. Wingate was still not happy and eventually Slim talked it over with him before indicating to Wingate that he, as Special Force Commander, should decide whether the operations should be mounted as planned or postponed.

The evidence is inconsistent: certainly Slim's own account indicates that Wingate passed the buck back to him as Army Commander. Later he wrote: 'Wingate was convinced that the whole plan of the operations had been betrayed and at first wished to postpone it. I was most averse to postponing the operation'. Whatever transpired, it seems certain that the final decision must have rested on the shoulders of Slim and if the fly-in had ended in disaster, then it would have been in his character to have taken the major part of the blame.

After some harrowing accidents during the early fly-in, Calvert established the Broadway stronghold and began what was, tactically, an almost flawless operation. He set off at the head of three battalions to block the railway between Myitkyina and Indaw. That raid led to some fierce hand-to-hand fighting with the Japanese. In the first clash at Mawlu, Lieutenant Cairns won a posthumous VC, gallantly leading an attack after his arm had been hacked off with a sword. The Japanese, so often used to seeing their opponents fleeing, fought hard before being routed themselves. Meanwhile, Calvert's White City stronghold had been organized to meet the worst that the Japanese could throw at its defenders. As at Broadway, the other 77 Brigade base more than 40 miles away, the Japanese found the wire, mines, booby traps, and excellently co-ordinated defensive perimeters too much for them, but the issue was in doubt for some time. The first few days of 77 Brigade's arrival in Burma saw much heavy fighting but their efforts were rewarded with success. Within two weeks their victories had stirred the Japanese into frenetic activity.

Meanwhile 111 Brigade had landed at Broadway and Chowringhee which meant that the raiding columns were widely separated from each other and their targets. In addition, Lentaigne had been ordered by Wingate to send yet another column east to the Bhamo district so that by the time the Brigade Commander had reached a position south of Indaw, there were only two-and-a-half battalions under his direct control. At that stage there were some 3,000 Japanese in the Indaw area, ready to resist. In retrospect, it seems odd that after Wingate had decided that possession of the Indaw airfields was the key to his whole plan – and that certainly is borne out by the available evidence – he then adopted a most circuitous approach to the target area. Why did

111 Brigade, for example, land on the east side of one of the great rivers of Asia and why was 16 Brigade, under Fergusson, made to begin its epic march from Ledo, miles away to the north, thereby increasing the chances of the Japanese discovering them as the long, spindly columns moved southwards to carry out their task?

Bernard Fergusson's intention was, first, to cut off Indaw from the west and south, then to use his other columns to strike from the north-east and north. Such an ambitious plan looked an extremely attractive one on the map but proved far too difficult to execute, especially when the Japanese were ready and waiting. Moreover, Fergusson and his men, exhausted after their long and arduous march, had been hustled into action by the impatient Wingate. Columns were ambushed, other groups ran into trouble, and after several rebuffs and defeats in detail, Fergusson had to order a retreat back to Aberdeen. For Fergusson, who had never commanded a battalion in a more normal type of operation, the ambitious dreams of Wingate were far too difficult to achieve. The gallant march had been in vain.

By that time the battle for the plain of Imphal had begun, and its story is taken up in another chapter. The part played by the Special Force in Slim's defence of Imphal had been variously assessed by historians. One view is that the Chindits helped to isolate the Japanese attackers from their base installations, while another maintains that only Stilwell's front derived any real assistance from Wingate's efforts. Slim believed that most of the hardships suffered by the three Japanese divisions near Imphal were caused by their own administrative shortcomings and were not the result of the interdiction raids carried out by the Chindits. In Slim's view, Wingate and his men had the primary mission of helping Stilwell, in order to fulfil the promise Slim had given the American general earlier that year. On 21 March, Slim categorically refused Wingate permission for his reserve 14 Brigade to be used in another role, stating that as far as he was concerned, 14 Brigade was to help Fergusson in the attack on Indaw. Unknown to Slim, however, different orders were given by Wingate to 14 Brigade's commander, Brigadier Brodie, and as a result the exhausted men under Fergusson made their abortive attack, unsupported by 14 Brigade. Not surprisingly, it ended in complete failure. The struggle for Indaw continued, with Wingate's brigadiers never really knowing what was in his mind. Certainly, his obsession about Indaw never wavered and to this end, 16 Brigade undoubtedly was committed to tasks beyond its resources and powers of endurance. It was as if Wingate wanted to prove his theories, even to the extent of risking men on the other side of the major river obstacle, the Irrawaddy, continuing with an inflexible plan that threatened to lose the whole force. What would have happened if he had lived? Would he have learnt from earlier mistakes and brought cohesion where little existed at a time when it was dearly wanted? No one can ever answer such questions, because, just after 77 Brigade had captured Mawlu, and the struggle for Indaw was going badly for Bernard Fergusson and his men, news came that Major-General Orde Wingate had been killed in an air crash in the hills near Silchar while on his way back from a visit to White City.

The death of Wingate shocked the British and sent waves of dismay through the Special Force. Not surprisingly the Japanese were openly jubilant because, for them, that controversial figure had threatened much, even if his sudden death now meant that his ambitious dreams would never be realized. Slim's tribute was generous: 'We could ill spare him at the start of his greatest adventure. The immediate sense of loss that struck, like a blow, even those who diffused most from him – and I was not one of these – was a measure of the impact he had made. He had stirred up everyone with whom he had come in contact'. When further evidence came to light after the war, showing that Wingate had been guilty of countermanding his superior's orders about the role of Brodie's Brigade, Slim changed his opinion slightly.

To attempt to sum up a man like Wingate in a few words is clearly impossible. But one thing is certain – Churchill's minute of 24 July 1943, was sadly awry: 'I consider Wingate should command the army against Burma. He is a man of genius and audacity and has rightly been discerned by all eyes as a figure quite above the ordinary level. The expression, "The Clive of Burma", has already gained currency'. If Wingate had been appointed to command 14 Army, it would have certainly led to a major disaster on the field of battle. He lacked the mental robustness of a great commander, having little in reserve when things went wrong. Wingate had a persecution complex, a contempt for professional staff officers, an inability to confide in his immediate subordinates, and was guilty of impulsive decisions, often without consulting those who were best placed to give him sound advice. Nevertheless, his sense of mission, unflinching moral courage, and fierce determination cannot be questioned. He was sometimes right and often wrong. He made all kinds of men believe in him and, equally, caused others to distrust him. Most important of all was his contribution to the technique of fighting in the jungle, his belief that troops could be maintained in enemy territory, without conventional logistic support and land communications. He taught soldiers to fight with a burning conviction, something that had been missing from the

British and Indian training methods of 1943 and early 1944. The Chindits never lost faith in Wingate and weeks later, when the ragged, exhausted survivors were finally relieved from their long ordeal, a typical comment was: 'We would be all right if he was here now'.

Wingate was dead, but the Chindits had to fight on. The selection of his successor had to be made quickly and Slim eventually chose Brigadier Joe Lentaigne, the most experienced of the Special Force brigadiers, one who was well known to him, being a fellow Gurkha officer. Later, Slim disclosed that Wingate had promised three Chindit subordinates that, in the event of his death, they would take over as commander Special Force.

Before Lentaigne could take up his new appointment, Slim had to unravel Wingate's plans and, in particular, to decide whether the brigades were to be used to cut 15 Army's communications or, as originally envisaged, to assist Stilwell's advance from the north. On 9 April a meeting between Mountbatten, Slim, and Lentaigne, finally reversed Wingate's plans and Special Force was irrevocably committed to the American and Chinese cause in Upper Burma. Much hard fighting as well as prodigious feats of physical endurance were to follow. Wingate's promise that Special Force would be on active operations for no longer than two months at a time was submerged by the needs of the moment, by the cries for help from Stilwell. In truth, it would be a mistake to think the death of their leader changed the individual circumstances of those who marched and fought in the Chindit columns after April 1944.

During the third week of March, 14 Brigade and 3 West African Brigade had been flown in, as previously arranged. The situation at the beginning of April was that 77 Brigade, strongly established at Broadway, had been making its presence felt at Mawlu by blocking the main road and rail communication to 18 Division facing Stilwell, as well as cutting the road south of Bhamo. As Calvert, their commander, said: 'We were fortunate in having a possibly more colourful role'. But 16 Brigade was not so fortunate because their clutching finger probes from all sides of Indaw were soundly defeated. The Aberdeen stronghold became the home base for Fergusson's columns as they, in turn, rested and refitted before returning to harass the Japanese west of Indaw. An unfortunate start was made by 14 British Infantry Brigade. The original orders were countermanded, changed, and then changed again several times during the first few days. The brigade marched far but achieved little. Meanwhile 111 Indian Infantry Brigade, with its columns spread far and wide, operated on more orthodox LRP principles, making raids and setting ambushes rather than making full-blooded attacks. Finally, the last of the Special Force brigades, 23 British Brigade, remained under 14 Army's control and later saw action in the fierce battles round Kohima.

The exploits of the Chindits and the encouraging gains made by Stilwell's forces, were completely overshadowed by the life-and-death struggle taking place for the Plain of Imphal. If 4 Corps had failed to hold the three Japanese divisions, then re-entry into Burma would have been postponed indefinitely, Stilwell's one major link with his supplies would have been cut, and latent unrest in India might have bubbled into open rebellion once more. While the battles raged round Imphal and Kohima, everything else was of minor importance. But captured Japanese records reveal how surprised they were by the landings – in spite of being forewarned by the LRP penetrations made the year before. It took the Japanese at least a week before they formed anything like a true assessment of the numbers that had landed in their territory. Indeed, those gliders that missed the target and crash-landed in various parts of the jungle only served to confuse the defenders even more. General Mutaguchi felt that the normal garrison units could cope with the situation, until fresh reports began to alarm him. Reserve units were rushed in haste from other parts of Burma to deal with the threat. By now, Mutaguchi appreciated that the landings might well be the start of an Anglo-American offensive, so that he was more than ever convinced that the U-Go offensive should be pressed home as being the most effective method of upsetting his opponents' overall strategy. East of the Chindwin a reserve force under the command of 15 Army was raised to conduct all operations against the airborne invasion.

To summarize: the Japanese operational strategy for the Central Assam Front and Northern Combat Area remained unchanged. But the airborne forces were undoubtedly a source of worry, being yet another burden on the overtaxed and indifferent Japanese administrative machine. After the war, Mutaguchi conceded that Stilwell's Chinese-American advance towards Mogaung and Myitkyina could not have succeeded without the intervention of the Chindits – who carried out the assignment originally agreed at Quebec, which was supported with enthusiasm by the Americans. Stilwell would never have agreed with Mutaguchi's assessment – not in public, anyway. His views on the Chindits were never favourable and became increasingly jaundiced as the summer of 1944 passed.

When the American version of the LRP, Merrill's Marauders, captured the airfield at Myitkyina on 17 May, Slim agreed that the Chindits would come under Stilwell's command but not be subject to his operational control. After 16 Brigade had flown out of Aberdeen and Broadway, the two strongholds were abandoned. In the meantime 14 Brigade remained with the West African Brigade at White City, while 77 Brigade marched northwards towards Mogaung. Although a more detailed account of Stilwell's operations is covered in the next chapter, some background is required to enable the story of the Chindits to be described. Myitkyina held out for many more weeks than Stilwell had expected. The frustrated American general berated the exhausted Chindits, claiming that they were not pulling their weight and that his orders were being flagrantly disobeyed. Lentaigne was equally furious, maintaining that Special Force had been pushed beyond the limit of endurance, that the maximum of two months on operations, without a period of relief, had now been doubled, as the fourth month began. The bitter war of words between Stilwell and Lentaigne in June led to Slim's being sent to the headquarters of NCAC in an attempt to pacify 'Vinegar Joe' and the irate Irishman, Lentaigne. A temporary peace was achieved but the trials and tribulations of the surviving Chindits did not end. The hot, wet, sticky monsoon added another unpleasant dimension to their discomfort with ill-health and sickness claiming countless victims.

The Japanese, too, did not let the Chindits have any rest. Apart from the early concerted attacks on White City, a bitter battle for Blackpool ensued, then under the command of Lieutenant-Colonel John F. Masters (later a well-known author). Eventually Blackpool fell but not until the defenders had been crippled by a lack of ammunition and a dearth of food, as well as suffering heavy casualties from the Japanese artillery and mortars. Probes by 77 Brigade towards Mogaung found that, contrary to the previous optimistic intelligence forecast, there were some 4,000 Japanese in the immediate area. The battle for Mogaung was long and fierce, and it was not until 20 June that Calvert's men were able to storm the town, while the Chinese 38 Division closed in from the north.

Subsequently, there was contention between Stilwell and Lentaigne, as well as misunderstandings with Mountbatten, as to who played the major role in the capture of Mogaung. It is extremely difficult to apportion the degree of success achieved by the Chindits and their Chinese allies; because partisan records vary considerably. 1 Battalion of the Chinese 114 Regiment played a sterling part, supported by 2 Battalion from the same regiment. Calvert, in overall control, pays them due tribute but points out that the Chinese, with good reason, had to be extremely chary about losing guns, equipment, and other combat stores. If they were lost, they could not be replaced. As a result, a general could find himself without the normal quota of fire power and organic support, and this could lead to demotion. The courage was there but the desire to survive was also strong. At Mogaung, a Chinese officer told Calvert that, 'they were there to please Stilwell' – which did not indicate that their heart was truly in the battle!

During the bitter, close-quarter fighting for Mogaung, individual feats of bravery on both sides were numerous. The VC was won by two members of B Company 3/6 GR. Captain Michael Almand, although suffering so badly from trench foot that he could barely walk, struggled alone through deep mud and charged a Japanese machine-gun post single-handed before he fell, mortally wounded. Meanwhile, Rifleman Tulbahadur Pun, accompanied by the two survivors of his section, had attacked another enemy outpost nearby. Firing a bren gun from the hip, Tulbahadur closed in on the Japanese, killing three and putting the other defenders to flight.

The courage of such men – British, Gurkha, Chinese, and Burmese – decided the unremitting struggle for Mogaung, but the Japanese more than matched their bravery with endurance and tenacity, until the extra firepower and overwhelming air superiority of the Allies won the final battle.

But 77 Brigade had shot its bolt. By now, the men looked like scarecrows, walking in torn and soggy rags. Weary, and depleted in numbers, they had played a notable part in Stilwell's campaign. So had the 111, 14 and the West African brigades. The fate of the Chindits had been inextricably bound up with the fortunes of Stilwell as the Chinese and Americans pushed towards Myitkyina. Stilwell had expected to seize the town in June, but his hopes were not fulfilled, and the agony of the Chindits continued throughout July and into August. Another posthumous VC was won by a young British officer with the Gurkhas, Captain Jim Blaker of 3/9 GR. Men of courage had never been wanting, but the days of the Chindits were numbered. They had been raised for a special role, trained and lightly equipped for guerrilla warfare, only to find themselves being used in normal operations for which they were not properly armed. The strain on officers and men was too much and was compounded by the psychological error in promising the volunteers that they would normally operate in Burma for a maximum of 90 days before being relieved to rest, and then if necessary, return for another short bout of active service.

In January 1945 Mountbatten told an assembled group of Chindit officers that Special Force was to be broken up and the battalions dispersed to other formations. The senior officers who had opposed Wingate, claiming that Special Force had been an expensive way of fighting the war, were delighted. Calvert, Tulloch, and others took a very different view and, with the benefit of hindsight, the Japanese tend to support them. For good reasons, therefore, it is fair to claim that the sacrifices of the Chindits, and the casualties they suffered, were not in vain and that they did play a significant part in 14 Army's return to Burma in 1945.

Nevertheless the decision to disband the Chindits when the tide of victory was beginning to roll inexorably forward was undoubtedly the correct one; Special Force was no longer needed at that stage of the Burma campaign.

CHAPTER 4

Stilwell returns to Upper Burma

The mission given General Stilwell in Asia was one of the most difficult of the War — General George C. Marshall

---

On 4 October 1943 the headquarters of the Chinese army in India was formed, with 22 and 38 Chinese Divisions under command, supported by 1 Provisional Tank Group and American led Levies, the Kachin Raiders. While the enthusiasm and keenness shown during training had been most impressive, the units were a mixture of raw recruits and the remains of a beaten army, and there was a marked difference in the standards of the two divisions.

Stilwell had received clear orders to push forward up the Ledo Road until it met up with the old Burma Road, which had run from Mandalay into China. The Ledo Road was started by the British in February 1942 when it was agreed that they would construct the road from Ledo through Shingbwiyang and Mogaung to Myitkyina. At the same time, the Chinese were to build from Myitkyina to their border, but the Japanese occupation of Upper Burma put paid to any construction work by the Chinese. The British found several reasons for postponing their part of the bargain. The logistical headaches alone were forbidding: a single archaic railway line, river communications that meandered by circuitous routes towards the front, both totally inadequate to meet the needs of 4 Corps around Imphal, the Chinese at Ledo, and the ever-rising tonnage required on the American airfields for the Hump operations.

All-weather roads were under construction during the autumn of 1943, from Dimapur to the central front, and from Dohazari, south of Chittagong, for 15 Corps in the Arakan. In British eyes the most important of these was that serving the main Imphal front, a road which climbed through the hills from Dimapur to Imphal, and one that was destined to become the land artery of 14 Army. Thousands of Indian labourers built these roads under the most arduous conditions of climate and terrain, using picks, shovels, and baskets. The roads they built not only had to penetrate the jungle, to cross mountain flanks and span huge rivers, but had to contend with the spate of water that descended during the monsoon season. Not surprisingly, therefore, the British viewed the Ledo Road with less than enthusiasm and produced reasons for postponing its construction. They maintained that the climate in the area was highly malarial as well as expressing deep apprehension about the engineering problems in cutting a way through the forbidding terrain between Ledo and Shingbwiyang. Fortunately for all concerned, on 10 December 1943 the Americans took over responsibility for building the road and in dynamic fashion their engineers pushed it forward until by 27 December they had reached Shingbwiyang, more than 100 miles from Ledo. It must be remembered that unlike their British counterparts, they were well stocked with modern equipment which they used with admirable vigour and to great effect. The result of their efforts was an impressive road of ambitious standards.

The driving force behind the road construction was Colonel (later General) Lewis A. Pick, called 'The man with the stick' by the Chinese as he chivvied the engineers and coolies on, stomping around with a pike in his hand. The Japanese were not caught napping. Radio Tokyo blared forth: 'The Americans will accomplish two things by building this road. In the first place they will teach the British how to build roads – a thing they have never learned – and second, the road will be finished just in time for us to use it to invade India'. The 18 Division, with victories in many battles behind it, was prepared, ready to live up to its proud designation of Ever-Victorious Corps.

To cover the construction work, 122 Chinese Regiment began the advance on 15 October 1943. A few days later at Sharaw Ga they encountered opposition for the first time and promptly dug in. Such a trend continued with the leading troops deploying and going to ground as soon as the Japanese outposts opened fire on them. It was a time for tough talking because, already, those who doubted the ability of the Chinese soldier to stand up to his Japanese enemy were openly deriding the over-cautious methods of the leading units. Stilwell's answer was to bring down the remainder of 38 Division and, after some very frank talks with the Chinese commanders, a concerted attack was launched on 28 December which dislodged the Japanese from their positions on the west bank of the Tarung Hka. The victory at Yapong proved the mettle of Stilwell's soldiers; it was, for the Japanese, a shock because they had tended to treat the Chinese with contempt. The effect on morale was of incalculable significance because China's army had not carried out any major offensive anywhere since the struggle for Shanghai. Throughout January, the three brigades from 22 Division continued to advance in the upper Mang-wan plain, while on the west flank of the Ledo Road, 65 Regiment from 38 Division moved towards the Taro plain. By the middle of February it had succeeded in clearing most of the area, except for isolated pockets of Japanese. The Kachin Levies were also in action; they operated well to the east, employing guerrilla tactics in skir-mishes round the Fort Hartz airfield. They successfully prevented the Japanese from reaching the only staging post for the C47s crossing into China, then harassed them so vigorously that they withdrew south-wards. By the middle of March the Japanese had withdrawn from that sector to the vicinity of Myitkyina. All told, Stilwell had good reason to be satisfied with the progress made during the first few weeks of 1944.

What had not gone according to Allied hopes and expectations was the move forward into Burma by the Chinese Expeditionary Force from the Yunnan. Chiang's failure to co-operate, which stemmed from his anger at Britain's inability to mount an amphibious operation in the Bay of Bengal, only served to postpone the inevitable humiliating reverse that the CEF eventually suffered: they were in poor shape and still short of vital equipment, as well as requiring more training time. Mountbatten's patience was taxed to the limit by Chiang Kai-shek's unpredictable statesmanship during this period. After a visit to Chungking he noted in his diary: 'I'm absolutely staggered that Chiang has once again rejected everything he'd recently agreed to.... I am delighted that the Prime Minister and the President and the Combined Chiefs-of-Staff have at least been given first hand experience of how impossible the Chinese are to deal with'.

Stilwell was content to concentrate on the military task in hand, leaving others to deal with Chiang and plead for promises to be fulfilled. The Generalissimo continued with his efforts to obtain more money from America, laying down terms before he would order his armies to cross the Salween River. He suggested the capture of the Andaman Islands, a seaborne assault against Rangoon or, alterna-tively, the capture of Mandalay. Wingate was sent to Chungking to explain the aims of his Special Force after Operation Thursday had begun, but Chiang's attitude had hardened to a simple statement: 'After you have completed the conquest of Burma I'm prepared to advance across the Salween but not before'. Even Wingate had to acknowledge failure, and after weeks of high level discussion, Mount-batten's far-reaching plans for 1944 had to be modified. Unless the Japanese struck first, then four smaller and less dramatic operations remained on the drawing board: Stilwell's drive towards Myitkyina,

Wingate's *coup de main* in the Indaw area, a limited advance in the Arakan by 15 Corps, and a modest offensive up to the Chindwin by 4 Corps on the central front.

Mountbatten did not find Stilwell easy to handle although the personal relationship between the two men was surprisingly good, taking into consideration the difference in age, background, temperament, and experience. Stilwell's comment on the young Supreme Commander's charm and persuasiveness was reported to be: 'Yes. That's what makes him so dangerous. Even I like him'. Mountbatten's tact, diplomacy and patience were stretched to the limit by Stilwell's erratic behaviour. At a heated conference held in Delhi on 31 January, Vinegar Joe, living up to his nickname, objected to the British proposal that the shortest, quickest way to defeat Japan was via Sumatra and Malaya rather than through Burma – which would raise the land blockade of China. At the conference it was decided that a SEAC deputation would be sent to explain the alternative proposals to the Combined Chiefs-of-Staff, the mission being headed by General Wedemeyer, an American who held the post of Deputy Chief-of-Staff under Mountbatten. Although Stilwell had been promised that his arguments would be represented by the mission, he took no notice and without informing the Supreme Commander that he had done so, sent his own representatives to Washington. By this piece of devious disloyalty he was able to influence his American superiors, sowing seeds of doubt and filling the Americans with alarm at Mountbatten's amphibious concept. Not surprisingly Mountbatten was very upset and signalled his displeasure to Washington: 'I regret that General Stilwell should have made representations in Washington without reference to me before General Wedemeyer had had the opportunity of presenting my proposals'.

Allied unity, although strained by the incident, was to have worse moments of dissension to face before the war was to end.

Mountbatten had never shared Stilwell's optimism that Myitkyina would be captured before the monsoon broke in May. On the other hand, the Chiefs-of-Staff were inclined to accept Stilwell's forecast that an overland route to China via Upper Burma could be opened with reasonable speed and asked Mountbatten to extend the scope of the air operations by increasing the tonnage flown over the Hump to China. Priority, too, was to be given to faster construction of the Ledo Road, first to Myitkyina and thence to Kunning in the wake of advances made by the American-Chinese forces.

Although Mountbatten, showing immense patience, avoided a showdown with the difficult Stilwell, the personal antipathy that had existed between Giffard and the American from their first meeting continued to bedevil command arrangements. A firm measure of co-ordination by land and air was essential; no longer could Northern Area Command move forward into Upper Burma in a vacuum, especially when it was envisaged that Wingate's Special Force would be operating behind the Japanese 18 Division's forward positions. Once again, Mountbatten recommended that Stilwell should come under Giffard's command. That proposal was tetchily turned down by his Deputy. Deadlock appeared to be inevitable until Stilwell himself made a face-saving concession, saying that: 'I am prepared to come under General Slim's operational control until I get to Kamaing'. As a solution it was far from ideal but it was preferable to any attempt at persuading Giffard and Stilwell to work together. Adversity would have strained and broken such an unhappy partnership. It was also another sign of Stilwell's respect for Slim, an admiration that began during the retreat when he noted, 'Good old Slim. Maybe he's all right after all'. In his eyes, Slim was one of the few British generals who relished a fight, and his feelings were reciprocated by the younger man – in spite of the fact that Stilwell never made any attempt to hide his deep distrust of 'limeys'.

Having won a tactical victory at the conference table in Delhi, Stilwell returned to his headquarters to see how his 32,000 Chinese troops were faring. On 9 February Force Galahad came into the picture for the first time, the code name for the unit with the official title of 5307 Composite Unit (Provisional). A war correspondent felt that the full military title was uninspiring and invented a bombastic nickname, Merrill's Marauders. In fact, Brigadier-General Frank D. Merrill commanded the Marauders only at intervals: the actual commander for most of the formation's time in Burma was a most able soldier, Colonel Charles Hunter. The Composite Unit consisted of three large battalions, each divided on the Chindit pattern into two combat teams. Like the Special Force, the Marauders were not organized to fight pitched battles or to hold ground, although as the weeks passed in 1944 they had to do both on many occasions. They were all volunteers who had been toughened by the same type of training as the Chindits had undergone. Stilwell had waited a long time for the only ground-force US combat unit in South East Asia to arrive and the last thing he was going to do was let them fight under a British general. Moreover Wingate was another person he disliked, partly because he distrusted the long-range penetration tactics – 'shadow boxing' he called them. After Colonel Hunter had organized and trained the unit, Stilwell immediately downgraded him to second-in-command and promoted one of his own staff, Merrill, to command with the rank of brigadier-general. Merrill's name went down in history, but the man who led by example, who held the force together in times of adversity to the bitter end, was Hunter. As will be seen, he was to receive scant justice, a hero who received a villain's reward.

Stilwell's method of using the Marauders was to send them off in flanking moves through the jungle, to bear down upon the Japanese rear while his Chinese units closed with the enemy frontally. His operational plan was simple and clear-cut – so was his mission for 1944. 'Clearance of the Japanese from the Hukawng and Mogaung valleys, leading to the capture of Myitkyina so that the US engineers could build a new road via Myitkyina on to China'. To achieve that mission the Chinese drove down the Hukawng valley with the American-led tank regiment in the van while the Marauders moved round the east flank to set up road blocks, behind the Japanese 5628 Regiment, in the neighbourhood of Walawbum. A spirited action followed, with the Chinese 22 and 38 Divisions together fighting their way into Walawbum on 7 March. Before that, the Japanese had made furious efforts to dislodge the Americans who, in a series of small, fierce actions, showed that the Marauders were fighters, well capable of dealing with their experienced opponents from the veteran 18 Division. On the command of General Tanaka, the Japanese broke off the battle and slipped away to the south.

The advance continued. On 15 March 22 Division occupied Tingkawk Sakan and four days later reached the pass between the Hukawng and Mogaung valleys. The first part of Stilwell's plan had been completed. Having cleared the Hukawng valley, elaborate plans were drawn up to eject 18 Division from the Mogaung valley. The manoeuvre did not meet with any marked success, chiefly because the two hook movements were carried out by Marauder battalions in the lead, followed by Chinese regiments. Such an arrangement led to problems of command with misunderstandings caused by political and linguistic difficulties. The inner short hook went according to schedule with 1 Battalion setting up a road block before handing over as planned to 113 Chinese Regiment. Meanwhile, Hunter, at the head of the remainder carrying out the long sweeping movement, had made reasonable progress bearing in mind that he and his men had to move through rugged mountains covered with dense forest, some of them as high as 5,000 feet. On 20 March Hunter was within five miles of his target, Kamaing, and sought permission to take it by a surprise assault, even though the Chinese were not near enough to give them any direct or immediate support. Merrill and Stilwell would not approve. In that instance their caution was wise, because unknown to them, the situation had changed radically. The Japanese had decided to make a counter-thrust.

A strong body of Japanese, after making a wide flanking movement to the east, were moving northwards in strength. Although 2 and 3 Battalions of Force Galahad had established a road block at Inkangahtawng, the town was too strongly held to be taken. Now the tables were turned. Three Japanese battalions were moving northwards to outflank the Americans. The Marauders were told to pull back from the Kamaing road and move eastwards in an attempt to intercept the Japanese. Thereafter a period of confused fighting followed. The position of 2 Battalion was on the key Nhpum Ga ridge, blocking the route selected by the Japanese counter-offensive force. Three miles to the rear of the ridge lay more than 100 sick and wounded Marauders, waiting to be evacuated from a newly constructed airstrip, so it was vital that 2 Battalion should hold fast until relief came. The defenders were bunched in a small, tight perimeter and had dug themselves in securely before 1,300 Japanese launched their first assault on 29 March and for ten long days and nights threw themselves at the position in vain. The courage shown by both sides was exceptional. The dwindling band of Americans stood firm against suicidal swarms of Japanese who scrambled up the steep slopes in an attempt to overcome their opponents by sheer weight of numbers. Meanwhile, 3 Battalion under Hunter's determined leadership, headed the remainder of the force in an attempt to relieve the position, fighting their way forward under cover of close air and artillery support, to eventually win through on 7 April. Force Galahad had been badly mauled during the fierce encounter. In the top executive post was another casualty: Merrill had a slight heart attack and, once again, had to hand over to Hunter. Unfortunately, Stilwell never realized what the operation had cost the Marauders. He recorded in his diary: 'Galahad is okay. Hard fight at Nhpum. Cleaned up Japs and hooked up. No worry there'. He could not have been more mistaken. The Marauders' effective strength had dropped from 3,000 to 1,400. The survivors were utterly exhausted, half starved, with many suffering from dysentery and malaria. The GIs had anticipated a period of rest and relief from operations but hopes were to be dashed immediately when it was learnt that they were about to move off on an even more ambitious venture. This time they were to move far, fast, and wide, to cross over 6,000ft mountains, emerge from the jungle and seize the vital airfield about three miles from Myitkyina. It was a daring and reckless enterprise, one that required fit, healthy soldiers.

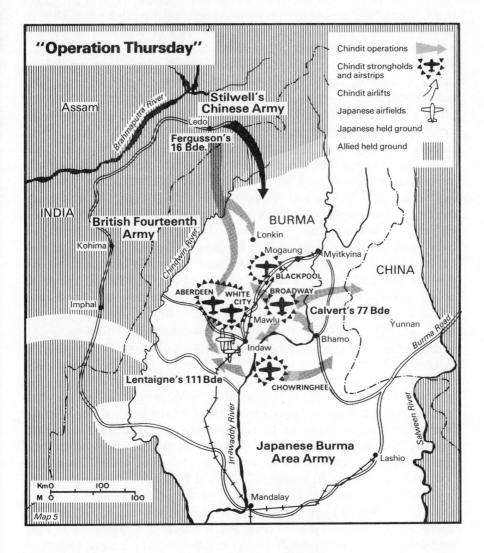

"Operation Thursday"

| Chindit operations |
| Chindit strongholds and airstrips |
| Chindit airlifts |
| Japanese airfields |
| Japanese held ground |
| Allied held ground |

Assam

Brahmaputra River

Stilwell's Chinese Army

Ledo

Fergusson's 16 Bde.

INDIA

Chindwin River

British Fourteenth Army

Kohima

Imphal

BURMA

Lonkin

Mogaung

Myitkyina

CHINA

BLACKPOOL

ABERDEEN

WHITE CITY

BROADWAY

Calvert's 77 Bde

Mawlu

Ýunnan

Indaw

Bhamo

Burma Road

Lentaigne's 111 Bde

CHOWRINGHEE

Irrawaddy River

Salween River

Japanese Burma Area Army

Lashio

Km 0 — 100
M 0 — 100

Mandalay

Map 5

Stilwell's driving, tireless energy was admirable but his man management could be appalling. Although he boasted that he was only a simple infantryman, he had strange blind-spots about the normal reactions of fighting men, irrespective of whether they were Chinese, British, or American. When Merrill's Marauders first arrived at the Ledo front after a long weary march from Assam, Stilwell did not bother to go out on the road to see them pass although he was nearby. Again, before the hazardous mission to seize the airfield at Myitkyina began, a visit from Vinegar Joe would have paid dividends; a short speech of praise, a few handshakes, and possibly the presentation of some well earned immediate awards for gallantry, would have sent the soldiers off in a different spirit. When his diary was published after Stilwell's death, a consistent pattern of childish disparagement revealed an inferiority complex of quite frightening dimensions. His staff, who were scared of his blistering tongue, tended to give him favourable news, and were ready to blow up anything that would fan his anti-British feelings. In the end they did their elderly commander a grave disservice by not keeping him in the picture. For example, when Calvert, Commander of 77 Brigade, visited Stilwell after the bitter fighting at Mogaung had ended, he found that the General had not realized that the Chindit Brigade had been constantly in action for four months, nor had he ever accepted reports about their heavy casualties as being true. His staff had told him about the failures and defeats but had concealed 77 Brigade's victories from him. On hearing the real facts, Stilwell belatedly showed a magnanimity that he was not to extend to his own countrymen – the survivors of Merrill's Marauders. Without knowing how near they were to exhaustion, he sent the Marauders off to seize the airfield near Myitkyina.

Under Hunter's inspired leadership, the Marauders set off on what was to prove a killing march, carried out while the heavy monsoon rain poured down upon them. The real struggle was against disease and fatigue, with malaria, amoebic dysentery and typhus claiming victims among the men, while half the pack animals died of sheer exhaustion. Somehow they made it, and on 17 May the first column emerged from the jungle to seize the airfield. But 150 Regiment, from the newly arrived 50 Chinese Division which had been flown into Assam for this operation, then displayed its complete inexperience. Some units mistook others from their own division for Japanese; there were a number of clashes during which regrettably heavy casualties were suffered, and this quickly led to a severe demoralization of the unblooded troops. Valuable time was wasted and during the resultant delay and disorganization, the Japanese force, consisting of nearly 5,000 men, dug in around and within the town, and prepared to offer savage resistance.

When he heard that the airfield had been captured, Stilwell, not unnaturally, was overjoyed – as he had every right to be. In spite of open discouragement and doubts expressed by his British allies, he had inflicted a startling, resounding defeat on the Japanese. He made the most of it. Accompanied by a handful of American war correspondents, he flew to Myitkyina airstrip, there to broadcast the news to the world. In his diary that night he wrote the oft-quoted words: 'Will this burn up the limeys!!'; printing the words in giant capitals. Stilwell exulted, but away in London, Winston Churchill was writing an angry note to the CIGS, enquiring why the Americans had liberated the first town in 'British Burma'. His irritation was understandable but it does show the desire to reconquer Burma was not based on strategic requirements only: British pride demanded that revenge should be exacted on the conquerors of Burma.

Japanese attention had been diverted from Myitkyina airstrip by their deep concern about the drive towards the key centre, Kamaing. The Chinese had made slow but steady progress during May and by 3 June, 65 Regiment from 22 Division, had set up a road block in the vicinity of Lachi, while 112 Regiment succeeded in cutting the Mogaung-Kamaing road. The Japanese garrison in the town was thus isolated. Although frantic efforts were made to succour the garrison, eventually heavy superiority in numbers enabled the Chinese to take the town. From there attention was switched to Mogaung where, as mentioned in the previous chapter, Calvert's 77 Brigade had marched northwards to come under Stilwell's overall control. The Chindits were pushed beyond the limit of endurance because Stilwell gave them no respite, nor did he ever send them a single message of encouragement. They did not actually mutiny, but they came very near to it. The unfortunate fact was that Stilwell had become a prisoner of his own publicity machine. He had promised that Myitkyina would be captured before mid-summer was over and whatever the cost might be, he was not going to eat his words.

The Marauders had captured an outlying airfield by a *coup de main* but the fortified town nearby which the Chinese and Americans had to invest was a very different proposition. The Japanese were determined to fight to the death and had converted Myitkyina into a series of strongpoints, with one flank of the town being protected by the Irrawaddy River. The garrison commander, Major-General Mizukami, had four 75mm guns, with mortars and heavy machine guns to support his garrison of some 4,500 men. To take such a position,

Stilwell badly needed fresh troops, adequately equipped with normal organic fire power and supporting artillery, all employed in a major co-ordinated attack, instead of the series of piecemeal efforts made throughout June and July. Those were repulsed with contemptuous skill by the Japanese defenders. During that stalemate Stilwell was seen at his worst, asking the Chindits to do the impossible, using two US engineer battalions in an infantry role without any special training, and refusing to release or relieve the three skeleton battalions of the original Marauders. Banal measures were even taken to comb hospitals, seeking out wounded or sick Marauders who were just fit enough to return to active duty, provided that they could stand or hold a weapon. American doctors vented their anger, and eventually the swell of discontent provided ammunition for the scandal which was about to break.

Mogaung finally fell to 77 Brigade, after which the brigade had to be relieved, although it was to take angry words from Lentaigne and a final confrontation between Calvert and Stilwell before the exhausted Chindits were allowed to return to India. Meanwhile at Myitkyina the Chinese divisions, disheartened by the courageous resistance put up by the resolute defenders, often preferred to remain in their foxholes and to fire volleys of bullets at their opponents' positions rather than risk a more dangerous confrontation at close quarters. Such tactics, patiently wearing down their adversary, biding their time until they felt the objective was ripe for the taking, had been a traditional Chinese way of waging war for centuries past. And so the long slogging match went on during June and July, while Morris Force, detached from Special Force, harassed the Japanese from the opposite side of the river. The fanatical defenders held on although their last land link with the outside world had been cut. Early in August raiding parties filtered through to the rear of the town to herald a concentrated attack from all sides which inexorably reduced the Japanese defences to rubble. On 3 August General Mizukami committed suicide, Stilwell became a 4-star General, and Myitkyina fell. One of the most stirring Japanese defences of the whole war had ended. Against impossible odds of ten to one, Myitkyina had been held for 79 days, an amazing feat of arms that has not been given the recognition it deserves. The casualties on both sides were heavy. Some 6,000 Japanese managed to escape and to cross the Irrawaddy, leaving behind 4,000, consisting of dead and wounded. Those who were captured had been wounded or were so ill that they could not fight – or even hobble to escape. The Chinese lost 4,300 while the American losses totalled 2,200.

The Marauders, however, had not remained as part of the task force that eventually captured Myitkyina. Like the Chindits, they had suffered from the continuous stress of climate, active service, and disease, having fought in pitched battles for which they were not properly equipped, and lacking the necessary organic supporting weapons. They, too, had been given to understand that their tours of active duty would be short and sharp, moving back for rest periods, then returning for another spell at the sharp end. The morale and discipline of the Marauders in the front line, in hospitals, and in rest camps broke down. Long before Myitkyina fell, the local commander, Brigadier-General Boatner, had to send a signal to Stilwell, 'US troops are shaky'. Stilwell did not share his view and said so. Shortly afterwards, the dejected men had to be withdrawn from the battle and when the final act came, the Chinese had the satisfaction of winning the day virtually on their own. The fine record of the Marauders, one that had been won by courage and self-sacrifice, by leadership and determination, must not be forgotten. Unfortunately, when the decision was made to disband 5307 Composite Unit, it led to much bitterness, backbiting, and unwelcome publicity. Hunter, who had held the men together through many trials and tribulations, who had never been afraid to stand up for his GIs' rights against Stilwell, was sent back to the US, summarily relieved of his command. An official enquiry followed, to bring to an end a sorry story of a gallant unit.

Stilwell's prestige was at its highest when the airstrip at Myitkyina was seized in May. That dramatic victory gained him world-wide publicity. His sweet hour of success then turned sour. The siege of the town dragged on, week after week, until events elsewhere in Burma made its final capture almost an anti-climax. By the time it fell the much maligned British had won the most decisive battle of the whole Burma campaign, that which had raged around Imphal. Thereafter the exploits of NCAC had less and less significance as Slim prepared for the final re-entry into Burma. Stilwell reluctantly accepted the British 36 Division in place of the Chindits and their example in battle was to be a stirring one for the Chinese when the next stage of the operations began. Meanwhile, in China itself, the overall position was beginning to look black. Japanese divisions were grouping, prior to beginning an offensive which was intended to overrun and destroy the newly constructed advance airfields – those used by Chennault's 14th Air Force – with the giant base at Kunning as their main target. Stilwell's forecast had been right and Chennault's optimism disproved. The importance of China as an ally had decreased, although Roosevelt and the US government continued to accept moral responsibility for the survival of the Chiang Kai-shek dynasty.

With the situation in China deteriorating, Chiang had lost interest in the campaign in Upper Burma and his relations with Stilwell worsened throughout September. Roosevelt tried to save Stilwell by stalling but in the end had to yield to the Generalissimo's firm demand that Vinegar Joe be recalled. The tired, embittered Stilwell went back to the US on 18 October, to be replaced by three American generals. Sultan took over NCAC, Wedemeyer left Delhi and went to Chungking as the Generalissimo's adviser, while Wheeler became Deputy Supreme Commander under Mountbatten. These generals were temperamentally far removed from the crusty Stilwell, all having proved that they could work amicably and efficiently in Allied headquarters. In effect, the dismissal of Stilwell was an admission by the Allies that there was no longer any urgent operational reason to supply China by an overland route. Ironically, when the road was eventually opened, its importance had become minimal. Only two complete convoys were to pass over it before the atom bomb persuaded the Japanese to surrender, and the need for the road disappeared.

Much has been written about Stilwell already and there is little more to add. Slim's view was, 'He was a first-class battle leader up to, I should say, corps level, an excellent tactician but a poor administrator'. As far as inter-allied relations were concerned, he was an unmitigated disaster. Testily pugnacious, he felt it necessary to tell the world, over and over again, that he was a simple soldier who could rough it without the necessary functional trappings of a headquarters and an efficient staff to support him. As it was, he was ill-served by one or two sycophantic staff officers who did not help the troops they were supposed to be controlling and administering on behalf of their superior general. Like other strong personalities – and he was one – his reputation and his place in history suffered badly when his diary jottings were published some years after his death under the title of *The Stilwell Papers*. The bitter comments and often cruel remarks, written down at the end of a tiring day, should have been edited out rather than left for the jibes of posterity. The unattractive side of Joe Stilwell has been remembered; the good 'has been interred with his bones'.

General Joseph Stilwell died in 1946, completely worn out by the way he had driven his thin, spare body during three years of campaigning in Burma. He had delighted in an exhibition of rough living, continually fostering the idea of the rough, down-to-earth, fighting general. In the end, nature caught up with him and hours of working under candlelight in badly organized command-posts left him half blind as well as a thoroughly disillusioned old man. Nevertheless the

Burma campaign without Stilwell – Wingate too, for that matter – would have been a very different one. For all his faults, Vinegar Joe never ceased to be a fighter. And for that we must salute him.

CHAPTER 5

The prologue – Ha-Go

Courage is like love, it must have hope for nourishment —
Napoleon Bonaparte

As 1944 opened, the Japanese continued with their plans for a counter-offensive from Burma which was to strike at their foes before it was too late. Their position was gradually becoming a dangerous one: it was obvious that large forces were preparing to advance against them from four divergent points. From the north the Chinese divisions, newly re-equipped, were waiting for the Generalissimo to give the order to move from the Yunnan; in the central sector stood 4 Corps which had been reinforced, openly preparing to go on to the attack from Imphal; Wingate's Special Force had been trained to fever pitch for another incursion; and to the south the British had never abandoned their plans to recapture the Arakan and Akyab. At such a time of crisis the Japanese High Command took a brave and optimistic decision. Their march on India was intended to forestall these attacks and to throw into disorder the aggressive plans being made by the Anglo-American commanders. In support of their diversions, 15 Army decided to deploy units of the Indian National Army.

The Japanese had formally recognized the Indian National Army at an inauguration ceremony held in Singapore during February 1942. The response was disappointing even though at that time Japan could rightly claim to be the patron of Free Asia. The arrival of Subhas Chandra Bose changed the situation; he was the obvious choice to spearhead and inspire a movement to liberate India from British rule. Bose was a Bengali who, like many of the pre-war Congress leaders, had been educated at Cambridge before entering the Indian Civil Service. A figure known throughout India, he had been president of the All-India Congress in 1938 and later became a successful mayor of Calcutta. Spurred on by the powerful emotional forces of Bengali nationalism, Bose lost patience with Gandhi's 'non-violence' campaign and this led to his imprisonment after the outbreak of war. A dramatic escape, followed by a daring journey from India through Afghanistan and eventually into Germany, where he was lionized and feted by the Nazis, ensured that he became a hero back in his native Bengal. In Germany, Bose's efforts to raise volunteers from the Indian prisoners captured in North Africa did not meet with much success, but when Japan entered the war he was quick to offer his services to the Japanese. He volunteered to be the leader who could organize a free India movement.

A very large number of the 115,000 Allied soldiers who surrendered during the Malayan campaign were Indians. The Japanese had much to offer the Indian captives – immediate freedom, reasonable wages, the resumption of their military careers and, possibly the biggest bait of all, exemption from the cruel forced labour squads for which the Japanese had already become notorious. If the initial response was poor it was simply because the Japanese themselves had a deep-seated contempt for all prisoners-of-war and even more for captives who were willing to be unfaithful to their original oath of service. Such disloyalty struck them as being so contemptible that they were unable to hide their feelings: they judged the prisoners by the same exacting standards they applied to their own soldiers – whatever the circumstances, in defeat as well as in victory.

Bose spent 13 weeks in first a German and then a Japanese submarine, before he reached Tokyo. He threw himself into the recruiting campaign with unbridled enthusiasm and on 23 October 1943 the provisional government of Free India (Azad Hind) was set up in Singapore, with Subhas Chandra Bose at its head. Nevertheless and in spite of his eloquent pleas, Bose did not succeed in persuading Japan to recognize a fully fledged government in exile. Like Ba Maw and the Burma nationalists, Bose found that the Japanese army did not relish working with opinionated, exiled governments and, as a prerequisite, waited to see what the INA could achieve in battle. As a result, units of the Indian National Army were included in their plans for offensives in Arakan and against Imphal. Bose and his provisional government were duly transferred to Burma in January 1944. Up to that point Bose had done well but thereafter his sense of reality deserted him. A slogan, 'Chalo Dehli' (on to Delhi) was proclaimed – he foresaw his army swelling in numbers, growing in strength supported by a popular upsurge in India that would enable him to dictate terms to the surrendering British. He had genuine doubts about what might happen if the Japanese Army invaded India, arguing that the invaders would bring the mass of the people solidly behind the British cause; in contrast, the appearance on Indian soil of an Indian army of liberation should have a rousing effect throughout the vast country. The world outside would hear for the first time about India's own National Army and thousands of young 'patriots' would rush to join it.

The Japanese took a cooler and much more realistic view about Bose and his ambitions. They had wanted to divide the INA into units of 250 men each, to act as liaison troops, guides, and intelligence agents, attached to a specific Japanese formation. In the end by dint of Bose's stubborn pleading, a compromise was attained. There were to be three organized divisions in the main invading force, each of about 2,000 men, while the remainder of the INA moved as auxiliaries. In effect, the Japanese army had reserved for itself the right of gaining the first major victory on Indian soil, a victory that was dearly needed because the war was going badly for them on other fronts in the Pacific. The INA's part in the Japanese diversion against 15 Corps in the Arakan was to be confined to propaganda only, to make known their presence and extract the maximum publicity from their first taste of action. Bose hoped that his main force would reap rich rewards when the U-Go phase began in mid-March.

After the British attempt in 1943 to drive the Japanese out of the Arakan had ended in failure, with early high hopes destroyed by reverses, it was perhaps surprising that plans for a second offensive were finalized towards the end of the same year. It was ideal country for defensive operations with the coast cut up into islands by muddy tidal rivers, with the hills and steep valleys covered in dense jungle, with few tracks and torrential rain falling during the monsoon season: for many reasons it was not the battlefield that a commander would choose unless he had the ability and means to launch amphibious operations, designed to unsettle or cut off tenacious defenders. No longer had Mountbatten the necessary landing craft to carry out such operations, so that the only other alternative, an overland offensive, was decided upon once more. In reality, the British offensive had defensive undertones because it was appreciated that the Japanese, from a base in the Mayu Hills, were in a position to threaten the port and airfield of Chittagong – and then from the Chittagong runways, key dock installations in the huge city of Calcutta would be well within bombing range. As a consequence, and in spite of the forbidding terrain with its meagre communications, Lieutenant General A. F. P. Christison, Commander 15 Corps, was given the task of clearing the Japanese forces out of the Arakan, and if all went well, to follow up with the capture of Akyab.

The Mayu Peninsula is bisected by a crested-spine of hills, the Mayu Range, with steep jungle slopes rising to 2,500 feet in several places. Crossing from east to west could be effected by three passes only: The Goppe and Ngakyedauk Passes were fit for mules and pack animals, while the Tunnels Road was suitable for mechanical transport. This, the key pass, connected the port of Maungdaw in the west with Buthidaung on the tidal Mayu River in the east. A road had been built, following the alignment of a narrow-gauge railway which crossed under the range by means of two short tunnels. Sixteen miles in length, the road was the line on which the Japanese, under Lieutenant-General Hanaya, sited and constructed their main defences, calling the area the Golden Fortress.

Christison began his advance using 5 Division under Major-General Briggs in the west and 7 Division under Major-General Messervy to the east of the Mayu Ridge. Christison's primary objective was to assault and destroy the Japanese concentration of troops in and around the Golden Fortress. Farther to the east, 81 West African Division had begun moving up the Kaladan valley on a pack-pony, mule basis.

British, Indian, and West African soldiers began to advance in a mood of cautious optimism built up during months of hard, realistic training in the province of Bihar. During the first few days, 15 Corps met with only token resistance, and by the New Year of 1944 Christison was poised to begin the first phase – a direct assault against the western end of the Golden Fortress, Razabil, just south of Maungdaw. Although it was a small port, Maungdaw was an important objective because its harbour was badly needed if the momentum of the operation were to continue. Without it, 15 Corps had to rely on a single supply line, the road that ran along the west following the coastal plain below the Mayu Range. While 5 Division had been ordered to take Razabil, 7 Division was to move in behind the buttress and seize Buthidaung. Closely co-ordinated with these attacks, 81 Division's task was to advance along the Kaladan River to cut the Japanese main line of communication – the road connecting Kanzauk and Htizweewe. Early tentative probes and light skirmishes continued until 161 Brigade (5 Division) met determined opposition near Razabil.

The Japanese there held firm and valuable time was lost, and although heavy air and artillery bombardment, combined with support from the Corps armoured unit (25 Dragoons), was used to full effect, little progress was made. For three days abortive assaults went in against the Japanese positions dug deep and sited in a series of low, steep hillocks under the keep of the fortress, soon to be known as the Tortoise. The small battered port of Maungdaw was taken but the Tortoise defences held out; pounded and bombed by the RAF, the Japanese did not waver. Even when some of their posts were taken, a few courageous defenders refused to give ground, fighting with fanatical fury against heavy odds.

Christison had reason to believe that his Corps still had local superiority over the Japanese. At the onset, his opponents were thought to have two divisions in the Arakan sector, 54 and 55. Gradually, intelligence provided the information that a new army headquarters, under Lieutenant-General Tadashi Hanaya, had arrived to take over operational control, while at the same time the first sounds of trumpeting slogans were heard from the INA. Slim, making one of his periodical visits to the Arakan, now agreed with Christison that a Japanese counter-stroke was more than a possibility.

For the moment Christison had to call a halt to the attack against the Razabil defences. Casualties had been heavy with, for example, an Indian battalion, the 4/7 Rajputs, losing 27 killed and 129 wounded. The weight of the offensive was switched to 7 Division's front. The tanks of 25 Dragoons, which had been most effective during the attack against Razabil, were moved over the Ngakyadauk Pass, which by then was capable of taking heavy vehicles as a result of magnificent work by the engineers. The sappers' efforts were immortalized when the British soldiers renamed the vital road, the 'Okey-Doke Pass'. The large-scale redeployment also involved the setting up of an administrative area near Sinzweya: grouped together were petrol and ammunition dumps, ration stores, medical supplies, and a hospital. Defence of the whole area was entrusted to a light anti-aircraft/anti-tank regiment, because the main threat was expected to come from the Japanese air force in hit and run raids.

By 3 February redeployment was almost complete, with the date for the second phase of the offensive being fixed for 7 February. As yet there was no firm indication of what the Japanese intended, although captured documents certainly revealed that a Japanese-Indian force had been concentrated for a major operation. Realizing that an attempt to outflank 15 Corps was a distinct possibility, Christison warned 5 and 7 Indian Divisions that they must be prepared to hold their ground against attacks from any direction, while 26 Division at Chittagong was placed at Scoones's disposal as corps reserve. Meanwhile, unimpressed by the fact that he was outnumbered, Lieutenant-General Hanaya decided to strike first.

The Japanese offensive in Arakan – code name Ha-Go – was to be a diversionary thrust to pin down 15 Corps and draw off British and Indian reserves from the main central front around Imphal. In executive command for Ha-Go was Major-General Sakurai (Commander 55 Divisional Group). Under his command there was a body of approximately 8,000 men, divided into three striking forces. The main one was led by Colonel Tanahashi who had already gained an impressive reputation by his leadership during the previous Arakan campaign. Tanahashi led his own 112 Infantry Regiment, supported by artillery and an engineer group: their task was to infiltrate through the advance posts of 7 Division, which were strung out along the eastern bank of the Kalapanzin. Then having wheeled to the left, the plan was to exterminate the bulk of the trapped 7 Division. It was an ideal moment to strike at opponents who were off balance, busily redeploying into jumping-off positions from where they could begin their own attacks.

The second column, consisting of only one battalion under Colonel Tai Kobe, was to march rapidly northwards, then wheel left near the Goppe Pass to cross the Mayu Range, and thereafter establish a road block astride the vital life line of 5 Division – the road between Bazar and Maungdaw. Finally, to pin down the forward troops while these ambitious movements were being performed, Colonel Doi was given a force consisting of two battalions which were to mount a series of holding attacks along the whole front. Such a bold plan had received the blessing of the Commander 15 Army, Lieutenant-General Mutaguchi. Unlike some senior British officers, Mutaguchi had been considerably impressed by Wingate's Loincloth operations of the previous year: now he decided to return the compliment with ambitious long-range penetrations behind 15 Corps. However, it is doubtful whether Mutaguchi ever accepted the optimistic predictions of Bose who had forecast that the INA would be received as liberators, heralding a rebellion in India – which if it had come to pass, would have been a major setback to Anglo-American hopes in Asia.

The Japanese had, in Sakurai and Tanahashi, selected ideal commanders to lead such a bold enterprise. Confronted by at least two British-Indian divisions, their soldiers set out with provisions for seven days only. Sakurai intended that his men should live off the spoils of war, and had even planned to use British weapons and vehicles as soon as these had been captured. Such a plan was based on the assumption that his opponents would not stand firm after being surrounded: moreover it failed to take into consideration the overwhelming air superiority enjoyed by the Allies, as well as underestimating the new spirit inculcated into their soldiers by the vigorous training carried out after the 1943 fiasco in the Arakan.

Tanahashi and his column, relying on surprise, set out from Kindaung just before midnight on 3 February. An amazing risk was taken when, 16 men abreast and accompanied by their mules, 112 Regiment

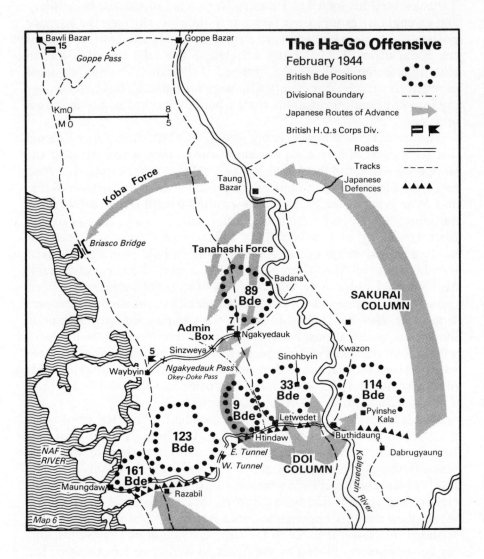

The Ha-Go Offensive

February 1944

British Bde Positions

Divisional Boundary

Japanese Routes of Advance

British H.Q.s Corps Div.

Roads

Tracks

Japanese Defences

Bawli Bazar
15
Goppe Pass
Goppe Bazar

Km 0   8
M 0   5

Koba Force

Taung Bazar

Briasco Bridge

Tanahashi Force

Badana

SAKURAI COLUMN

89 Bde

7
Admin Box
Ngakyedauk

Kwazon

5   Sinzweya
Waybyin

Ngakyedauk Pass
Okey-Doke Pass

Sinohbyin

33 Bde

114 Bde

Pyinshe Kala

9 Bde

123 Bde

Letwedet

Buthidaung

NAF RIVER

Htindaw

DOI COLUMN

Dabrugyaung

161 Bde

E. Tunnel
W. Tunnel

Maungdaw

Razabil

Kalapanzin River

Map 6

moved down a narrow valley, fully aware that units of 114 Brigade (7 Division) were in position on the ridges on either side. Heavy mist blanketed and muffled the sound while the night was dark and moonless. Nevertheless, sounds of movement were duly reported by brigade headquarters but it was assumed that the noise had come from an Indian supply column moving up during the night. At first light the few troops stationed at Tong Bazar were wiped out after a quick, surprise attack by the Japanese. The first blow had been struck. An air of euphoria was noticeable in 15 Army headquarters, which led Tokyo Radio to announce a string of victories according to a pre-planned timetable – and it continued to do so, irrespective of what was actually occurring in the Arakan jungles and swamps. Early in the morning strong frontal attacks were launched by Doi Force which enabled Tanahashi and his men to cross over to the west bank of the Kalapanzin River and, after some indecisive skirmishes with the divisional reserve (89 Brigade), the Japanese reached the Okey-Doke Pass by 7 February. Meanwhile Kobe Force debouched on the coastal road to overrun two administrative units near the Briasco bridge. Kobe's early success was soon nullified by a strong counter-attack that sent his small party reeling back into the foothills. With only a weak battalion he could not hold captured ground and the vital road was reopened, even though convoys were often under direct fire. Meanwhile, Tanahashi was now firmly astride the Okey-Doke Pass and had succeeded in severing all links between 5 and 7 Divisions.

Sakurai and his soldiers had done well, but the long-term value of their infiltrations depended on their opponents' retiring as soon as land links to the rear were threatened. This did not happen. In 7 Division area the three brigades, 33, 89, and 114, were ordered to dig in and hold firm within their localities. Pre-planned arrangements for supplies by air were set in motion. Everything that the brigades required, from medicine to weapons, from rations to clothing, had been pre-packed and was now flown to the 'boxes'. In spite of some early spasmodic interception by Japanese fighters, the daily volume of supplies delivered by air continued to increase: during the course of the battle more than 700 sorties were flown, with some 2,300 tons of supplies being air-dropped. Even so, the strain on the air forces was severe and Mountbatten had to seek the American government's permission before he was able to use some of the C47s, normally employed on ferrying stores to China over the Hump route, to augment the RAF in their supply-dropping missions. The air supply organization of 14 Army became more and more efficient as lessons were learnt and new techniques devised, after operational experience had been gained.

But without the complete air superiority won by the fighter aircraft of the RAF, none of this would have been possible nor could the 'boxes' have been held for very long.

From the start Christison had appreciated the vital importance of retaining his administrative area at Sinzweya, the title of which was to be changed by the Press to the Admin Box. While 26 Indian Division moved from army reserve at Chittagong, Christison also ordered 5 Division to send 9 Brigade, under its commander Brigadier Geoffrey Evans, to move immediately to the Box and hold it to the bitter end. The area selected, although an ideal place for an administrative base, was particularly vulnerable because all the advantages of the terrain lay with the attacker. It had been chosen for its flatness, a bowl devoid of jungle, scrub, and trees. The open clearing was a tactical trap with its sides encircled by a rim, covered in jungle. Everyone and everything in the Box was under direct observation, while the Japanese found that they were able to approach unseen to the edge of the perimeter from any direction they wanted. Even if every man, from muleteer to cook and from storeman to clerk, had been free to take his place in the defences, there would not have been enough defenders to provide an unbroken line around the 1200-yard perimeter.

Time was short and vigorous attempts were made to prepare some defences before the Japanese attacked. Late in the afternoon of 6 February, Major-General Messervy, with a number of his staff from headquarters 7 Division, arrived. Earlier that morning divisional headquarters had been overrun and as the afternoon passed, more and more stragglers dribbled back, many with hair-raising stories of brushes with or narrow escapes from Japanese patrols. Messervy resumed command of his own brigades by radio but wisely left the defence of the Box in Brigadier Evans's hands. That evening Evans's instructions to his miscellaneous force were brief: 'Stay put and keep the Japanese out'.

Later that evening other units, which had been temporarily lost or detached in the jungle, came into the Box, including a mortar battery and a battery from a medium regiment, as well as two companies of the 4/8 Gurkha Rifles.

At midnight the Japanese struck for the first time at a sector held by an Indian mule company but the muleteers, many of whom were Pathans with a martial tradition behind them, held their fire until the screaming assailants were almost on top of them – then they hit hard and drove them back. It was to be the first of many such encounters. At dawn Sakurai's artillery began to shell the area, keeping up a fire programme that rarely ceased throughout the next ten days. A life-and-death struggle had been joined which was to continue until the siege ended. During daylight hours Japanese shells struck ammunition dumps, which exploded in lethal fashion, setting on fire large patches inside the perimeter as well as peppering all parts of the area with deadly missiles. At night Sakurai's troops attacked, probing and seeking weak spots: the ordeal continued by day and night without any respite. The nightly assaults usually began with cat-calls, shrieks, and shouts, designed to upset the defenders, calculated to make them panic in the hope that they would open fire, thus disclosing their positions. Then waves of Japanese armed with swords, bayonets, and grenades would follow up, smashing a way through the outer perimeter, until they were on top of the defenders. Only by the stoutest and fiercest hand-to-hand fighting were the defenders able to hold their own, but the strain was increasing because the advantages were very much in Sakurai's favour.

One of the most notorious incidents occurred when a strong raiding party infiltrated the forward positions to enter the Box hospital. Their first act was to bayonet a number of the badly wounded while they lay helpless on stretchers. Then six doctors were lined up and shot. When, at dawn, a counter-attack was successfully organized, the retreating Japanese withdrew behind wounded patients and medical staff, using them as human shields. As a final act of barbarity they murdered the hostages in cold blood. Such a horrific incident only served to heighten the defenders' resolve to stay put, to fight it out to the bitter end. Next morning, a handful of clerks under the RSM, B Echelon 9 Brigade, exacted a partial revenge for the hospital murders. They allowed some 50 Japanese infiltrators to approach to within a few feet of a well-sited ambush position; on a perfectly timed word of command from the RSM, all the intruders were wiped out at point-blank range.

The tanks of the Dragoons played an important part throughout the struggle for the Admin Box. One of the most notable incidents occurred when during the darkness the Japanese manhandled their 70mm howitzers to the crest of a ridge and as dawn broke on 9 February, opened up at point-blank range at exposed ammunition stores. Soon chaos reigned. The situation was restored when the Lee-Grants, supported by the heavy AA troop, engaged the Japanese guns in a duel in the open. The tank armour was proof against the 70mm shells and in the end, the enemy batteries were silenced. This encounter was one of many successful interventions made by armour and showed how mistaken some officers had been when they had scoffed at the use of tanks in Burma.

The first phase of the battle was over by 11 February. The Japanese had failed to destroy 5 and 7 Divisions; indeed, they had not taken full advantage of the initial confusion caused by their surprise moves. Now Kobe Force faced starvation, powerless to stop British and Indian convoys getting through the vital coastal road. The Box, despite furious attacks and onslaughts, showed no signs of being overrun or being deprived of critical supplies. Although still cut off, 114, 33 and 89 Brigades were holding fast and hitting back at their adversaries. Contact with detachments of Sakurai's column at Tong Bazar had already been made by 26 Indian Division, while 36 Division, the army reserve, had embarked in Calcutta en route for Chittagong. All told, commonsense dictated that Hanaya withdrew what was left of Sakurai's original force, back to the main defences around the Golden Fortress. Hanaya hesitated and left the decision to Sakurai. From available evidence, it now seems clear that if he had pulled out as soon as the signs showed that his gamble had failed, Sakurai might have saved the majority of his soldiers from death and starvation. But both commanders prevaricated until the British were able to turn the tables on them by surrounding pockets of Japanese before they could retrace their steps back to safety.

Unlike the British and Indian troops who had received badly needed supplies and necessities by air, the outlook for Tanahashi and his soldiers was grim. They could not fight without food and ammunition; they had counted on living off their enemy but in spite of a long, bitter siege, the rich prizes within the Admin Box had not been captured. It was impossible to bring even a modest share of their requirements along the same jungle tracks as had been used for the Ha-Go strikes a few days before. They were trapped and soon for the first time in South East Asia, a handful of Japanese soldiers began to surrender. Emaciated men gave up because they were ravenously hungry, they lacked ammunition, and were bitterly upset because their once powerful airforce had deserted them. They had lost faith in the glowing propaganda which proclaimed that the British and Indian troops would collapse as soon as they had been encircled. Only a few Japanese surrendered, however, because in the Bushido tradition, to die in battle for the Emperor was an honour, infinitely preferable to becoming a despised prisoner-of-war. Even now, in the blackest hour, there was no retreat. On the contrary – Sakurai was ordered to press home his attacks against the Box with even greater vigour, and from 10 to 18 February he obeyed the order with loyalty and stubborness, so that the fate of the box hung in the balance on more than one occasion. Sometimes it was the bravery of a few men that foiled an enemy penetration to the core of the defences: on several occasions the margin was perilously close.

To describe the many spirited actions that took place would require a longer account than this short chapter. Magnificent fighting spirit was shown by the veteran 2nd Battalion The West Yorkshire Regiment, the squadrons of 25 Dragoons, 4/8 Gurkha Rifles, and officers and men from the various supporting arms and services. One VC was posthumously won by Major Ferguson Hoey, a company commander in 1 Lincolnshire Regiment (26 Division): the gallantry of countless others was unrewarded but like Major Hoey, their sacrifices contributed to the final victory, because precious time was passing, which added to Sakurai's administrative headaches.

On 19 February, when two battalions fought their way into the Box, much needed relief was given to the exhausted garrison. By that time conditions had deteriorated badly. The hospital was a shambles, with the wounded piled up; flies by the million infested the wards, while two weary surgeons worked in the most unhygienic surroundings imaginable. Ammunition dumps had been repeatedly hit by Japanese shells. The defenders were at the end of their tether when, on 24 February, the main relief column from 5 Indian Division was able to get through the Okey-Doke Pass, following the capture of Point 1070 by 2/1 Punjab Regiment. The commander, 5 Indian Division, Major-General Briggs, drove into the Box at dawn on 24 February to meet Messervy. More than 500 wounded were evacuated without delay – the ordeal for Evans and his gallant men was over.

Ha-Go, which had started with such high hopes, ended in disaster for the Japanese. Of Sakurai's selected 8,000 men, fewer than 3,000 scrabbled a way through the jungle to the Golden Fortress – and most of them trickled back in a starving, exhausted condition. Although 15 Corps had lost 3,506 men, it was the first time that Japanese jungle tactics had been successfully countered, due to the air supply techniques and the new spirit that Slim and his commanders had instilled into their British and Indian troops. There was no dramatic end to Ha-Go because extensive mopping up had to be completed. This was a slow and difficult operation since the Japanese resisted with courage and resolution, and it was not until 5 March that 15 Corps was ready to continue with the original offensive that had been so dramatically disrupted by Sakurai's men. The British made the most of the victory, the first they had won in the war against Japan. Without any doubt Public Relations in Delhi over-reacted and magnified the importance of the battle. In reality, five British/Indian divisions supported by an enormous air effort, had been fully stretched to withstand the invasion of 8,000 Japanese. It had ended in defeat for the Japanese but it was not nearly as great a victory as was claimed in the glowingly phrased communiqués issued in India. The INA also joined in the propaganda war when Bose's Azad Hind Radio described how 7 Division had been completely destroyed, claiming that dozens of Indian troops had deserted to join the ranks of the INA, contemptuously called the JIFC (the 'Japanese-Inspired Fifth Column') by the Indian Army. After the collapse of Ha-Go, the desertions were invariably in the other direction, with dejected INA men seeking to surrender whenever a convenient opportunity occurred to slip across to a British or Indian unit.

How important was this, the second struggle in the Arakan? When he wrote *Defeat into Victory*, Slim claimed that it represented 'one of the historic successes of British arms. It was the turning point of the Burma Campaign'. There was no doubt that the legend of the Japanese superman, the soldier invincible in battle, had been smashed and, as a consequence, the morale of 14 Army rose in a remarkable fashion. From the Japanese point of view, in spite of early tactical successes, their infiltration did not continue long enough to remain a diversion for the next phase in their campaign, the major onslaught aimed at the Imphal Plain. While it is true that Slim had committed five of the twelve divisions available, plus another in reserve, in order to meet the crisis on the Arakan front, nevertheless by the beginning of March the situation there had not only been stabilized but had been restored to what it had been before Sakurai had thrown down his challenge. It is fair to say that Slim took a risk, but retrospective knowledge of Japanese intentions makes it easy now to be critical about his cautious decision to move 36 Division from Calcutta, to build up a sledgehammer to confront a striking force of little more than 8,000 men. At the time, Slim's reasons for over-reacting to the Arakan crisis were sound and logical, based on incomplete information available at that particular juncture. The most honest and candid of generals, Slim conceded that he had been guilty of over-optimism about the impending battle for Imphal. Whatever view critics may take, the complete defeat of the Ha-Go attack in the Arakan meant that when Imphal and Dimapur appeared to be in peril, two experienced divisions from 15 Corps were moved by air to save a dangerous situation. That fact alone must surely vindicate Slim and his handling of the crisis in the Arakan.

When 15 Corps resumed its offensive in early March, the defences around Razabil, the bastion that had held them up at the end of 1943, fell to 5 and 36 Divisions; while Buthidaung was taken by 7 Division on the 23rd of the month. Even when events on 4 Corps front dictated the transfer of 5 and 7 Divisions to the Imphal sector, fighting to improve the forward tactical positions continued throughout April. Christison lost yet another formation when 36 Division was pulled out of the Arakan, to rest and refit, before eventually joining Stilwell's NCAC to replace the Chindits during the late summer.

By the end of May, the monsoon season had brought large-scale operations in the Arakan to a virtual standstill, with 25 and 26 Indian Divisions and 81 (West African) Division holding the front, attempting little that was ambitious in deplorable conditions. The Japanese were content to do likewise: both sides in the Arakan realized that the U-Go offensive aimed at Imphal would dictate the course of their own activities after the monsoon rains had ended.

CHAPTER 6

Imphal and Kohima in peril

Now I am convinced that victory was within my grasp—
Lieutenant-General Renya Mutaguchi

The advances made by NCAC, the grim struggle in the Arakan, the imaginative penetrations by Special Force, all these were preliminary but important sideshows to the death struggle that was to be waged with relentless fury around Imphal between March and July of 1944. It was to be the most decisive battle of the campaign in South East Asia.

For the Japanese the tide was turning. Their commanders in Burma could see the gathering strength of the British around Imphal, fully realizing that a major offensive was about to be launched which would be difficult to withstand. The plan made to counter this threat was sound in conception, even if its execution relied on an over-optimistic approach to administrative problems. The Japanese were confident that they could capture the towns of Imphal and Kohima before moving to the border of Bengal – although no specific measures were prepared for an advance that would have taken them any farther into that province. However, it suited Mutaguchi's purpose well to fall in with Bose and his cries of 'Dehli Chalo' for a general invasion of India, as those had a stirring propaganda appeal. The tough, ruthless 56-year-old army commander was in a confident mood when the dramatic onslaught against the British/Indian 4 Corps was launched on 7 March, under the code name, U-Go.

On the face of it, Mutaguchi had little cause to be optimistic. His army was made up of three experienced infantry divisions – 15, 31 and 33 – about 100,000 front-line troops in all. In support was the INA 1 Division, nominally 7,000 strong, but only a handful of the rank-and-file shared the fervent hopes of their leader, Bose. The majority had been coerced into enlistment as a way of escaping the horrors of Japanese prison camps, and after they had reached the front line, their loyalty and enthusiasm for the cause of Nippon soon evaporated. In other respects, too, Mutaguchi had meagre support compared with 4 Corps holding the Manipur sector. For every gun he could bring into action, the British could produce four; his tanks, based on a pre-war British design, were outnumbered, outgunned, and soon to be out-manoeuvred by those in the opposing 254 Indian Tank Brigade. Finally, the cardinal factor in the struggle for Imphal, the Allied air forces ruled the sky – as had already been clearly demonstrated during the abortive Ha-Go attacks made against 15 Corps a few days earlier.

After the war, Mutaguchi claimed that the U-Go offensive came very close to success and stated that there were two reasons for its eventual failure. He blamed the unwieldy command structure in Burma, which led to inflexibility while, in addition, there were grave differences of opinion between the Army Group Commander, Lieutenant-General Kawabe, and himself as to how the operation should have been conducted. His views are respected and not disputed but there were other major factors. In essence, Mutaguchi staked the previous invincibility of the Japanese soldiers against the over-whelming odds which confronted them, and this mistaken belief so blinded him that he failed to appreciate the hard logistic realities which faced his men. Surprise, speed, the diversion in Arakan, and a deep-rooted contempt for British and Indian soldiers lay at the heart of Mutaguchi's U-Go operation. Two years before, in their drive through Malaya and Burma, Japanese soldiers using superior mobility and well supported by their air force, had repeatedly surrounded British forma-tions or units and whenever that occurred their opponents withdrew, usually in considerable disorder. But 15 Corps in the Arakan had shown that times had changed; now there would be no abject with-drawal even when formations were surrounded or in danger of being encircled. An elaborate air supply organization, coupled with the greatly improved strength of the RAF in the area, had radically altered the situation. Once again the Japanese found their enemy, whom they thought had been trapped, had dug in and was ready to fight to the end instead of running away in disarray.

The opening phase of the offensive began with Lieutenant-General Yanagida's 33 Division advancing in two columns. Their immediate opponents were 17 Indian Division holding positions in the Chin Hills, with Major-General 'Punch' Cowan's HQ located at the town of Tiddim, some 8,000 feet above sea level. In almost daily contact with Japanese patrols and out-posts in the forward areas, 17 Division were located in a lonely and perilous mountain perch, and they had to rely on a single narrow road that corkscrewed its way more than 160 miles to the north as their only land link with Imphal. Not only was Cowan and his division out on a limb but the division was also under strength, consisting as it did of 48 and 63 Brigades only. Although plans had been made to withdraw 17 Division as soon as it became apparent that the long-awaited Japanese offensive had begun, executive orders to do so had been delayed, possibly because of some confusion between Lieutenant-General Scoones at 4 Corps HQ and Cowan, forward at Tiddim. Slim had agreed with Scoones's appreciation that U-Go would probably be launched on or after 15 March so that higher HQ did not exert any pressure on Cowan to begin the tactical withdrawal. It was understandable that Cowan would prefer to hold on until the last moment, being well aware that the officers and men under his command did not want to hand over hard-earned gains – unless it was absolutely clear that the Japanese were about to deploy vastly superior numbers against them. However unavoidable the delay might have seemed, it was to have dire consequences when 17 Division faced disaster and only narrowly avoided extermination. Unknown to Cowan, Yanagida's men began their penetration on 7 March with columns making for the Tuitam Saddle and Milestone 109, where the road snaked up and down over steep ridges and crossed deep valleys in a series of hairpin bends. A rough-and-ready bridge near Milestone 109 spanned the Manipur River where it rushed through a gorge. It was an ideal place for the Japanese to cut off 17 Division's retreat.

Ironically, two young riflemen on patrol from 1/10 Gurkha Rifles, reported on 9 March that they had seen more than 2,000 enemy soldiers with guns and mules, moving towards the west, having crossed the Manipur River. Although other pieces of information had come in indicating that something was afoot, that particular item had been treated with open disbelief by Intelligence at Divisional HQ – although Cowan himself suspected that the attack would come at an earlier date than the one predicted by his superiors. He was right, because the Japanese not only struck at 63 Brigade's forward positions on the 13th but reports soon confirmed earlier rumours that their enemy had established blocking positions at Milestone 109 and at three other points along the road back to Imphal. Cowan received the order to withdraw later that day, with the Japanese astride his line of retreat and without any means of resupply by land. The actual withdrawal did not begin until 5 p.m. on the following day – on 15 March Tiddim itself was evacuated and the long trek back began.

The clearing of the first two enemy positions between Milestones 128 and 132 was achieved by some fierce fighting by 48 Brigade, which consisted of two Gurkha battalions and one British. The brigade ejected units of 214 Regiment from the Tuitam Saddle, then shortly afterwards cleared the road block at Milestone 130. Meanwhile, the vital Manipur Bridge was being guarded by the Jat MG Battalion

1 Joseph Stilwell being greeted on his arrival by (Major General) Idwal H. Edward

2 Orde Wingate

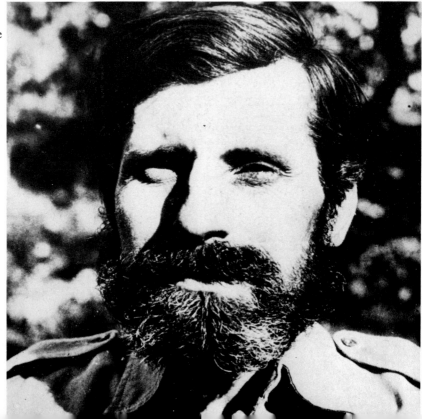

3 Those that returned; sick and wounded Chindits being evacuated from behind the Japanese forward positions

4 Mule handlers in 'Merrill's Marauders'

5 Stilwell with Merrill

6 Mountbatten, Leese and Slim

7 The West Tunnel on the Maungdaw-Buthidaung road. (The inverted cross is above the Razabic Ridge.)

8 Gurkha wounded in the Arakan

9 Troops wading ashore from landing craft on Akyab Island

10 The winding road to Tamu

11 Air oblique view of Kohima defended area

KEY:

1	Deputy Commissioner's bungalow and tennis court	10	GPT (General Purposes Transport)
2	Garrison Hill	11	Norfolk Ridge
3	Kuki Piquet	12	Rifle Range
4	FSD (Field Supply Depot)	13	Two Tree Hill
5	DIS (Detail Issue Section)	14	Jetsome Track
6	Jail Hill	15	Pulebadze Peak (7532 ft)
7	Road to Imphal	16	South end of the Pulebadze Ridge
8	'Pimple'	17	Top end of the Aradure Sput
9	Congress Hill	18	Japvo Peak (9890 ft)

12 A sepoy of the Madras Regiment in action, with Sita Hill in the background (Imphal front)

13 Hats and smiles—RAF airmen receive mail from home

14 Amphibious DUKWS sliding into the Chindwin, prior to moving forward with reinforcements and supplies

15 The 360-yard long pontoon Bailey bridge over the Chindwin, guarded by a balloon

16   Meiktila—after the battle was over

17 Bill Slim addressing troops of the Indian Army, near Meiktila

18 Some of the Japanese who died in an unsuccessful attack on the Cantonment area of Meiktila

19 General Slim telling the world, by means of the BBC, that Mandalay has been recaptured

20 The fruits of air superiotiy. The Myitinge Bridge, on the railway from Mandalay to Rangoon, after being attacked by RAF Thunderbolts

21 General Mud! The RAF Regiment manhandling a 20mm Ack-ack gun on the landing beaches, off the Rangoon River

THE JAPANESE GENERALS IN CAPTIVITY **22** General Kimura

23 (Left to right) Lieutenenat-General Hayashi (55 Division), Major-General Koba (54 Division), Lieutenant-General Honda (GOC 33 Army)

which had been rushed up from Imphal; and after 48 and 63 Brigades had withdrawn over the bridge, it was blown on 26 March. Thus 17 Division escaped the first dragnet: for them to have crossed the river at all was a setback for Yanagida, but their situation remained highly precarious because other groups of Japanese blocked the road back to safety. At this critical hour, Scoones took the brave and momentous decision to send up two brigades from 23 Division, thus ominously depleting the corps reserve at a time when danger threatened elsewhere especially from the direction of Ukhrul. It was a calculated risk, but 17 Division faced annihilation and only decisive action of this nature could have saved them.

Moving quickly, 37 and 49 Brigades were able to push aside the blocking positions, thus opening up the line of escape as well as enabling badly needed supplies of food, ammunition, and medicine to get through to the retreating 17 Division. The Japanese followed as Cowan and his men steadily withdrew and although they pressed them hard, the Black Cat Division eventually reached the Imphal Plain. It had taken them three weeks at a cost of about 1200 casualties. Yanagida had won half a victory only, because his mission had been to stop 17 Division from taking any further part in the next phase of the concerted assault against the town of Imphal, the crux of the U-Go operation.

Historians have tended to point critical fingers at Slim for his failure to recall 17 Division until it was almost too late. Typically, he never ducked the issue although he could have done so or blamed his chief subordinates. He and Scoones had been expecting an attack although the advance timing caught them unawares. Far from accusing Scoones, Slim gave him unstinted praise: 'His appreciations could be reread after the event and found uncannily accurate, and he had, too, a steadiness in crisis that was, for the coming battle, to be invaluable. He had, in accordance with the overall plan for the theatre, been preparing for an advance and the whole layout of his area and the dispositions of his fighting formations were designed with this idea'.

Slim had decided to concentrate 4 Corps on the Imphal Plain and fight there to destroy Mutaguchi and his 15 Army, accepting that such a course meant giving up ground even if this entailed risking a sharp drop in morale. In his words: 'I was tired of fighting the Japanese when they had a good line of communications behind them and I had an execrable one. This time I would reverse the procedure'.

The timing of the withdrawal was obviously of crucial importance and on this Slim subsequently admitted that he had been in error. With the benefit of hindsight, it is clear that he misjudged his enemy's

ability to mount a major attack so swiftly, but based on the information available at the time to his intelligence staff, 15 March appeared to
be the most likely date by which the Japanese could be ready to sally
forth over the Chindwin. The carefully considered plans that Scoones
had drawn up were thus in jeopardy from the very start. Moreover,
the Tiddim road was not the only approach to Imphal: there were two
other routes for the Japanese divisions to move along, one from Tamu
in the south-east over the Shenam Pass and the other from the north-
east down the track from Ukhrul. And 17 Division was not the only
formation in an isolated position – on the left guarding the road which
led from Tamu into the unhealthy Kabaw valley was 20 Division
under Major-General Douglas Gracey. That sector had been a quiet
one, although after the first few days of March, evidence began to
indicate that the Japanese were about to strike. In the rear of Gracey's
Division stood a range of mountains dominated by the 6,000-foot
Shenam Ridge which separated the Manipur Plain from the Kabaw
valley. It was vital that those mountains should remain in British
hands in order to bar any entrance to the Imphal Plain along the road
from Tamu.

The Japanese force commanded by Major-General Yamamoto, consisting of a regiment of 33 Division with two tank battalions and some
artillery in support, moved north-west up the valley to attack Gracey's
right flank. Contact was made on 14 March, and in accordance with
prearranged plans, 20 Division was told to pull back, barring the way
to Imphal. Gracey's line of retreat was very much easier than that
which tormented 17 Division: the road covered a distance of about 50
miles and was far less exposed to infiltration, ambushes, or road blocks
by the invaders. Moreover Yamamoto and his men met with a sharp
rebuff on 17 March, when they had the worst of a fierce action fought
with the rearguard of 20 Division, which included tanks of 3rd
Dragoon Guards. But the respite gained was short-lived. An attack
against Tamu, where tanks were used by both sides, was an indication
that the Japanese were continuing their build-up, with more units
arriving, until 26 March saw them in occupation of the Tengnoupal
Ridge which ran at right angles to Shenam. For three days a fierce
struggle was waged while 80 and 100 Brigades from 20 Division dug in
firmly along the ridge, thus effectively barring the road through to the
plain behind them. That part of 4 Corps' withdrawal strategy had gone
as planned.

During this phase of the fighting one significant action occurred
when B Company of 4/10 GR ambushed a brigade of the INA 1
Division. The Japanese version of the encounter was as follows: 'The

Gandhi Brigade advanced south and met a strong counter-offensive by the Indian Army, together with attacks from the air: they retreated thereafter and were very cautious in their advance'. The Gurkha battalion's account was far less complimentary: 'Never were so many so utterly routed and put to so disorderly a flight by so few!'

The preliminaries were now over – the chosen battleground lay before the invading columns. Seventy miles from the Indo-Burmese border lay the city of Imphal, capital of the small state of Manipur, which covered some 700 square miles. About 3,000 feet up, Imphal is set in the middle of a high plateau surrounded by a rim of jungle-clad mountains. The Imphal Plain was where some of the bloodiest fighting of the whole war was to be fought. Entrance from Assam to the plain was via Dimapur along a tortuous road that wound its way up to Kohima, before continuing on to Imphal. The road had been significantly improved by the engineers of 14 Army until it had become the life line for 4 Corps, weaving an erratic course like a squirming snake north to the army rail head and major supply base of Dimapur. On the map the distance between the two towns was about 80 miles but because of precipitous gorges and steep jungle-covered hills, the actual distance was a precarious 140 miles. Undoubtedly the most vulnerable point on the road was where it crossed the summit of a 4,700-foot pass. There lay the village of Kohima, with lofty, awe-inspiring ranges of mountains dwarfing the road as it went over the crest of the pass. The road was the only feasible route between Manipur and Assam for large-scale movement by mechanical transport and heavy weapons.

The village of Kohima is in the heart of the Naga country. The Nagas, a tough and cheerful people, had originally viewed the British with grave distrust during the 19th century but since then strong bonds of affection had grown up between the proud hill folk and the tiny band of dedicated British administrators who lived in their midst. If the Japanese could seize the pass at Kohima, then Imphal would be completely cut off: if they could capture Dimapur as well, then it would mean that Stilwell's supply line to Ledo and beyond would wither and die. However important Kohima was, Dimapur with its railway and major installations was of far greater significance and, not surprisingly, Slim was certain that Dimapur would be the primary objective for Sato. In the event, he was to be proved wrong and, as a result, Kohima was left relatively unguarded until the eleventh hour.

The second phase of U-Go began on 15 March when Lieutenant-General Yamauchi's 15 Division and 31 Division under Lieutenant-General Sato poured across the Chindwin by raft, ferry, and boat. For

Sato the target was Kohima which he had been ordered to seize 'with the speed of wildfire'. He and his men had been given the toughest of assignments because the country between the Chindwin and Kohima was almost trackless, with forbidding jungle-covered mountains rising to 7,000 feet, barriers to mechanical transport and difficult for man and beast to traverse. Sato was expected to advance at least 20 miles a day, with 5,000 oxen following and some of his soldiers acting as porters, helping to carry rations for 50 days. On his left flank Yamauchi had been ordered to bulldoze a way through 4 Corps' positions on the east of the Imphal-Dimapur road and thereafter to strike at Imphal itself. Mutaguchi expected to capture the state capital within a month.

It was a day or two before Slim could be sure about the target selected by Yamauchi and the strength of the enemy force. Moreover, Scoones had committed all his infantry reserves when he had taken the brave decision to send two brigades to save 17 Division during its withdrawal from Tiddim. At this critical hour, Slim turned to Mountbatten, stating that he needed 25 to 30 Dakota aircraft, between 18 March and 20 April, to move up reinforcements by air from the Arakan sector. Mountbatten did not hesitate: permission was given and before the end of March the whole of 5 Division, including guns, mortars, jeeps and regimental mules, had been air-landed in the middle of the Imphal battlefield. Mountbatten's decisiveness and moral courage at a time when disaster faced 4 Corps, undoubtedly played a major part in the successful outcome of the battle. As Supreme Commander he had been authorized to divert transport aircraft from the Hump airlift in order to meet emergencies but after doing so during the Ha-Go campaign, he had been warned that he must not do so again, or take it for granted that authority would be given by the American Chiefs-of-Staff in Washington. As it was, 5 Division arrived in the nick of time – the Japanese were about nine miles from the airfield as they were landing. Some of the units were whipped straight into action, with battalions from the same brigade moving to different sectors and companies from the same battalion being rushed to meet whatever crisis needed urgent remedial action. Mutaguchi had badly underestimated the flexibility of air power, and the dramatic arrival of 5 Division, with its 161 Brigade being ready to defend Dimapur within a matter of hours, was something that he had never anticipated.

Although the U-Go attacks had been foreseen by 14 Army – and measures to meet them had been drawn up and promulgated down to the formations concerned – the speed of the onslaught, and the unexpected strength of the thrust towards Kohima, posed severe problems for the British commanders and their soldiers. Although 17 and 20 Indian Divisions had withdrawn from their respective limbs, their return to the Imphal Plain was achieved only by costly fighting, with considerable danger threatening during the withdrawal. Critical though the early situation was around Imphal, the most dangerous threat of all was being aimed at the hill station of Kohima. In addition, the left column of 31 Division, 58 Regiment under Major General Miyazaki, was making for Ukhrul – an important place, with its supply dumps set at the confluence of roads. By 16 March when Scoones had decided that there was little chance of holding Ukhrul, he ordered 50 Parachute Brigade to form a defensive box round the villages of Sangshak and Litan, between Ukhrul and the main road, then to hold fast and buy time. In addition to its two parachute battalions, the Brigade included the 4/5 Marathas and a battalion from Nepal, the Kali Bahadurs. On the outbreak of World War II, the Maharajah of Nepal had unhesitatingly offered help to his country's old ally, Great Britain; so here were soldiers from the Nepalese Army in action for the first time against the Japanese. Unlike their fellow countrymen serving in the Gurkha Brigade of the Indian Army, these Nepalese soldiers did not have a long tradition of heroic feats won in numerous campaigns from 1815 onwards. Moreover their standard of training did not match that of the famous Gurkha Brigade so that the battle inoculation near Sangshak was to be a cruel and searching one, indeed.

On 22 March Miyazaki's regiment hurled itself at the Parachute Brigade within its tight perimeter measuring only 600 by 3,000 yards. The Brigade, although outnumbered and outgunned, held on for four days until the Japanese had overrun the only two water points available: on the following day the survivors were told to break through the Japanese positions and split up into small groups, before trying to make their own way back to Imphal. Although this was a severe setback, the sacrifices of the Brigade were not in vain. Miyazaki had appreciated that his real mission was to press hard for Kohima but at the same time he knew that he could not ignore the Brigade box or leave it to become a running sore in his flank. Hence much valuable time was spent in trying to eliminate Sangshak; equally, the sudden evacuation caught the Japanese off balance just when they were preparing for yet another attempt to bulldoze a way into the heart of the defences. It took the survivors from the Parachute Brigade four days to reach a safer refuge after an action that had cost them more than 600 men. On the other side of the hill, Miyazaki subsequently admitted that 'the loss of 580 first class men including a company commander greatly affected the Kohima battles' – which were about to begin!

It was at this critical juncture that Major-General Briggs' 5 Indian Division really made its presence felt. As already mentioned, 161 Brigade raced to Dimapur while, to the east, 9 and 132 Brigades moved towards Ligaun so that 31 Division did not find an open road to Imphal after capturing Sangshak; instead, they encountered a numerically superior and fresh foe. Moreover, they were poised to enter open country where the British could use ample superiority in armour, artillery, and air power to maximum effect. Cloaked by the jungle canopy, Mutaguchi's soldiers had been able to move with comparative immunity towards selected objectives: thereafter the British, Indian, and American pilots would be able to see their targets. As a result, on 29 March a Japanese battalion was decimated after being trapped in the open, being pounded mercilessly by guns as well as straffed without pause by the RAF.

Nevertheless, the threat in the north continued to grow, especially when on 30 March a column from 15 Division reached the Dimapur road and established a strong blocking position, some 30 miles north of Imphal. From that moment 4 Corps lost its sole land link with Dimapur and had to depend on the air forces for all its supplies – indeed, for its very survival. It is worthy of record that the Corps strength, including non-combatants, was estimated to be more than 155,000 men. For some anxious weeks ahead the amazing Operation Stamina kept 4 Corps alive and in the battle, much to the surprise of Mutaguchi. During the opening phases miscalculations had been made by the British commanders but now their opponents began to take decisions which, in the end, made a humiliating and crushing defeat as inevitable as the last act of a Greek tragedy.

As the Japanese advanced farther and farther to the west, so did their logistical arrangements become more and more tenuous. The capture of Dimapur would have provided the bulk of Mutaguchi's requirements with food, ammunition, and weapons for many weeks to come. Its loss would have been a crippling blow for 14 Army as well as for the American/Chinese divisions pushing towards Myitkyina. Why then did the Japanese hesitate? As indicated earlier, Mutaguchi commented on this episode as follows : 'Failure was due partly to our command structure and partly to the differences that existed between myself and the Army Group Commander, Lieutenant-General Kawabe as to how the operation should be conducted. His cancellation of my order to the divisional general at Kohima to make a dash for Dimapur changed the whole prospect. British success was due to the ability of their commanders to select a promising course of action and then pursue it with resolute intent'.

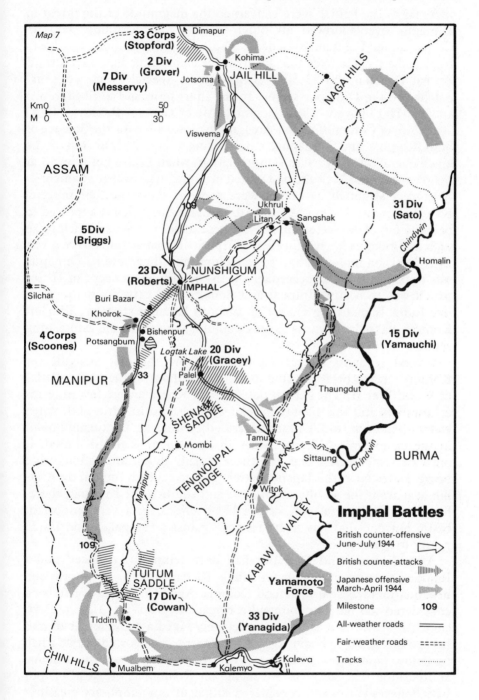

Map 7

Imphal Battles

British counter-offensive June-July 1944	⟹
British counter-attacks	⫴
Japanese offensive March-April 1944	➜
Milestone	109
All-weather roads	═══
Fair-weather roads	══
Tracks	·········

As far as the British were concerned the magnitude of the threat to Dimapur overshadowed all other tactical considerations. HQ 33 Corps, under Lieutenant-General Stopford, was summoned in haste from India to take over that front while as an immediate measure, 2 British Division and 23 LRP Brigade from Special Force were dispatched to the Dimapur sector. In the short term and until Stopford and his HQ arrived, Slim appointed Major-General Ranking, GOC 202 Lines of Communication Area, to be responsible for the defence of both Kohima and Dimapur, emphasizing that Dimapur was to be given overall priority. Slim's appreciation, when he did not know that the over-cautious Kawabe had reined in Mutaguchi, was fundamentally correct although as events were soon to show, he had misread Kawabe's mind. U-Go was such a daring enterprise that it appeared to be quite out of character for the Japanese to hesitate when a rich prize such as Dimapur lay within their grasp. Strict instructions were given to 31 Division under Sato to seize Kohima and then hold it: Dimapur was to be left alone in accordance with the original concept of U-Go, which was to occupy Imphal and dominate all exits from the plain into India. In guarding against the obvious Japanese strategy, Slim left Kohima nakedly open as Sato's columns moved at an astonishing speed towards the small town.

Several accounts have been written about the epic struggle for Kohima – it has been elevated to the status of one of the major battles of World War II. The gallant defenders of Kohima were few in terms of numbers and the disputed area was measured in yards, but when victory had been won, Giffard described Kohima as 'the turning point in the campaign'. Although such an assessment is not disputed, it must be remembered that elsewhere equally important actions were being contested as the Japanese attempted to capture Imphal by striking at it from the south, south-east, and south-west. Kohima, therefore, was an integral part of the U-Go offensive, a very important battle but one that has to be viewed against a campaign that lasted nearly four months.

After Kohima and Dimapur had been temporarily placed under Ranking's command, Colonel Hugh Richards with an improvised headquarters was sent to defend Kohima. Aged 50, Richards had been considered too old to command a brigade in 81 West African Division. An ordeal that would have severely taxed a commander of half his age was about to begin. Initially his garrison consisted of two small battalions and some administrative troops. Based on the original appreciation that Sato was advancing on Kohima at the head of four battalions only, this was considered sufficient as a temporary measure:

it was thought most unlikely that the Japanese could move a larger body of troops through the rugged and forbidding Naga Hills. Only on 29 March did it become evident that the whole of 31 Division was moving at top speed towards Kohima. Although numbering about 2,500, the garrison contained only one regular unit, 1 Assam Regiment, which had been raised recently and this had no experience of active service. An undertrained Nepalese State Battalion, the Shere Regiment, and 3 Assam Rifles made up the infantry element of Richards' fighting force – and 3 Assam Rifles had been raised originally as local gendarmerie.

As the Japanese closed on Kohima, valuable time was bought by sub units of 1 Assam Regiment which fought some stirring actions before withdrawing to bolster up the garrison. By now the danger was abundantly clear and 161 Brigade was ordered to move up the Manipur road to reinforce the tiny scratch force under Richards' command. But the order was countermanded when it was feared that 31 Division would switch direction and strike for Dimapur. Fortunately for Richards, that second order was changed and a battalion group under command of the CO 4 Royal West Kents was able to reach Kohima on 4 April at a most opportune moment – the Japanese attacked that night. Meanwhile the other units of 161 Brigade reached a point some four miles west of the village, only to find themselves tangling with the Japanese and unable to fight their way through to join the garrison. The Royal West Kents' arrival coincided with a heavy attack against the perimeter and as a result within minutes they were in action without any chance to familiarize themselves with the ground or acquaint themselves with the local situation. Their timely appearance saved the garrison but they were not able to stop a prominent feature known as Jail Hill from being overrun. A tantalizing narrow strip of three miles separated the puny garrison from the rest of Brigadier Warren's brigade but from dug-in positions his artillery was used to good effect against the Japanese besieging Richards and his men.

Sato's soldiers mounted unremitting attacks and, on 8 April they cut the water supply. Water rationing was instituted, and this meant that each man was restricted to half a pint a day, a meagre amount in the hot, humid pre-monsoon climate. Fortunately another source of water was discovered five days later. The onslaught continued and by 9 April the perimeter had become so restricted that a savage battle developed around and for possession of the District Commissioner's tennis court. Grenades were hurled where once tennis balls had bounced in harmless fun. The ordeal of the exhausted defenders worsened when, on 13 April, the Advance Dressing Station was hit several times, killing two doctors and several patients as well as wounding many others. That was a day of bleak misfortune because several outposts round the perimeter were overrun by the Japanese. Richards issued what he thought might be his last Order of the Day, ending with the words: 'Put your trust in God and continue to hit the enemy wherever he may show himself'.

The tired, undernourished survivors courageously responded to their commander's rousing appeal but were being pushed relentlessly back by sheer weight of numbers. By dawn on 18 April their perimeter had been reduced to a little square with each side being no more than 350 yards. A thick morning mist clouded the rising sun but when it lifted, it was not the Japanese who were revealed but the welcome sight of relieving troops from 1/1 Punjab Regiment. On 20 April the siege was over; the tiny scratch force had fought with epic gallantry and those that survived left for Dimapur in motor transport, knowing that no men could have fought with more resolution or unflinching courage than they had done.

The first phase of the Kohima battle had ended. There was still much bitter fighting to come because Sato had not given up hope of winning. Unfortunately for Sato, Mutaguchi then ordered him to send a regimental group to 15 Division's sector, an order that the Divisional commander chose to disobey. Worse still, a copy of Mutaguchi's written order was found on the body of an ambushed dispatch rider, on the day that Richards' garrison had been relieved. Armed with this knowledge, Slim ordered the newly arrived Stopford to redouble the pressure being exerted on the hard pressed 31 Division, an order which he obeyed so effectively that Sato, in turn, refused to weaken his force by sending away a third of its strength – thus flagrantly disobeying his superior officer's instructions.

Meanwhile the furious struggle for Imphal continued without any slackening of tempo. Mutaguchi's hope that the State capital would fall in a month was receding. Moreover, the gathering dark clouds indicated that the monsoon was about to break. South of Imphal heavy pressure was exerted by 33 Division, with the column under Yanagida covering prodigious distances to bypass the Tuitam Saddle, then striking north to Bishenpur which was astride the road running west from Imphal to Silchar. The fighting there rose to an even greater pitch of fury. Nevertheless, in spite of the fluid situation, the unfortunate Yanagida was replaced in mid-April by the able and dedicated Lieutenant-General Tanaka: Mutaguchi had been enraged by Yanagida's 'regrettable miscalculation' which, he claimed, had allowed 17 Division to escape disaster and withdraw back to the plain. Tanaka did not promise his soldiers an easy victory when exhorting them to capture Imphal: 'You must accept that the Division will be almost annihilated. . . . Regard death as something lighter than a feather'.

In a sense such rousing words were almost justified because at that time the best part of four British divisions had been pushed back into the Imphal plateau and appeared to be bottled up, devoid of exists and access to India. The Silchar track, the last link to Assam, had been closed to the defenders. The front defended by 4 Corps was no more than 100 miles in circumference and it was in danger of being reduced yet further. From the hill village of Ningthaubang, Tanaka was only 21 miles from his final destination, Imphal, which appeared to be within his grasp. It was for that reason that he prevailed upon the demoralized Japanese air force to make one of its rare appearances over the front line, providing short-lived encouragement for his soldiers who were constantly under attack from RAF Hurricanes and Vengeance dive-bombers.

As the fighting continued, the strain it imposed was aggravated by the ordeal of the opening rains of the monsoon. In late April there were spasmodic but heavy rain storms: by the middle of May the main monsoon began to rage, making life miserable for all concerned. Dry water-courses became torrents. Paddy fields were swamped and weapon pits and foxholes on the hills were soon full of muddy water. The Japanese alone could take some consolation from the thick white mist that rose from the sodden soil in the mornings because this blanket hid them from the prying eyes of the Allied pilots.

The moves and counter-moves made by Cowan (17 Division) and Tanaka during late April and early May involved both sides in days and nights of violent costly fighting. Spurred on by Tanaka, the Japanese fought with such suicidal fanaticism that the hard-pressed Cowan had to call on Scoones for reinforcements, which duly arrived in the shape of 50 Parachute Brigade. The survivors of Sangshak had formed the nucleus of the reconstituted brigade that now entered the cauldron raging around Bishenpur. Deeds of valour abounded. Three Gurkha soldiers and a British sergeant from 1 West Yorkshires each won the Victoria Cross during those battles, two of the Gurkhas serving in 3/5 Gurkha Rifles and the third, Rifleman Ganju Lama, 1/7 Gurkha Rifles, who rose to extraordinary heights of courage by winning the MM and VC in two separate actions within the space of a few days. It was the bravery of such men, British, Indian and Gurkha, that restored the situation around Bishenpur. The cost to both sides was distressingly high: when Slim visited the battlefield he had the macabre experience of watching bulldozers disposing of 'a carpet of corpses'. It was estimated that during the engagement Tanaka lost about 1,000 men and Cowan about half that number.

On 13 May, 48 Brigade Commander, Brigadier Cameron, led his two Gurkha battalions supported by medium batteries, in a wide sweep which came behind the forward Japanese positions at milestone 33, near Torbang, on the Tiddim road. The flanking move took 33 Division by surprise and roused them to fury: with the majority of the division on the wrong side of the Torbang defiles held by the Gurkhas, vital supplies required for an all-out bid to capture Bishenpur could not get through the road block. Thus the first part of Cowan's plan had been achieved but the second phase met with a setback when 63 Brigade were unable to join Cameron's men and, as a result, 48 Brigade had to be ordered to fight their way back. In vile weather and after many skirmishes that cost them dearly, they eventually rejoined the rest of the division. Although decisive results had not been achieved by the bold manoeuvre, 33 Division's aggressive ambitions had been dampened and, as a result, the direct threat to Imphal from that sector had been staved off. Nevertheless, a bitter battle of attrition for Bishenpur continued without a break and for the Black Cat Division there was to be no relief.

By the first week in May, Mutaguchi's advance had been checked on most fronts and, in some places, his soldiers had had to give ground. Looking back at the situation with access to records of both sides, it could be claimed that the plight of 15 Army had been sealed by the time this stage in the struggle had been reached. However, the overall picture that faced Slim and his subordinate commanders was still far from encouraging: 20 Division had been forced to give ground slightly as they struggled to hold the Shenam Ridge: The Imphal Plain was virtually encircled and all its ground links with the outside world remained cut. Against those black clouds, Mutaguchi's original miscalculation in starting the Ha-Go diversion too quickly had allowed 14 Army time to recover its balance, seeking aid from first, 5 Division, then the veteran 7 Division, both of which arrived on the scene of battle at crucial moments – instead of being tied down in the Arakan by Hanaya's offensive. And once Slim had stabilized the situation, albeit by the narrowest of margins, then the administrative problems facing the three Japanese divisions became more and more acute. Mutaguchi's rash gamble had been based on the assumption that lucrative spoil would be available when the supply depots and dumps around Imphal had been captured. Even though circumstances were grim and dangerous, Slim was able to assert that by the middle of May, 'My worst anxieties were over'. Others remote and far away from the plain pressed for an urgent relief of Imphal but, rightly, the Army Commander was concerned with scheming the long-term destruction of 15 Army. Time plus the ready availability of reinforcements augured well for 14 Army; in contrast, Mutaguchi could only switch units from one threatened sector to another. The courageous 15 Army was withering away while the stubborn refusal of its commander to admit defeat or at least adopt a face-saving withdrawal, contributed to the terrible casualties suffered by the Japanese soldiers during the closing weeks of the U-Go operation.

North of Imphal, on the very rim of the plateau, the Japanese seized Nungshigan Hill, the nearest they ever came to the city they were striving to capture. The feature was recaptured only after violent air strikes had paved the way for determined infantry assaults. Tanks played a notable part, being winched up steep slopes until their crews were able to fire at point-blank range at the Japanese bunkers. On Shenam, 20 Division's two brigades had been subjected to unrelenting attacks for more than seven weeks by Yanamoto Force and eventually 80 and 100 Brigades were forced to give ground slightly – in engagements where, in proportion to the size of the battlefield and the number of troops engaged, it has been claimed that more casualties were suffered than in any other single engagement during World War II.

Against such rugged determination Yanamoto's offensive lost its momentum, and during a lull in the fighting, Scoones was able to relieve the two exhausted brigades, replacing them with the whole of 23 Division. When the torrential monsoon rains began to fall on 18 May, Yanamoto found that his fresh opponents were more than ready to withstand anything that he could hurl at them – but he continued to mount assault after assault until finally forced to give up early in July.

The Japanese generals began to lose their jobs. Mutaguchi had already sacked Yanagida. At the end of May another general went: Lieutenant-General Sato lost command of 31 Division when he addressed a plea to his Army Commander, asking that his division be allowed to withdraw while there was still an opportunity to do so. Sato's appeal was a realistic one because by that time Stopford's 33 Corps had been heavily reinforced with 7 Indian Division as well as 23 and 268 LRP Brigades coming under command. Outnumbered by at least five to one, with a tenuous supply line which the heavy rainstorms had almost closed, the soldiers of 31 Division were woefully short of ammunition, food, and medical supplies. Sato's request was, of course, against all Japanese military traditions. Mutaguchi's angry order to replace him came too late because by that time Sato had begun leading the survivors in a withdrawal towards the Chindwin. In truth, that march back was a nightmare with scores of men dying from malaria and dysentery, from starvation, exposure, and utter exhaustion. The struggle for Kohima was over, the road to Dimapur was open – and the once formidable 31 Division had been reduced to a disorganized rabble. Some of the survivors were able to join up with 15 Division in the Ukhrul sector, escaping death from starvation in the jungle only to undergo yet more ordeals in battles to come.

In spite of these major disasters, the individual Japanese soldiers continued to fight to the death although the majority of their so-called allies, the INA, were quick to surrender after a token struggle, selecting the most opportune moment to slip across to the nearest British or Indian unit.

A phenomenal strain was imposed on the Anglo-American air forces by the heavy daily demands of 4 Corps: every available aircraft in South East Asia Command had to be used to meet the emergency. At the height of the air supply operation—in fact, at the most critical moment—Mountbatten on his own responsibility had to refuse to release aircraft back to the Chiefs-of-Staff. The Chiefs-of-Staff were not being deliberately unsympathetic about the needs of 4 Corps but, nor surprisingly, their thoughts and fears dwelt on the impending invasion of Normandy. When Slim was informed about their request, his comment was that, if the 79 transport aircraft were removed, he could not be responsible for the successful outcome of the battle. In the event, Mountbatten stuck to his guns and refused to release the aircraft. The firm stand was warmly commended by Churchill, who backed him to the full. Since taking over as Supreme Commander, Mountbatten had grown in stature and confidence, which allowed the three Service commanders under his jurisdiction to concentrate on their tactical responsibilities. Mountbatten's contribution to victory was far greater than was realized at the time – he was far more than a handsome, youthful figurehead, engaged in morale-raising visits to the men serving in various parts of the SEAC theatre.

Another architect of victory was the AOC Third Tactical Air Force, Air Marshal Sir John Baldwin. After Imphal had been surrounded and 4 Corps was completely reliant on air supply, the daily requirement was for about 540 tons of supplies as well as reinforcements to replace casualties. Fortunately excellent pre-planning meant that there were six airfields in operation, two of which had been lengthened and improved to allow transport aircraft to land within 4 Corps area.

Nevertheless, the spectre of starvation constantly haunted Scoones who initially had estimated that ground links with India would have to be reopened by mid-June at the latest, unless extreme measures were taken to reduce daily needs and vital supplies. By dint of imaginative reorganization, and by making maximum use of the aircraft available with full utilization of airfields, Baldwin confounded the prophets of doom: not only was 4 Corps fed and supplied but reserves of most commodities had been amassed before the ruptured ground links were opened once again. It was not surprising, therefore, that Mountbatten signalled the US Joint Chiefs-of-Staff, strongly advocating the retention of the transport aircraft at that crucial juncture. Later he relayed another message: 'There is no doubt that these aircraft turned the tide of battle, and have altogether altered the outlook in Northern Burma'. To which Giffard added an even more direct postscript: 'Had we not had air supply we should have lost the Imphal Plain and the position on the eastern frontier of India would have been very grave'.

The turning point had been reached and passed: 2 and 7 Divisions in 33 Corps debouched to reopen the road to Imphal as well as pursuing the stragglers from 31 Division, making vigorous efforts to stop them reaching the Chindwin. The latter task proved to be a most difficult one; the rain-sodden jungle was a formidable barrier and progress was slow. Even with 23 LRP Brigade's assistance, the ambitious plan to intercept and destroy the Japanese did not wholly succeed. At the same time, 2 British Division pushed its way down the Imphal road. Rearguards under Major-General Miyazaki fought stoutly but under constant pressure their resistance became sporadic and gradually weakened. During these actions, an immense amount of help was received from the gallant Nagas whose loyalty to the British cause never faltered. In Slim's words: 'They guided our columns, collected information, ambushed enemy patrols, carried our supplies, and brought in our wounded under the heaviest fire – and then being the gentlemen they were often refused all payment'. The hard-earned victory at Kohima was to have immense prestige value in the eyes of the Nagas, and swept away any lingering doubts about an eventual British victory.

Nine miles south of Kohima, the Japanese fiercely defended Viswema for five days but after their ejection, progress towards Imphal became easier. Miyazaki, who had remained behind on Sato's orders to command the rearguard, found that the task of evacuating more than 1000 wounded, all stretcher cases, through thick jungle and along muddy mountain trails, posed immense problems. Delaying tactics along the road, including a liberal use of mines augmented by a series of sturdily fought ambushes, could not postpone the inevitable for much longer. On the night of 21 June, 6 Brigade from 2 Division had reached Milestone 102 and was preparing to continue its advance early next morning. At dawn, it was not the Japanese that they spotted when movement was seen and engaged by artillery. A furious message came over the radio from units of 5 Indian Division that had moved up the road from Imphal into the line of 'friendly' gunfire. The siege of Imphal was over: the road through to Dimapur was open. That very evening a convoy with headlights blazing roared its way to the capital of Manipur carrying badly needed supplies.

With the Imphal road open to 4 Corps and groups of 31 Division in headlong flight towards the Chindwin, or fleeing through Ukhrul to join 15 Division, even the redoubtable Mutaguchi knew that his army could not win. Nevertheless, being the man he was, in public he continued to exhort his tired soldiers to make one final effort: 'If your hands are broken, fight with your feet .... if there is no breath in your body, fight with your ghost. Lack of weapons is no excuse for defeat'. At the time that he made this dramatic appeal, Mutaguchi was asking his superior, Kawabe, for permission to withdraw, to pull back behind the Chindwin. Cautious as ever, Kawabe did not make a decision but consulted Field Marshal Hisarchi Terauchi, Commander South East Asia back at his HQ in Singapore. As a result it took another fortnight for permission to reach Mutaguchi, and by that time the obstinate army commander had decided to make one more despairing bid to capture Imphal.

For this offensive 15 Division, now without its commander, Yamauchi who had been evacuated to hospital with severe malaria, attempted to capture Talel, in conjunction with probes made by the remnants of 31 Division from the north and a regiment from 33 Division attacking from the south. On paper, the plan had some merit but in reality both supporting formations were already engaged in rearguard actions and at the crucial moment could not disengage themselves. At the centre of the contested area was the main Japanese supply base of Ukhrul, guarded by one of the INA brigades, but once the Indians realized that they were no longer on the winning side, they deserted in ever-increasing numbers, leaving Ukhrul open at a vital moment. Mutaguchi's forlorn last fling was doomed to failure.

The longer Mutaguchi's men remained west of the Chindwin, the better it suited Slim's overall strategy. A shattered, defeated 15 Army would mean that Kawabe would be hard-pressed to hold the outer perimeter of Burma until he had time to regroup and refurbish Burma Area Army. Although Slim was ill with malaria for some days during the closing stages of the pursuit battles, 14 Army continued to carry out the overall directives given them by Giffard. Having cleared the Japanese pockets from the Imphal Plain, 14 Army advanced up to and then across the Chindwin. The mission was not made easier by two factors. The country ahead contained a series of mountainous ridges, interspersed by rivers that flowed from the north down to the sea in the south; the advance was to be against the grain of the land, contending with steep ascents and slippery decents of up to 4,000 feet. Moreover, the heavy monsoon made the difficult ground almost impassable because the rains had not ceased to pour down since the middle of May. The rivers became swollen floods which could only be crossed with difficulty at one or two selected points. The low, heavy monsoon clouds meant that even the most experienced of pilots could not carry out resupply missions because the heavy mists made flying in the hills or mountains an extremely hazardous business.

On 2 July official permission was given for Mutaguchi to withdraw the remainder of 15 Army, to seek refuge behind the Chindwin. Operation U-Go had ended. Slim summed it up with cogency 'as a battle which swayed back and forth through great stretches of wild country ... columns, brigades, divisions, marched and countermarched, met in bloody clashes, and reeled apart, weaving a confused pattern hard to unravel'. Intricate though the patterns were, the result was clear-cut. About this the Japanese had no doubts whatever, with one verdict declaring that: 'The disaster at Imphal was perhaps the worst of its kind yet chronicled in the annals of war'.

Before we label that judgement a gross exaggeration, the numerical losses of the contestants should be considered. When the offensive began, 15 Army had approximately 100,000 front-line soldiers of whom 53,000 became casualties. The official figures show that 30,000 were killed in battle, while hundreds died after the defeat became a rout, victims of sickness, malnutrition, and exposure. Every tank and gun with Mutaguchi's invading force when the offensive began was lost – not a single heavy weapon was recovered across to the east bank of the Chindwin. The staggering figure of 17,000 mules and pack ponies perished during the operation. After the remnants of the once proud army had trickled back over the river, 15 and 31 Divisions were virtually out of battle until reinforcements had been received and integrated with the sparse numbers of veterans who had survived the long and bitter ordeal. The whole structure of 15 Army from top to bottom had been severely shaken. Generals had been sacked in the midst of battle, including Sato, Yanagida, Yamauchi (from ill health), and then finally, Mutaguchi himself. Following the Imphal débâcle, Mutaguchi was attached to the General Staff in Tokyo before being placed on the reserve in December of that year. Not surprisingly the changes in the hierarchy of 15 Army had grave repercussions on the morale of the dejected soldiers. Nevertheless, the Japanese troops had fought with immense bravery and almost snatched victory against impossible odds. Even in defeat the majority had chosen death either in battle or from starvation, with typical stoicism and courage rather than accepting the ignominy of surrender. The spirit of bushido still ruled the soldiers of Nippon.

The dreams of Bose had been shattered. Apart from the increasing number of deserters, those INA members who saw action did not cover themselves in glory. The grandiose concept of 'Chalo Dehli' had come to nought. Those who hesitated and remained in the INA became disillusioned and homesick, fully realizing that their old comrades in the Indian Army regarded them as traitors, the lowest of the low. There were about 7,000 INA soldiers when the Imphal battle began but only 2,600 returned to Burma, still capable of fighting – the others had been killed, or had deserted, or just disappeared into oblivion. Thereafter the INA ceased to play any significant part in the military struggle for Burma, and only after the war was over did they once again assume any importance. In the heady atmosphere of independence the returning members of the INA found themselves being hailed as patriotic heroes by the Congress Party. It was a sad and puzzling time for the million members of the Indian army who, after fighting with such loyalty and distinction in four theatres of war, found themselves ignored by their own politicians while the traitors of the INA were lionized to become objects of adulation. Fortunately it did not last forever: after 1947, independent India soon found that most of the ex-INA were not men of substance and appreciated that they were not the sort of men to be entrusted with responsibility in an emerging nation.

While the Japanese generals suffered shame and personal misfortune, their British counterparts emerged with enhanced reputations after the Plain of Imphal had been cleared of the enemy. For Slim it had been an exhausting, taxing time which he had faced with unruffled calm, even when the strain had been immense. After the initial miscalculation, his direction of the battle became increasingly confident and sure: while he grew in stature as Commander, so did the confidence of his army increase as victories were achieved under his leadership. It should be remembered, too, that there were considerable burdens on his shoulders when the battle was at its height. He had to resolve 'Operation Thursday' with its complicated mounting problems, cope with Wingate's erratic behaviour prior to his tragic, unexpected death, and give encouragement and tactful direction to Stilwell, especially when the American was deeply disturbed at the possibility that the Japanese might cut his supply line from Dimapur to Ledo. He had more than his share of problems but fortunately worked in harmony with the stolid, reliable Giffard and enjoyed unhesitating support from Mountbatten especially in the darker hours. The fact that even in a major crisis, Giffard and Stilwell could not work together, made it imperative to find a suitable person who could co-ordinate NCAC and 14 Army – and be acceptable to the Americans. Once there was an overall Land Forces Commander, Slim could concentrate on commanding his own 14 Army.

The Japanese view of the brutal, primitive battles for Kohima and Imphal, when savage hand-to-hand fighting often decided local issues, was 'those fierce battles are comparable to Verdun in the last World War'. Mutaguchi and 15 Army lost after a remarkable gamble for high stakes: they were defeated so conclusively that a successful re-entry by the Allies into Burma became a certainty.

CHAPTER 7

Over the Irrawaddy to victory

A Man Surprised Is Half Beaten—Thomas Fuller

The news of the defeat reached Tokyo on 4 July, a black day for the Axis partners because Allied troops entered Paris on the same day. The reverse astounded the Japanese public, who had grown accustomed to a string of victories by their soldiers and had been fed with glowing reports about progress around Imphal and Kohima. The despised British, who had been swept aside with contemptuous ease in Malaya and in the early fighting in Burma, had not retired in disorder – or melted away when surrounded. Mutaguchi and his generals had openly derided British troops, asserting that Indian sepoys fought with more heart than their white rulers. Defeats around Imphal had torn their theories to shreds. In such a bitter loss of face lay the seeds of an acrimonious public debate that ended in senior officers losing their posts and a complete reappraisal of strategy in Burma having to be carried out.

At a lower level, morale can best be illustrated by the following order issued by a junior commander: 'A decisive battle is the only battle known to a Japanese soldier, or fitting to the Japanese spirit, but now other methods may have to be adopted'. In short, withdrawal had to be accepted as inevitable, certainly until Burma Area Army had stabilized the overall situation. At General Headquarters the possibility of a complete withdrawal from Burma was examined, only to be firmly rejected in Tokyo: it was pointed out that the western flank from Burma to Sumatra had to be held for as long as possible, in the hope that the Anglo-American forces would be deterred by ever-mounting casualties from trying to force a way through the outer curtain, in order to strike at the Japanese homeland.

The veteran 66-year-old Lieutenant-General H. Kimura, who had a high reputation as a strategist, took over from the discredited Kawabe as Commander-in-Chief, Burma Area Army. His task of reorganizing the defeated 15 Army was made somewhat easier by the monsoon, which played a vital part in delaying the follow-up by 14 Army: if the pursuit had not been hampered by torrential rain, very few Japanese would have left India and crossed the Chindwin to survive and fight again. Kimura's problem was that he did not have enough troops to hold the Allied divisions ready to enter Burma, from NCAC in the north to 15 Corps in the Arakan. His rearguards tenaciously bought time by defending certain points along the main routes to the Chindwin. Nevertheless by the first week in August the leading British patrols had reached the western bank, while behind them, 33 Corps under Stopford closed up to the river, having advanced 330 miles to Tiddim and 276 miles to Iazabyo in the Kabaw valley. Firm plans were made to establish a bridgehead at Kalewa across the Chindwin, this to be seized early in December.

While the Japanese underwent a period of severe demoralization, their untrustworthy partners, the INA under Subhas Chandra Bose, virtually ceased to be active comrades-in-arms. Those who remained with the Japanese found themselves being treated with contempt, never to be entrusted with an important operational role again. Bose became depressed, disillusioned with his patrons, and increasingly disenchanted with his own countrymen who had carried such high hopes into the U-Go offensive. His overall concept had been sound and if the INA units had won an early success in action, then the story of Bose's enterprise might have been a different one. At the time, the authorities in New Delhi had viewed the INA with apprehension: rigid censorship concealed the facts from the Indian public; and few Indian civilians had any inkling about the considerable numbers of their fellow countrymen who had joined the INA, voluntarily or under duress. It was impossible to conceal matters when the INA began surrendering and deserting in droves during the Imphal battles but by then the threat to East Bengal had disappeared. Those who abandoned the INA cause were an embarrassment for the government of India because, technically, they were guilty of desertion, of being traitors to their own country as well as inciting rebellion. For any one of those major crimes they could have been shot, but fortunately wiser counsels prevailed and they were left to languish in jail. With victory in sight it would have been the height of insensitivity to have risked politically dangerous trials – in the words of Winston Churchill: 'The grass grows quickly over the battlefield. Over the scaffold never'.

Only when peace came did the handling of the ex-INA prisoners prove too difficult, culminating in a complete fiasco when trials were held at the Red Fort in Delhi. But by that time, Bose had perished: On 8 August 1945, after deciding to risk his fortune with the Russians, he perished in a plane crash after take-off in Formosa. That he died in the crash is certain, but a legend persisted, especially within his native Bengal, which claimed that Bose survived the crash and had withdrawn from the active world to become a *sadhu*.

The Japanese, therefore, aided by the monsoon and protected to some extent by the wide river barriers of the Chindwin and Irrawaddy, could only hope that Slim would overstretch himself and leave a substantial part of his army open to a counter-thrust. The overall position in South East Asia Command had changed substantially since 8 June 1944 when the directive given Mountbatten enjoined the Supreme Commander: 'To develop, maintain and protect the air link to China in order to provide a maximum and timely stock of petrol, oil and lubricants, in support of Pacific operations; so far as is consistent with the above, to press advantages against the enemy by exerting maximum ground and air effort, particularly during the monsoon season, and in pressing such advantages, to be prepared to exploit the development of overland communications to China. All these operations must be dictated by the forces at present available or firmly allocated to SEAC'.

There had been no let-up during the monsoon in spite of the appalling conditions. The sickness rate had been kept at a reasonable level thanks to the new forms of treatment and medical techniques that Mountbatten had master-minded: preventative measures were enforced with strict discipline so that offenders were punished for laxity and non-compliance of orders. But once again the Combined Chiefs-of-Staff had spelt out the top priority – air and land links with China, although the second part of the directive implied that they no longer ruled out an overland thrust across the Chindwin, striking at the very heart of Burma.

The necessity to have an overall land commander who could co-ordinate the drive towards Akyab with 14 Army's advance in Central Burma and NCAC near the Chinese border, was belatedly recognized when, on 11 October, General Sir Oliver Leese took over from Giffard, adopting the new title of Commander Allied Land Forces South East Asia (ALFSEA), with his headquarters at Barrackpore. Although Slim strongly defended Giffard when writing *Defeat into Victory*, the truth of the matter was that Giffard did lack the necessary quickness of intellect and was often at variance with Mountbatten. On more than one occasion he had opposed the Supreme Commander's views: during 1944 it had become increasingly discernible that such two incompatible personalities could not continue to work together. Matters came to a head when, in accordance with the overall directive, operations continued throughout the monsoon. Giffard protested, claiming that he did not have enough divisions available to ring the changes, with his jaded troops badly needing rest and rehabilitation as soon as the Imphal battles had been won. Mountbatten decided to check his statement, whereupon Giffard was extremely angry. As a result, a more co-operative subordinate was sought, a move that was welcomed by the Americans, who had never found Giffard an easy person to work with. In came General Sir Oliver Leese with a high reputation as a Corps Commander won in the Western Desert and later as 8th Army Commander in Italy. Slim commented: 'The staff, which he brought with him, and which replaced most of our old friends at General Giffard's headquarters, had a good deal of desert sand in its shoes and was rather inclined at first to push 8 Army down our throats. No doubt we provoked them but while we had the greatest admiration for the Eighth Army, we also thought that the 14 Army was now quite something'.

Mountbatten now had a tidier and more efficient command set up with the American Lieutenant-General Dan Sultan at NCAC, and Christison's 15 Corps in the Arakan, both directly under Leese's command. The reorganization enabled Slim to devote himself to the impending offensive, due to be launched into Central Burma, without being burdened by distractions elsewhere. Meanwhile Leese's opposite number, Kimura, had reorganized Burma Area Army so that by November of 1944 he was able to deploy three armies in the field.

In the north, facing the Chinese-American divisions, was the 25,500 strong 33 Army, consisting of two depleted divisions under Lieutenant-General Honda. In central Burma Lieutenant-General Katamura commanded the remnants of the original four divisions of 15 Army, while in the Arakan, Lieutenant-General Sakurai commanded 28 Army which consisted of three strong divisions. At first sight, the strength of the Arakan army may seem surprising but the Japanese were not to know that the Combined Chiefs-of-Staff had stripped SEAC bare of landing craft: thus, the series of amphibious landings they expected, and feared, had to be shelved by Mountbatten.

In the Arakan, Christison was soon to learn that battalions from the tough but battle-weary 55 Division had moved northwards, in anticipation of a 14 Army thrust across the Irrawaddy aiming for Mandalay. When the monsoon rains ended, both sides moved forward to take up the tactical positions which the appalling weather had forced them to abandon. It fell to 15 Corps to take advantage of the weakened Japanese position and, once and for all, clear the enemy out of North Arakan as soon as possible. Clearly it was uneconomical to keep four divisions in a sector which promised no real long-term rewards, especially when their efforts were opposed by comparatively few Japanese soldiers. If Sakurai's troops could be driven out of the Arakan, then at least two divisions could be released to 14 Army at a vital stage in its offensive.

15 Corps' next operation was called Romulus, which began on 14 December with vigorous probes on either side of the Mayu Range: on the left was the 81 West African Division, in the centre 82 West African Division, while on the right 25 Indian Division started advancing up the coastal plain, with 26 Indian Division and 3 Commando Brigade in immediate reserve, ready to be used for the next phase, code word Talon. That operation entailed the assault and capture of Akyab. Against such a formidable force, Sakurai could do little except move back, deploying rearguards which offered spirited resistance in order to buy time. With generous Royal Navy support on the sea flank and 224 Group Royal Air Force roaming the skies at will, the end was never in doubt. Indeed, as the latter half of December approached events had moved more quickly than Mountbatten and the Joint Force Commanders had ever anticipated. Buthidaung was captured on 15 December, the much disputed Donbaik, where intrepid Japanese defenders had thrown back so many British and Indian attacks with contemptuous ease in 1943, fell eight days later; a direct landing on Akyab then became an immediate possibility.

But unknown to Mountbatten and his subordinate commanders, the Japanese had pulled back from the Mayu Ridge into the Kaladan valley and, as a result, Akyab was ready to be 'taken' by the first Allied soldier who arrived on the island. This was an artillery observation officer who, seeing no evidence of Japanese activity, landed on 2 January 1945, to be told that all the defenders had fled. The elaborately organized attack scheduled for 3 January, which was to involve all three services, preceded by a mighty effort from 224 Group RAF, was no longer necessary. The capture of Akyab was an anti-climax but the planning, on a tri-Service basis, served as an extremely useful rehearsal for similar subsequent operations. Why did the Japanese abandon Akyab? The explanation was that Miyazaki, commanding 54 Division, did not have enough men to defend Akyab and, at the same time, protect the vulnerable left flank of 15 Army under Katamura. The West Africans' advance down the Kaladan valley had been the final straw, the danger sign that caused the Japanese to send away two of the three battalions originally earmarked to defend Akyab.

By the end of January other islands were captured, the most important being Ramree and Cheduba. The task of taking Ramree was given

to Major-General Lomax's 26 Indian Division. The initial landings
went well, being assisted by heavy naval and air bombardments but
the defending 121 Regiment pulled back behind a *chaung*, which virtually bisected the island from east to west. A deception plan was put
into effect: 'D' Force, a trained decoy unit with British, Punjab
Muslim, Sikh, and Jat companies, held the attention of the defenders
while a left hook was thrown through the jungle parallel to the *chaung*.
The ruse was successful, and complete surprise was achieved by 26
Division.

Now, at last, a measure of reward was reaped from the much-
maligned Arakan campaign which in the past had seemed valueless,
particularly when small groups of Japanese soldiers had successfully
defeated 15 Corps' attempts to extricate them from some of the most
unpleasant fighting country in the world. Strenuous efforts were made
to set up a new network of supply bases, to bring into operation major
airfields, using the resources available in Akyab and Ramree. Christison's victories made an important contribution to the drive on Rangoon, which was to become a race against the 1945 monsoon. By the
end of March Akyab began to function and less than a month later
Ramree became a base from where air supply operations could cover
14 Army's advance up to and beyond Rangoon. A penalty had to be
paid, however: 15 Corps had its teeth drawn by Leese, when he drastically cut the air supply available to Christison's depleted corps. As a
result, local operations had to be curtailed and when the monsoon
rains began, some of 15 Corps' units were withdrawn to Akyab and the
coast.

One major battle that occurred earlier in the year deserves to be
mentioned because it involved two amphibious landings, the first on
the Myebon Peninsula – the approach to Kangaw and the second, ten
days later, near Kangaw itself. The second landing led to furious
opposition and although the Japanese had but one brigade, their resistance was so strenuous that, initially, Christison was under the impression that a complete enemy division had been waiting for his troops.
The earlier landing south-west of Kangaw was carried out by 3 Commando Brigade, with follow-up troops and reinforcements from 25
Division being landed to exploit the situation. Eight days later on 30
January, after Kangaw had been captured, the soldiers who took part
in the operation paid a warm tribute to the air force pilots for the
unceasing support they gave throughout all phases of the fighting.
Without their sustained efforts the casualties on land would have been
very much heavier.

Although 15 Corps did come within sight of completely closing the final escape route of the Japanese force left behind in the Arakan, fanatical resistance by rearguards enabled some of Sakurai's men to make their escape to the north. During last ditch battles certain key features were captured, lost, and retaken. One such battle was waged for a steep ridge nicknamed 'Snowdon'. Occupied on 4 March by 3/2 Gurkha Rifles, with barely a shot being fired, that very evening the Japanese decided to fight for its recovery and by next morning at least half the hill was in their hands, although the defending Gurkha platoon fought with the greatest gallantry until more than half their number lay dead or severely wounded. Next morning 3/2 Gurkhas sent in a company to attack and its exploits were both overshadowed and enhanced by the supreme gallantry shown by a young rifleman, Bhanbhagta Gurung. Bhanbhagta's stirring example which enabled his section to reach the top of the hill, won him the Victoria Cross. When the fighting died away, the grim count of casualties revealed that the company had lost a third of its number: on the battle-scarred ridge more than 60 Japanese bodies were recovered. This was the climax of that stage in the Arakan campaign – apart from a few suicide squads which clung to fox-hole warrens in the jungle, refusing to surrender and meeting death in the traditional bushido manner.

In the north, NCAC under its new commander, Sultan, still had a significant part to play, especially as the last directive issued by Giffard, before he handed over, categorically stated that 'other missions to destroy or expel the Japanese forces in Burma at the earliest date were not to prejudice the security of existing air supply routes to China, including the air staging post at Myitkyina and the opening of overland communications'. But, even as the directive was being promulgated, events in China were taking a turn for the worse, with Japanese advances threatening to overrun airbases and under-trained troops. While the Chinese divisions with Sultan looked over their shoulders at events in their own land, 36 British Division had made excellent progress from Mogaung in their advance southwards, assisted by efficient American fighter and light bomber cover. Indaw was seized on 10 December and early in 1945 the division continued to move at speed, crossing the Sweli River at Myitson before eventually joining up with the American Mars Brigade at Kyaukme.

On 1 April 1945, Slim's request that 36 Division should return to 14 Army's control was granted. He paid a generous tribute: 'Festing and his division besides a good fighting job, had done a great deal to dispel the cloud of uninformed criticism that at one time threatened to darken Anglo-American relations. Instead of only hearing secondhand and often malicious stories, soldiers of both nations had now seen one another fighting the enemy. The result was mutual respect. The Division was given a great farewell by its American friends as it turned south-west to Maymo to rejoin 14 Army'. Although the quotation refers specifically to 36 Division's record and the reputation its soldiers earned with the American and Chinese forces, it also highlights the biased opinions frequently expressed by contemporary writers, some of which became accepted without question in later accounts of the campaign in Burma. It is plain that 14 Army did not win back Burma on its own. It is equally true that NCAC, even though supported by the wholehearted efforts of the US Air Force, and by new techniques employed by American engineers in road-building and in the rapid construction of airfields, plus numerous unsung administrative marvels, could not have defeated the Japanese on land. Only a combination of all these agencies made possible the crushing blows that were struck by 14 Army after Allied troops crossed the Irrawaddy.

Sultan's divisions, in trying to effect a quick junction with the Chinese Expeditionary Force after it had crossed the Salween River, had been involved in severe fighting without achieving notable success. As mentioned earlier, the political situation in China had become very unsettled. Chiang Kai-shek depended on the support of his war lords, buying their allegiance with American guns and money but never being completely certain that some of his generals, particularly in the south-east, would not turn and stab the Nationalist government in the back, with the object of forcing his resignation. No one ruled China during the last year of the war; the Japanese held the north-east and key points in central China, while Mao's communist armies controlled the north-west, without owing any allegiance to Chiang and his government in Chungking.

All told, General Wedemeyer had a difficult path to tread after he became Chief-of-Staff to the Generalissimo. Nevertheless, there was one bright spot because the opening of the Myitkyina staging post meant that the tonnage carried by the American Air Transport Command had so increased that the equipping of freshly recruited Chinese armies no longer caused deep apprehension. What concerned Wedemeyer most at the end of 1944 was the possibility that the Chinese armies, resisting the Japanese approach to Kunning, might disintegrate under pressure, a danger which caused the Generalissimo to warn Mountbatten that after Bhamo had been captured, then at least two of the Chinese divisions under Sultan's command in NCAC would be withdrawn. Mountbatten remonstrated strongly, ending his dispatch with the words: 'I am quite clear that the removal would endanger the accomplishment of my directive and undermine the whole policy of aid to China which had governed Allied strategy in South East Asia'.

The matter was referred back to the Chiefs-of-Staff who told Mountbatten that they had no option but to agree to the withdrawal of two Chinese divisions from Upper Burma. The ones to go were 14 and 22 Divisions, following the capture of Bhamo at the end of December 1944. The veteran 22 Chinese Division had fought with mixed fortunes in many actions since 1942 and had achieved a measure of renown. Sultan continued his advance, although he was under the everpresent threat from the Generalissimo to withdraw the American Mars Force and other Chinese formations. Invariably the momentum slowed down after the two divisions had been airlifted back to China, just at the time when 14 Army was striving to reach, first, Mandalay, then Rangoon before the monsoon season began. The Japanese were thus given the chance to retire in reasonable shape, as well as switching troops to oppose Slim's 14 Army. A notable success was achieved when on 7 March, the Chinese 1 Army under that most able leader, General Sun Li (late commander 38 Division), captured Lashio. During the fighting in the early part of 1945, the American Mars Force had played a significant part, taking over the role that 22 Chinese Division had been assigned before its departure for China. In addition, Force 136, composed of irregular Burmese tribesmen under British officers, infiltrated nine special groups behind the Japanese forward positions during this period, groups that sent back intelligence of operational value as well as raising a strong force of Shan and Lahu Levies who harassed the Japanese as they retreated along shaky lines of communication. Fortunately for Sultan, the weakened state of NCAC was not as serious a matter as it might have been because the dramatic advances made by 14 Army in Central Burma forced the Japanese to concentrate the maximum strength there rather than striving to drive a wedge between the Chinese Expeditionary Force in Yunnan and their comrades, serving under American command in NCAC. Furthermore, possibly under instructions from the Generalissimo but certainly given without Sultan's knowledge, from February onwards the Chinese 1 Army adopted dilatory tactics by avoiding direct confrontation wherever possible, so that only 36 British Division continued to strike south-eastwards with dash and vigour during that period.

Behind the scenes there were countless political moves and counter-moves. Chiang Kai-shek wanted the American Mars Force (475 Regiment) to be flown to China as soon as possible so that it could help in the reorganization and training of newly raised Chinese divisions: in addition, he recommended to Mountbatten that the NCAC stopped at Lashio and advised that Supeme Commander to limit 14 Army's advance in central Burma to the capture of Mandalay. With the hour of complete conquest fast approaching, it was an unrealistic suggestion to rein in 14 Army at Mandalay. Mountbatten, while refusing, did agree to compromise by transferring Mars Force to the China theatre – although on purely military grounds Leese strongly advocated its retention in Burma. Other points of issue had to be thrashed out, too: for example, Who would have the overall responsibility for the security of the Burma Road? Who would provide the aircraft to transport the Chinese and Americans back to China? With 14 Army operating more than 900 miles from its main railhead at Dimapur, and with the battle around Meiktila at its height, few, if any transport aircraft could be spared, especially as the majority of the planes already were working at about two-thirds above the normal sustained rate. A bitter and exhausting wrangle followed in which the British Prime Minister, General Marshal, and the Chiefs-of-Staff, were involved, with Mountbatten showing admirable firmness and patience until eventually he obtained the assurance that he would have available all American aircraft and reserves at his disposal in South East Asia, until at least 1 June – by which time it was hoped and assumed that Rangoon would have been reoccupied. (It actually fell on 3 May.)

NCAC no longer had a significant role to play after 38 Chinese Division, which had moved slowly down the Burma Road from Lashio, made contact with 50 Chinese Division as it advanced southwards from Nanto. The Burma Road from Mandalay to the Chinese border, which had been in Japanese hands since April 1942, was once more under Allied control. It was for this and no other reason that the Americans had recognized the Burma campaign as being one worthy of their support. Ironically the famous, almost mythical, Burma Road, the goal for which thousands of soldiers had died, proved to be a complete white elephant because it had no part to play in the course of the war in China or South East Asia thereafter.

Let us now return to Central Burma after putting the clock back to the last few weeks of 1944. Slim's 14 Army was closing up to the Chindwin, prior to making preparations to cross the river in strength and re-enter Burma, some two-and-a-half years after Burma Corps had been thrown out. Kimura's overall strategy was to retire behind the Irrawaddy, hoping to entice Slim across, there to fight a decisive action in the Mandalay area. He expected to be afforded the chance to stage-manage a U-Go type of operation in reverse, with his own troops fighting with their supply depots close at hand, while 14 Army would have to operate with a long, difficult line of communication, one that would stretch across two major rivers back to Dimapur. Against a different background, Kimura followed Mutaguchi by completely underestimating the capacity of the Allied air forces to sustain and supply the land battle, irrespective of the situation, and regardless as to whether formations were surrounded by the enemy or rapidly moving as a spearhead of an advance. The lessons of the Ha-Go and U-Go offensives had not been learnt, so that Kimura expected 14 Army to be in dire straits when it began to operate in the arid region of Central Burma. Moreover, he ignored the likelihood that the areas of semi-desert would offer wonderful opportunities for British and Indian tanks to be used to full advantage, thus to play an even more important part than they had done on the plain of Imphal, earlier in the year.

Although the Japanese reshuffled the generals holding key appointments in the Burma theatre, they were not able to bring about an efficient technique of command and control or achieve the relatively high standard of teamwork that existed in the Allied headquarters that opposed them. The Japanese divisional commanders tended to plan and fight their battles in a vacuum, as if they were the only ones that mattered, obsessed by the problems that beset them rather than taking into consideration the overall situation. Their infantry continued to fight with stoical courage and blind obedience to orders, but the support they were given in the air and from their few light tanks was pitifully inadequate. Bravery alone could not win the day against such terrible odds. For example, the Japanese 5 Air Division with less than 100 fighters and bombers had to contend with 650 front-line Allied fighters and 700 bombers.

Apart from excellent close support from well-drilled mortar teams, the Japanese infantry had to rely on their ability to dig deep and quickly, allied to undoubted expertise at camouflage and concealment. Finally, to add to their problems, radio communications were unsophisticated, unwieldy and unreliable, while the logistical support system, even with supply depots relatively close to the front line units, was inflexible once the battle became a fluid one. Provided that 14 Army could resolve its own considerable administrative problems, and bring the Japanese army to battle where it could be hit by concentrated blows from the air and strong armoured formations, then the chances of the offensive going awry seemed most unlikely. In short, Slim had most of the trump cards that were denied to his unfortunate but stalwart opponent: considerable air power, which gave him freedom of movement while, conversely, the Japanese had to wait for the hours of darkness before attempting anything ambitious tactically or in resupply. The terrain favoured Slim because, after crossing the Chindwin, 14 Army would emerge from close jungle into open country where the much-practised co-operation between air, armour, artillery, and infantry could reap the dividends richly earned by the officers and men, who had spent several exacting weeks in rehearsing such techniques in India, in preparation for the new type of environment. While the vanguard of 14 Army had been closing up to the Chindwin, the other divisions were carrying out ambitious retraining, designed to fit them for the different style of warfare they would encounter after the river barrier had been crossed.

Although 33 Corps' operations that took place during and immediately after the 1944 rainy season were not dramatic, the pressure exerted on the Japanese never relaxed as, superbly assisted by 221 Group RAF, Stopford's men moved relentlessly forward. Sittaung was reoccupied on 4 September by 11 East African Division to stop the Japanese from using the Chindwin as a means of escape, thus preventing any large-scale movement north and south. Stubborn pockets of resistance continued to be eliminated west of the Chindwin. During this phase, the Lushai Brigade rendered sterling service in conjunction with the two infantry divisions then operating under HQ 33 Corps: 5 Indian and 11 East African Division. The battle-scarred 17 Division was one of several formations taking a breather back in India – re-equipping, retraining, and snatching a few days of well earned rest.

The Lushai Brigade came into its own operating as guerrillas. Previously it had been based around Tiddim and Fort White, carrying out local actions in the Chin Hills on a minor scale. After the Japanese began their general retreat from Imphal, the Brigade, consisting of Indian soldiers and local levies stiffened by a handful of British NCOs, all under the command of British officers, undertook a series of highly successful raids against the flanks and rear of the Japanese, as they retreated to the east along the Tiddim road. The Lushai ambushes accounted for enemy vehicles as well as killing many Japanese soldiers. The progress of 5 Division along the Tiddim road owed much to the Lushai Brigade and the influence its members exerted throughout the region. The Chins, like the other hill tribes, had stubbornly opposed the Japanese invaders from 1942 onwards; now their spirit of resistance changed to open aggression until it was not long before the more easy-going Burmese were influenced into turning on the Asian conqueror whose 'Co-Prosperity' concept had brought them so few benefits apart from the top collaborators who had toadied their way to favour for personal gain.

Tiddim was not to fall into the laps of 5 Indian Division: instead the veteran 33 Division resisted with stubborn skill, using every advantage given them by a succession of hairpin bends as the road wound and climbed about 4,000 feet in some ten miles. From dug-in positions east of Tiddim, the defenders threw back assaults and repulsed early attempts to outflank them. In the end, it required a full scale operation, involving tanks and Hurribombers, and even then the elements played a significant part in the outcome of the battle. A heavy morning mist lay over the hills as the tanks moved towards the Japanese positions at MS 156, 5,600 feet above sea level. To start a well co-ordinated programme, the Hurribombers dived through the mist, their noise drowning the rumble of the armour until it was too late for the defenders to recover from complete surprise. Tiddim fell on 10 October and although the advance along the Kalemyo road continued to meet resistance, especially near Fort White, the way to the Chindwin was open.

The progress of 5 Division along the Tiddim road was more spectacular than 11 East African Division's advance through the Kabaw valley. Sickness and exhaustion had taken a heavy toll during the last few days of the monsoon and even with the better weather in October, the track down the valley remained covered in a sea of mud, often up to 18 inches deep. It became a struggle against the terrain, which imposed a heavy burden on everyone, especially the engineers and the drivers of all types of vehicles. Only in early November did the conditions begin to improve and allow the thrust towards the southern end of the Kabaw valley to make headway, the immediate aim being to occupy Kalemyo and Kalewa. On 24 November the Africans entered a deserted, ruined Kalemyo. A few days later Kalewa was occupied when the last Japanese withdrew to the east bank of the Chindwin.

These successes by 33 Corps enabled an ambitious programme to begin, aimed at concentrating the striking force of 14 Army close to the Chindwin. The single track through the Kabaw valley had to be repaired, strengthened, and enlarged; forward airfields and landing strips had to be constructed; bridging and other heavy equipment had to be brought forward: and this hectic programme had to take place while the whole of 4 and 33 Corps moved eastwards, ready for the next step – the reconquest of Burma under the code name, Capital.

That this would not be easy was borne out by the remarkably few Japanese prisoners taken during the pursuit to the Chindwin – some 600 were captured of whom no more than 150 were physically capable of fighting at the moment of capture or surrender. The bushido tradition still held sway.

Under the original concept of Capital, Slim had anticipated that the Japanese would make their main stand defending Mandalay on the plain around Shwebo, north of the confluence of those two giant rivers, the Chindwin and Irrawaddy. Slim's appreciation that Kimura would fight a major action at Shwebo was based on earlier intelligence assessments, coloured by a degree of wishful thinking. The Shwebo plain would have been an ideal killing-ground for the powerful Allied airforces and vastly superior British-Indian fleet of tanks and armoured vehicles. Unknown to Slim, however, Kimura had no intention of fighting a lengthy battle of attrition west of the Irrawaddy, especially when he was outnumbered and badly wanted the protection afforded by the wide river, which ran between the key points in central Burma and the enemy that threatened him. By holding positions east of the Irrawaddy, his forces could wait and see where the British intended to cross the river, then crush them before any bridgeheads had been consolidated and strengthened. If he could strike before the armour and heavy weapons had crossed, then the troops holding the early footholds might be eliminated or be forced back to the opposite bank.

There had been plans for an airborne operation to be mounted with a view to seizing Shwebo by a *coup de main*, but these had not found favour in Slim's eyes, chiefly because every available aircraft was urgently needed in support of 4 and 33 Corps while they prepared for and then executed crossings, prior to the major breakout. He certainly did not want to risk precious aircraft in any other hazardous undertaking. As a result, 7 Division was held back while 19 Division from 4 Corps set off on 4 December, crossing the Chindwin to the north of Sittaung. The plan was that if 19 Division found the going easy and the route suitable to its first objective at Pindebu, 7 Division would be ordered to follow the same course rather than being landed near Shwebo. Scoones, who with Slim and Stopford had been knighted by the Viceroy (Lord Wavell) after the Imphal battle had ended, had handed over 4 Corps on promotion - to be replaced by the enterprising Frank Messervy, who had commanded 7 Division with dash and vigour whenever he had led them into action. Messervy's optimistic temperament made him an ideal choice for the open, fluid warfare that was to come, especially as 19 Division had a mercurial Welshman, Major-General Pete Rees, a veritable human dynamo who led from the front. Soon Rees was to so inspire 19 Division that its exploits made newspaper headlines in the United Kingdom – a remarkable feat at a time when 14 Army was still The Forgotten Army, because the war in Europe continued to grip the imagination of the British public. The

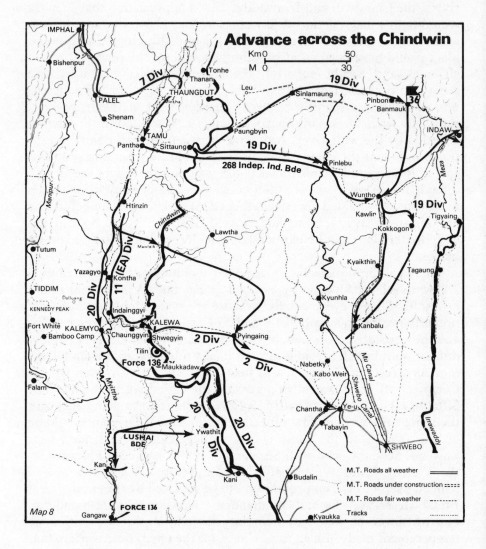

Advance across the Chindwin

Map 8

emblem of 19 Division was a dagger: now the Dagger Division plunged its way forward with remarkable speed to capture Pindebu on 12 December. By then Slim realized that he had misread Kimura's intentions, that the Japanese commander had decided not to fight a major battle north and west of the Irrawaddy. The original concept of destroying the Japanese on the plain of Schwebo had to be drastically revised without further ado. Slim admitted later that: 'I expected he [Kimura] would have had much the same characteristics and faults as his predecessors. In this I was wrong. General Kimura was to prove himself a commander with a much higher degree of realism and moral courage'.

Slim had been on the verge of falling into Kimura's trap but being the commander he was, he worked out a revised plan in record time after firm policy decisions had been taken. On 17 December Leese received a summary of the hastily conceived operation, Extended Capital. By that time intelligence reports from many sources enabled 14 Army to glean a far more accurate picture of the disposition of the divisions under Katamura, Mutaguchi's replacement as 15 Army Commander. Rees's men had captured highly revealing enemy documents which, augmented by reports from Burmese agents, showed that 15 Army was grouped round Mandalay like a clenched fist, with its main road and rail communications extending 60 miles to the south linking up with the important centre of Meiktila. In Kimura's eyes, the retention of Mandalay was all-important and 15 Army's divisions had been marshalled accordingly. Slim was quick to appreciate that if Meiktila were seized by a sudden thrust, 15 Army would be deprived of vital supplies, separated from reinforcements, and starved of its life blood. By such a blow, a lengthy battle of attrition round Mandalay would be avoided because Kimura would be compelled to divide his forces in an attempt to reopen the vitally important lifeline with Meiktila.

Extended Capital saw 33 Corps seizing bridgeheads north and south of Mandalay, with Stopford's role being to draw Katamura's divisions into making costly counter-attacks against the two main bridgeheads. Meanwhile, with the attention of the Japanese fully engaged by the battle raging in the north, Messervy's 4 Corps would move through the Kabaw and then Gangaw valleys, marching under strict radio silence and cloaked by deception measures in order to ensure maximum secrecy. After emerging from the Kabaw valley, 4 Corps would swing eastwards and bounce a crossing over the Irrawaddy near Pakokku, just below its confluence with the Chindwin. From Pakokku the vital target of Meiktila lay less than 90 miles away. The concept was a daring one and only by dint of imaginative deception devices, plus rigorous discipline, was the whole corps able to cover a march of more than 300 miles at speed and without being detected, before establishing a bridgehead over the Irrawaddy. Thereafter little time was lost before launching a striking force towards Meiktila while the Japanese still laboured under the impression that 4 Corps was waiting to follow 33 Corps across the Shwebo Plain. Although the battles for Mandalay and Meiktila had yet to begin, the fate of Katamura's army (and Honda's in the north), was sealed by 4 Corps when it made its presence felt on 10 February: secrecy was cast aside as the fight for a bridgehead opened on the east bank of the Irrawaddy. Even then Japanese intelligence believed that this landing constituted another Chindit-type diversionary operation - a mistake that had the gravest consequences for Kimura. Before following Messervy and his corps towards Meiktila, let us observe a chronological sequence and return to 33 Corps.

On 9 January 1945, 19 Indian Division established a foothold when two small battalions crossed the Irrawaddy at Thabeilyun, a point some 60 miles north of Mandalay. Three days later another brigade from the same division landed a few miles to the south, using nothing more sophisticated than powered assault boats and rafts, a remarkable feat of watermanship when it is remembered that the river there is twice the width of the Rhine. Katamura was convinced that 14 Army's main assault had begun and immediately sent his tried and trusted 15 and 33 Divisions against Rees's bridgeheads, launching one attack after another in a desperate attempt to throw the Indian Division back into the river. But 19 Division stood firm, until on 12 February the Japanese received another piece of disconcerting news when they heard that 20 Indian Division under Gracey had also crossed the river and secured a bridgehead, south-west of Mandalay. Again Katamura was determined to drive these new arrivals back into the Irrawaddy but his inadequate resources were stretched yet again when, on 21 February, 2 British Division established another foothold on the east bank of the river. By this time 15 Army no longer had any reserve units left so that the British bridgeheads were consolidated and made ready for exploitation. All that the Japanese could do was to adopt a defensive posture in an attempt to delay the British and Indian soldiers as they began to advance towards Mandalay. During the heavy fighting that occurred round all the bridgeheads the Japanese lost far more casualties than their opponents, chiefly because Allied armour had been transported quickly across the river, and in the more open country tank guns were used to maximum effect,

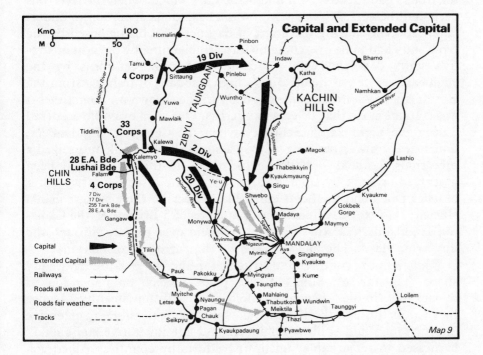

Map 9

devastating and demoralizing the brave but relatively unprotected Japanese infantry.

Although these crossings of the Irrawaddy have been dismissed in a few words, certain facts should be borne in mind. The width of the river varied between 800 and 1,500 yards; the current was usually about 2 knots but flowed considerably faster along certain stretches; in many parts of the river there were large sandbanks with shifting shoals; the western approaches often tended to be open and overlooked by steep cliffs on the east bank of the river; and, finally, the majority of the troops had to cross on home-made rafts which, when the river was deep and the current ran swiftly, was a hazardous operation to undertake, especially during the hours of darkness. Problems posed by the Irrawaddy had to be overcome by forward planning by the administrative staffs concerned and ingenuity and resourcefulness by the engineers, as well as demanding a high standard of training from the assault troops – with a degree of good fortune thrown in. Sometimes it was courage alone that saved a local crisis. One such example occurred during the night 24/25 February when the Cameron Highlanders, under heavy fire, stormed a way up a steep 30-foot bank and seized a precarious foothold – while behind them all their boats had been destroyed or sunk by enemy action. When the assaults on two other beaches failed and the Scots clung like limpets to their meagre gains, efficient staff work switched two battalions of 5 Brigade to the Cameron Highlanders' sector, transported them over to pass through the tiny bridgehead. The day was won by the narrowest of margins.

While Kimura continued to struggle for 'the battle of the Irrawaddy shore' (his phrase), Slim's master plan – which on paper looked remarkably simple – began to unfold. The swift but stealthy advance by 4 Corps through the Kabaw valley was made possible by extensive improvisation and skill by engineers and administrative staffs alike, harnessed to remarkable, unstinting efforts by countless Allied aircrews. Those airmen maintained a minimum of some 7,000 sorties a day – and without question, were the main architects of Extended Capital, one of the truly great master-strokes of World War II. The Japanese continued to be jittery about the Mandalay front while paying scant regard to the crisis farther south, looming up west of Meiktila. The most successful noisy diversion carried out by Stopford was the prologue to the unexpected, dramatic crossings, effected during the night 13/14 February at Nyaungu, when 7 Division, under Major-General Evans, crossed the Irrawaddy, to strike at the relatively unguarded boundary between 15 and 28 Armies. Moreover, that traditionally vulnerable boundary was guarded by a small contingent of reluctant Indian National Army. Within hours the INA defenders of the ruined city of Pagan had surrendered without a fight. Slim later commented with wry sarcasm: 'This instance was, I think, the chief contribution the Indian National Army made to either side in the Burma War'.

As 7 Division strengthened its bridgehead, Messervy prepared for the next phase to his plan. 17 Indian Division supported by 255 Tank Brigade, was to make the breakout before dashing on to Meiktila. At the height of the emergency there was divided counsel among the senior ranks of the Japanese officers about the significance of the landings in the south. Honda was one who immediately recognized the threat to Meiktila but Kimura at Burma Area headquarters continued to believe that the new bridgehead was merely a diversion from the struggle with 33 Corps for Mandalay. Nevertheless, resistance against Messervy certainly strengthened, and 28 East African Independent Brigade, which had landed at Lesse as a diversion from 7 Division's thrust, had to fight extremely hard to hold its own against vigorous counter-attacks delivered by 28 Army under Sakurai. Sakurai saw more significance in the 'dummy' bridgehead than in the one which 7 Division consolidated until the striking force, required for the next phase, had successfully crossed the river. On 21 February under Major-General 'Punch' Cowan, the veteran 17 Indian Division, spearheaded by 255 Indian Tank Brigade, broke out to begin its dramatic dash for Meiktila. Famous Indian Army cavalry regiments drove Sherman tanks instead of horses – Probyn's Horse and the Royal Deccan Horse – with 116 Regiment RAC (Gordon Highlanders) being the other unit in Brigadier Pert's Tank Brigade. For the first time in Burma, tactics akin to those adopted in the Western Desert were seen as the fast-moving armour raced ahead. This was closely supported by fighter-bomber squadrons under the control of RAF liaison officers travelling with the leading units or sub-units, using radio to call in fighter aircraft against any pockets of resistance encountered by the leading armoured units.

Now that the Irrawaddy had been breached on a wide front, Leese issued an overall directive to Slim, Sultan and Christison, co-ordinating the next moves. In effect, NCAC and 15 Corps were to continue probing forward on the flanks while 14 Army had the mission of destroying 15 Army in the Mandalay area prior to capturing Rangoon before the monsoon rains began. In contrast, Kimura had to gamble and gamble fast. He was prepared to risk NCAC moving forward; he accepted that the Arakan could no longer be held; he recognized that he would have to strip the other fronts if he were to have even a remote chance of smashing 14 Army before it had expanded bridgeheads eastwards away from vulnerable footholds with the Irrawaddy at its back. By dint of energetic reorganization, Kimura had rustled up eight divisions but this total included two formations from the INA so that the balance of power still lay very much with Slim. Fanatical courage was not enough when fighting against an enemy who had overwhelming air superiority, whose tanks had devastating hitting power and which could be used to maximum effect in ideal open country. Moving swiftly and purposefully, 17 Division and 255 Tank Brigade brushed aside rearguards, raced through pockets of defenders and avoided hurriedly placed minefields en route. The Japanese High Command was confounded and their shocked surprise was intensified by an incredible blunder when the communication net reported that the British advance was being made by 200 vehicles instead of 2,000 – which the originator of the message had intended. His had been an accurate assessment. The garbled message received at HQ Burma Area Army appeared to confirm that it was still a hit-and-run raid and no major steps were taken to deal with the attack until it was too late.

Only one thing slowed up the vanguard – the Japanese administrative troops in the rear areas proved that they were just as prepared to die for their country as were their comrades in the crack infantry divisions. For the first time in Burma, *Nikuhaku Kogeki* (human combat destruction squad), whose sole purpose was to blow up an enemy tank, made an appearance against the Rajputs. These fanatics hugged explosive charges to their chests and weaved their way towards the target selected for destruction. Many such suicide missions were encountered by 255 Tank Brigade but although such fanatics were respected they had little deterrent effect. While Cowan closed in on Meiktila the garrison commander, Major-General Kasyua, belatedly appreciated the danger posed by 4 Corps. Although ordered to send 168 Infantry Regiment northwards to the Mandalay front, he disregarded the instruction and galvanized the 3,500-man garrison into activity, converting buildings into strong points, and even detailing the wounded to man a portion of the perimeter and fight to the death. The battle for Meiktila began at the end of February.

Meiktila lies between two lakes, with the town centre at the head of the larger lake in the south. To the north-east lay an important airfield, while on the eastern side of the southern lake stands a large hill, Point 860, on which, in 1945, a golden pagoda stood. This was a well known landmark for both sides because it was visible for miles around. At dawn on 28 February Meiktila was attacked from four directions and although the broken country to the west did not help the assailants, by nightfall the town had been surrounded. While the advance across the plain to Meiktila had been an exhilarating experience – especially after countless weeks of cautious, silent movement in the jungle – progress from now on was to be measured in yards instead of miles, with the Japanese defending the town with courage and tenacity. Clearly defined sectors of responsibility were allotted to 48 and 63 Brigades in 17 Division. 63 Brigade was to attack the western defences while 48 Brigade was ordered to move round and strike from the north. Neither brigade found the going easy. Together with tanks from The Deccan Horse, operating under the command of 48 Brigade, 1/7 Gurkha Rifles advanced slowly against the north-east corner of the town, gradually overcoming pockets of resistance. Slim subsequently wrote about the exploits of the 7th Gurkha Rifles company: 'It was one of the neatest and most workmanlike bits of infantry and armoured minor tactics I have ever seen'. It was by such tactics that the attackers eventually triumphed. Meanwhile in the western half of the sector, 63 Brigade, using similar methods, advanced with little difficulty at first, although the Japanese with callous brutality deliberately and needlessly defended an area surrounding a hospital that housed many of their own sick and wounded. Although every effort was made by the British commanders not to bombard the area, eventually and inevitably a direct assault had to be launched against the converted strongpoint and the majority of the unfortunate Japanese inmates were killed. Pressed back by hand-to-hand fighting which raged in the blazing town, General Kasuya and his indomitable force died to a man. Meiktila had fallen but only after some of the hardest fighting seen in the whole campaign.

The news that the town had been seized by the British was a devastating blow to Kimura. He immediately ordered Honda to leave the northern front and with his 33 Army HQ move southwards at full speed. His mission was to recapture Meiktila at all costs. To help Honda, reinforcements destined for the Mandalay battles were diverted, while units holding a line along the eastern bank of the Irrawaddy were dispatched in haste to swell the counter-offensive. Gradually, but in a piecemeal manner, the Japanese began to surround Meiktila until 17 Division found itself besieged. The divisional supply line was in enemy hands and the British hold on the important airfield at Thabukton was contested with unabating ferocity. By that time Honda had succeeded in concentrating 18 and 49 Divisions against Meiktila, but there was no direct radio link between the two divisional commanders and, as a result, each formation fought its own battle in a vacuum. On the face of it, the Japanese were in a strong position but inside the perimeter Cowan met the emergency with confidence, knowing that he could rely on daily supplies by air. It was for just such an emergency that Mountbatten, in answer to strong pleas from Leese and Slim, had decreed that all Allied transport aircraft had to be available, and could not be diverted to less urgent assignments in support of China.

From outside the city, the Japanese could see 17 Division's gun area, wheeled transport, and daily supply drops – all tantalizingly near – without being able to stop even the light aircraft taking off to return to India with the seriously wounded aboard. It must have been a daunting prospect to witness such an organization operating with obvious efficiency, in spite of the fact that they had surrounded the whole perimeter. Moreover, Cowan had decided that passive defence was not the answer to this crisis. Instead, he organized strong columns of infantry and tanks, heavily supported from the air, which sallied forth to harass and attack enemy concentrations wherever they were reported. These sweeps often lasted up to 48 hours and continued to be a thorn in the Japanese side throughout the three weeks of the siege, smashing their preparations for a co-ordinated assault, and preventing them from reaching the jumping-off positions required for an effective all-out attack on 17 Division. A further cruel blow for Honda and his men occurred when, on 17 March, Cowan was reinforced by the arrival of 9 Brigade from 5 Indian Division. The Brigade was flown into the fiercely contested Thakukton airfield. Now Honda had to stake everything on a final attempt, fully appreciating that defeat was staring him in the face. During the night of 20 March Honda hurled his soldiers against the defenders of the airfield. Courage and gallantry ensured that a lodgement was secured but heavy, devastating fire halted the attackers until the following morning – then during the daylight hours, the Japanese survivors were hunted down mercilessly by combined tank and infantry teams. The siege of Meiktila was over when Honda pulled back the remnants of his shattered force.

Slim paid Cowan a stirring tribute for the way he conducted the battle. He ended by stating: 'His firm grip on his own formations and on the enemy never faltered. To watch a highly skilled, experienced, and resolute commander controlling a hard-fought battle is to see, not only a man triumphing over the highest mental and physical stresses, but an artist using his effects in the most complicated and difficult of all the arts'. (*Defeat into Victory*).

During a visit, Slim saw Cowan at close quarters controlling opera-

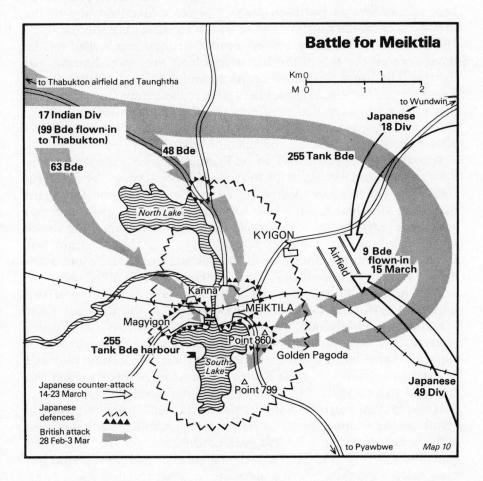

Battle for Meiktila

Km 0   1
M 0   1   2

to Thabukton airfield and Taunghtha

to Wundwin

17 Indian Div
(99 Bde flown-in
to Thabukton)

**Japanese
18 Div**

48 Bde

255 Tank Bde

63 Bde

North Lake

KYIGON

Airfield

**9 Bde
flown-in
15 March**

Kanna

MEIKTILA

Magyigon

Point 860

**255
Tank Bde harbour**

*South
Lake*

Golden Pagoda

Point 799

**Japanese
49 Div**

Japanese counter-attack
14-23 March

Japanese
defences

British attack
28 Feb-3 Mar

to Pyawbwe   *Map 10*

tions around Meiktila, but at no time did he interfere with the divisional commander's control of the battle. Cowan's capture and subsequent defence of Meiktila enabled Slim's overall strategy to end in complete success because Katamura's Irrawaddy line, starved of reinforcements and with its divisions sucked into the struggle for Meiktila, then began collapsing like a crumbling wall. In the north, Rees at the head of 19 Division had been pushing towards Mandalay and by the first week of March his troops were within gunshot range of Mandalay Hill. Thereafter for several days, a bitter struggle was waged for the monastery on the top of the hill overlooking the town. During that fighting The Royal Berkshire Regiment and 4/4 Gurkha Rifles played a notable part: many Allied soldiers were to die before the Union Jack flew once more over Fort Dufferin. By the end of March all Slim's divisions were pushing forward as enemy resistance slackened, thereafter to become spasmodic and unco-ordinated.

Kimura lost the battle for Central Burma when he was outwitted by Slim's master stroke, the feint towards Mandalay while the lightning right-hook delivered by 4 Corps buried itself under the Japanese guard by seizing Meiktila. Kimura later admitted that the Meiktila operation was the 'master stroke of the whole campaign in Burma – the stroke which sealed the fate of the Japanese armies in that Theatre'. Considering the scale and the bitterness of the fighting for Meiktila and Mandalay, 14 Army's casualties – which amounted to 10,500 – were not unduly heavy. The result meant more than just the capture of two important towns; of far greater significance was the fact that apart from the élite 33 Division, the other Japanese formations had so disintegrated that they were forced to seek an escape for the south-east of Burma in small parties, fully realizing that their defeat could only end in death or captivity. For the British, the next prize was Rangoon and they had to race against the ever-approaching monsoon clouds.

If the Imphal battle had shown the world that Slim had grown in stature as the commander of 14 Army, then Extended Capital proved without any doubt that he had entered the ranks of the truly great generals of World War II. The original concept had been sound but even more impressive was his imaginative, swift reaction when Kimura decided to withdraw over the Irrawaddy. Slim's decisive generalship was of a high order and for many reasons, Extended Capital has been called his masterpiece. While praising Slim, the constructive support given to Slim by Mounbatten must not be forgotten. Mountbatten had the personality to withstand pressure from the highest level, which meant London, Washington, and Chungking. His firm touch, combined with natural charm and tact, allowed him to make necessary concessions, provided they did not upset the overall strategy that he and his subordinates considered essential for total victory. Mountbatten also made an outstanding contribution by helping to uplift the morale of those serving in SEAC. He did this by visiting commanders and formations, by meeting thousands of Allied sailors, soldiers and airmen fighting in forward areas, or serving on lonely airfields, or engaged in mundane but all-important administrative duties. The Allied cause in South East Asia owed much to Lord Louis Mountbatten after he had been appointed Supreme Commander. Under his overall guidance, central Burma had been recaptured: Rangoon now lay within the British grasp.

The Allied Land Forces, in a matter of about six months, had crossed the gigantic mountain barrier between India and Burma and followed that achievement by crossing two great rivers – in spite of determined opposition. No one can doubt the merit of those deeds. What can be questioned – and will be examined later – was Britain's purpose in ejecting the Japanese from one well defended post after another, in continuing to follow up the withdrawl when there might have been far more fruitful ways of using its armed forces in the Far East. And the Japanese, too – were they justified in expending so many lives in an attempt to hold the outer curtain of western Burma – or indeed, Burma as a whole? Perhaps, the Americans' limited aim of keeping China in the war, and only using the Indian bases and Upper Burma to do so, was not so shortsighted after all when weighed against the really decisive fighting elsewhere in the Pacific, fighting that did far more to weaken Japan's position than did the prolonged struggle in Burma.

CHAPTER 8

Rangoon – monsoon permitting

The good rain like a bad preacher does not know when to leave off – Ralph Waldo Emerson

The overseas adventures of the soldiers of Nippon were nearly at an end. The Japanese had stirred up opposition from all corners of the world. Even in the comparatively small Burma theatre of operations, men from Britain, the United States, India, China, and Nepal, as well as from East and West Africa, joined together in the final pursuit of Kimura's broken armies. Unlike 1942, when the Burmese population sided with the Asian invaders, support had switched to the British, and even units of the Burmese Army – which had been raised and trained by the Japanese – revolted, turning against their masters at a critical stage in the campaign. Prior to early 1945, the hill tribes – Karens, Chins, Kachins – had rendered substantial assistance to the Anglo-American forces. Indeed, the Karens had raised an efficient force of about 1,000 men, who served under British officers. The change of heart undergone by the Burma National Army (BNA), which came to a head at the end of March, posed a problem that was Mountbatten's responsibility to resolve. Should those traitors – patriots in Japanese eyes – serving under the command of Aung San, be accepted into the Allied fold or not? As far as Slim and his subordinate commanders were concerned, the BNA could play an important military role by harassing the Japanese as they fell back, first towards Rangoon, and then to south-east Burma. Tactical and military expediency won the day and on 16 May Slim met Aung San at Meiktila. Following frank discussions between the two men, the BNA cooperated with 14 Army on a realistic day-to-day basis. A decision on their future was deferred until final military victory had been achieved.

By early summer, operations in NCAC and the Arakan had virtually ceased because the Japanese had concentrated all available reserves in forlorn attempts to withstand 14 Army's drive over the Irrawaddy. Planning for the capture of Rangoon had started at the height of the struggle, well before Mandalay and Meiktila had fallen. Slim issued his final operational instruction for the advance to Rangoon on 23 March but the Japanese counter-offensive around Meiktila delayed 4 Corps' move southwards and, as a result, the Army Commander had grave misgivings as to whether the city could be captured overland before the monsoon broke. Rangoon appeared to be within 14 Army's grasp provided that the momentum of the advance could be maintained and, an even bigger imponderable, assuming that the monsoon did not begin in early May, before the port had been secured. After he had launched his two corps, Slim knew that he would have to rely on favourable weather because the land line had already been dangerously over-extended; only supply by air could keep his troops moving forward. If the aircraft were grounded, the Japanese would have time to pull themselves together and resist with more cohesion, thus postponing the inevitable end as well as condemning to death countless men on both sides in a pointless struggle.

The earlier campaigns in Arakan had been criticized in scathing terms by the Americans, and certainly the results achieved by the numerically superior British forces had been meagre, and of little value. Now, at last, dividends were being reaped when under Leese's co-ordination, the important airfield at Akyab, followed by that on Ramree, began to function: transport aircraft could now supply 14 Army with its needs up to and beyond Rangoon. The tremendous feat of opening up those airfields, establishing vital communications, stock-piling supplies, and drafting in the technicians and ground crews for round-the-clock supply operations, was an outstanding landmark in a campaign which had already witnessed miracles of administration. Without this assured means of supply by air, the decision to capture Rangoon before the monsoon would have been a dangerous gamble. As it was, there were still significant risks in the race against time. In his book Slim specifically mentions worries about his mechanical transport, which was on its last legs – his tanks and armoured cars being long overdue for replacement. And the most daunting fact of all, the drivers of those venerable and tired vehicles would have to cover some 300 miles in no more than 30 days – an ambitious timetable that did not include the possibility of serious delays caused by stubborn Japanese defenders. The imponderables were many and for that reason the original operation Dracula, which envisaged sea and airborne assaults against Rangoon, was resurrected and reviewed against the changed circumstances. In the modified version, 14 Army was to link up with the amphibious force as quickly as possible.

Slim's fear was that the Japanese garrison in Rangoon would be

given ample opportunity to fortify the city, to turn it into another
Meiktila or Myitkyina where the defenders had resisted with fanatical
fury for days on end. Originally, there had been much argument about
the feasibility of taking Rangoon by an amphibious assault combined
with an airborne landing, rather than launching a land campaign
across central Burma. The original Dracula plan envisaged Rangoon
being captured from the sea and sky by ambitious, large-scale landings. But such an operation would have required far too many aircraft
and precious landing craft at a time when other theatres of war had a
much higher priority strategically. For this reason, Extended Capital
became the blueprint for the reconquest for central Burma. The pros-
pects of Rangoon being seized before the rains began appeared to be
slim. The old Dracula was dusted, revamped, and brought into line
with the current situation. No longer was it viewed as an alternative
method of capturing Rangoon; the landing was to be launched as an
adjunct to the overland thrust being made by 4 and 33 Corps. Its aim
was to prevent the Japanese setting up defences or preparing strongpoints manned by suicide parties, to unsettle the formations trying to
hold up 14 Army, and to link up with Slim's men as soon as possible
thereafter.

Slim had changed his mind because early in the year he had been
convinced that his troops could reach the city before the rains came,
without being embroiled in a slogging match while doing so. That was
before Honda failed in his attempt to recapture Meiktila, but the
Japanese action retarded 4 Corps' plans for a breakout – and a dash for
Rangoon. On 19 March Slim recommended to Leese that a revised
Dracula would be necessary, with an amended version being mounted
in the first few days of May. For reasons that have not been satis-
factorily explained in official narratives, Leese and his staff took
11 days to formulate a plan – and even then, Mountbatten had to inject
some ginger into the proceedings before detailed operational instructions were finally produced. To 15 Corps under Christison fell the task
of seizing Rangoon by a *coup de main*, using 26 Indian Division
and 50 Indian Parachute Brigade, supported by a naval assault
force (Force W), in close concert with 221 and 224 Groups RAF,
operating from Toungoo airfields. For Christison time was indeed
short. The planners were given eight days only to complete the multitudinous preparations and briefings required for a complicated
assault involving all three services. Provided that the weather con-
formed to optimistic expectations, the landing was scheduled for 1
May, a date earlier than the one suggested by Slim but selected on
naval advice. It was very much to the credit of Rear-Admiral Martin,

Lieutenant-General Christison and Air Vice-Marshal the Earl of Bandon, the three commanders concerned, that the assault force was ready to move from the islands of Akyab and Ramree, sailing in six convoys at various times between 27 and 30 April. There was to be nothing stealthy or silent about Dracula: two battleships, four cruisers, two aircraft-carriers, and a small destroyer escort sallied forth into seas devoid of enemy warships. At the same time British and American bomber squadrons from the Strategic Air Force opened the prologue to the landing by carrying out heavy bombing raids on known defences along both sides of the Rangoon River. Dracula had begun. But how was 14 Army faring as 15 Corps began its descent on Rangoon?

Two axes of approach were open and possible – the first down the Irrawaddy, and the second astride the railway that ran southwards from Meiktila. The river route was taken by 33 Corps and for this purpose the corps was reduced to two formations only, 7 and 20 Indian Divisions. Meanwhile Messervy, commanding 4 Corps, controlled the bulk of 14 Army for the main thrust down the axis of the railway track to the distant goal of Rangoon. There were three Indian divisions (5, 17 and 19), while 255 Tank Brigade was to be used like a battering ram, a fast moving armoured element which would have to blast a way through, without delaying or worrying about open flanks. This was not to be a conventional advance to contact: speed was absolutely essential, combined with the ability to hit hard at any opposition encountered. A heavy punch was recognized as being of paramount importance so that in the order of march, guns of 18 Field Regiment RA found themselves travelling behind the leading Sherman tanks, ready to give instant fire support to the armoured units as they smashed through any opposition on route. Not surprisingly after the long arduous struggle to reach such a point in the campaign, there was friendly but deep-seated rivalry between 4 and 33 Corps as to who would win the race to the city and port of Rangoon. At 14 Army HQ, too, there was a mood of confident optimism with all 'raring to go'. But the race was more than just a question of accepting hazardous administrative risks. In Bill Slim's words: 'Whatever the risks, we were winning. We had kicked over the anthill, the ants were running about in confusion. Now was the time to stamp on them. My soldiers were out for Rangoon and anyone who was with them and had seen them fight could not doubt that they would get there'.

The more spectacular role fell to 4 Corps. Messervy, with two motorized divisions and 255 Tank Brigade under his command, was given the chance to apply blitzkrieg tactics and chase the surviving units in Honda's force once they had been dislodged by 17 Division and its supporting armour at Pyawbwe. The leading units set off in an attempt to cover 300 miles in 30 days, first with one division then the other in the lead, seizing airstrips which would be prepared for immediate operation by engineers travelling behind the armour. Honda was not allowed to regroup his men or gather any semblance of organization out of chaos. Honda himself had a series of hair-raising escapes. He was fortunate to get away from Pyawbwe where his own staff were forced to join the HQ defence unit in an attempt to hold up the Indian infantry. The harassed general was able to make his escape in the confusion that reigned in the town. The defeat at Pyawbwe meant that the right sector of Kimura's defensive line was crumbling. This presented a most serious threat to Sakurai (28 Army), most of whose troops were still in the Arakan. While Kimura still firmly proclaimed his intention of holding Rangoon to the end, Sakurai obtained his superior's reluctant permission to make necessary adjustments and by this foresight, saved 28 Army from complete destruction at the hands of 4 Corps in the Irrawaddy valley.

Japanese survivors, brushed aside by the lightning advance, attempted to infiltrate back behind the leading British and Indian units and at the town of Yamethin succeeded in cutting the road, thus stopping all movement. From dug-in positions protected by houses, they used anti-tank guns to halt the vehicles in support of the leading armoured group moving with 5 Indian Division. Eventually the 400-strong Japanese party was winkled out and destroyed but 4 Corps' ambitious timetable could not afford such checks, for time was a precious commodity. Delays of a few hours caused grave concern – anything longer was quite unacceptable.

The next target was Pyinmana, which the Japanese had hurriedly prepared for defence, using troops from 55 Division who had been rushed up in haste from south-west Burma. With the minimum of delay, the leading column at the head of 161 Brigade bypassed obstacles and overcame stiff resistance at a hill feature, Shwemyo Bluff. On 20 April the airfield at Lewe, an important prize, was captured. The fighting that developed for Pyinmana utterly destroyed the last vestige of control exercised by HQ 33 Army; once again Honda was forced to make an escape, this time across paddy fields on foot. Only a self-sacrificing stand made by the defence company enabled the commanding general to flee to safety. Now it became a race for Toungoo.

Belatedly, the Japanese tried to occupy the town before 4 Corps could reach it. If they had done so, there would have been the usual inevitable delay while the town was cleared, house by house.

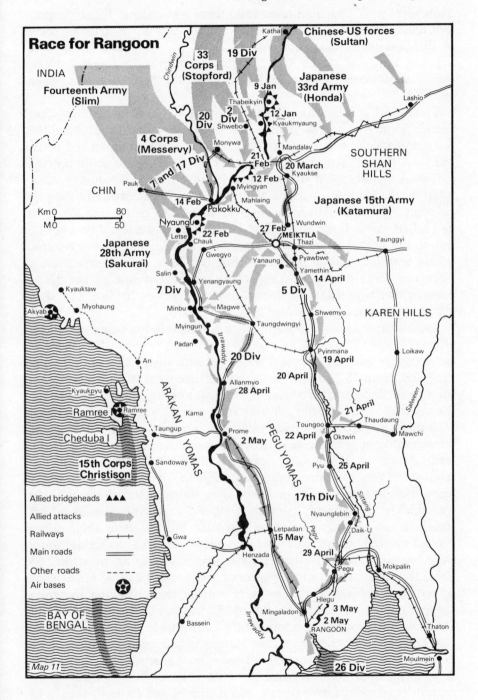

Race for Rangoon

INDIA

**Fourteenth Army
(Slim)**

Katha

**Chinese-US forces
(Sultan)**

Chindwin

**33
Corps
(Stopford)** **19 Div**

Thabeikyin

9 Jan

**Japanese
33rd Army
(Honda)**

Lashio

**20
Div** **2
Div** Shwebo

12 Jan
Kyaukmyaung

**4 Corps
(Messervy)** Monywa

Mandalay

SOUTHERN
SHAN
HILLS

7 and 17 Div

21
Feb

20 March
Kyaukse

CHIN Pauk

12 Feb
Myingyan

14 Feb
Pakokku Mahlaing

**Japanese 15th Army
(Katamura)**

Km 0   80
M 0   50

Nyaungu
Letse 22 Feb
Chauk

27 Feb **MEIKTILA**
Thazi

Wundwin

Taunggyi

**Japanese
28th Army
(Sakurai)**

Gwegyo

Yanaung

Pyawbwe

Salin

Yenangyaung

Yamethin
14 April

Kyauktaw

Myohaung

7 Div

Minbu Magwe

Shwemyo

5 Div

KAREN HILLS

Akyab

Myingun

Taungdwingyi

Padan

20 Div

Pyinmana
19 April

Loikaw

An

20 April

Kyaukpyu

Ramree Ramree

Kama

Allanmyo
28 April

21 April

Thaudaung

Cheduba I

Taungup

Prome
2 May

Toungoo
22 April Oktwin

Mawchi

**15th Corps
Christison**

Sandoway

Pyu **25 April**

Allied bridgeheads ▲▲▲

Allied attacks

Railways

Main roads

Other roads

Air bases

Gwa

Henzada

17th Div

Nyaunglebin

Letpadan
15 May

Daik-U

29 April

Pegu

Pegu Mokpalin

BAY OF
BENGAL

Bassein

Mingaladon

Hlegu
3 May
2 May
RANGOON

Thaton

Irrawaddy

Map 11

26 Div

Moulmein

ARAKAN YOMAS

PEGU YOMAS

Irrawaddy

Sittang

Salween

Moreover, with Dracula impending, there was another highly important reason for the early seizure of Toungoo. A group of airfields, some of the best in Burma, were situated near the town and these were urgently required by the Strategic Air Force in order to give round-the-clock air cover to Dracula, before and after the landings had been effected.

Thus 255 Tank Brigade, closely followed by 123 Brigade Group, set out for Toungoo, and so swift was their advance that by 22 April the town and its three airfields had fallen after some ill-organized resistance. Although Kimura had ordered 15 Division to reinforce the garrison, matters went wrong when it moved through country inhabited by the Karens – because the tribesmen repeatedly ambushed its columns so that the division never arrived. The news that Toungoo had fallen was a devastating blow for Kimura and a few days later he moved his headquarters from Rangoon to Moulmein in lower Burma, taking with him Subhas Chandra Bose. As Bose moved farther away from the scene of the fighting, the entire 1 Division of the INA, numbering about 3,000 men, surrendered without firing a shot as 4 Corps approached the town of Pyu.

As 15 Corps' assault on Rangoon was scheduled to begin on or just after 1 May, 4 Corps had only six days in which to cover the 144 miles between Pyu and Rangoon if it was to earn the distinction of capturing the port. From 25 April onwards the advance went at such a pace that some of the light armoured elements ran out of fuel and had to wait for the arrival of petrol lorries, thundering up in the rear. Although faced with disaster, Japanese suicide parties continued to cause delays at the wrong moment – as far as 4 Corps was concerned. On 27 April the leading units at Byinbongyi, nearly 70 miles from Rangoon, encountered some very tough customers in the shape of engineers who really knew their business. They had used their time to good effect: the area was thickly mined with cunningly placed explosive charges which knocked out or disabled several Sherman bulldozers as their crews probed around, trying to locate the deadly devices. Valuable hours were lost until early next morning when, following an air strike, 63 Brigade entered the town. In spite of lost time, 4 Corps' hopes continued to run high. The odds were still on their reaching Rangoon before Dracula was launched, but on the last day of April, Cowan's 17 Division was brought to a temporary halt outside the town of Pegu.

What had happened was that Rangoon had been stripped of its defenders in order to stop the advance by 4 Corps from the north. A hastily raised force consisting of 24 Independent Brigade, supported by administrative troops, stood firm in the eastern suburbs of

Pegu. Probing attacks were launched on 30 April, but once more mines delayed the tanks and the Japanese infantry succeeded in holding up the attack until 1 May. Then, after blowing up the important bridge over the Pegu River, the Japanese withdrew from the eastern half of the town during the night. By 2 May the town itself had been cleared while engineers began with feverish haste to construct a Bailey bridge to span the river. By superhuman efforts, the sappers enabled a column under the command of Lieutenant-Colonel J. N. Chaudhury, 16 Light Cavalry (later to become Chief-of-Staff Indian Army), to cross the river and continue the advance once more. On 2 May, when 48 Brigade was about 40 miles from the town the first torrential rains came down, slowing the advance in a matter of hours. Eight miles further on, the long advance halted when contact was made with Shermans from 19 Lancers, the spearhead unit from 26 Indian Division pushing their way out from Rangoon. After covering 300 miles in three weeks, living off half rations, and taking risks with petrol and ammunition, Messervy and his men had good reason to feel cheated of the prize they had so richly earned. It was a sad anticlimax. In a sense, the rain had won because the final swift thrust had become a crawl through mud and torrents of rain.

When the sound of naval guns was first heard, deep disappointment was felt in 4 Corps, as the comments of a battalion commander reveal: 'It was a thrilling, and at the same time, depressing sound reverberating in the distance because we now knew that 15 Corps would be in Rangoon before us, a race we had set our hearts on winning'.

While the world's attention had been focused on 4 Corps' dramatic advance, 33 Corps, never the favourites for the race to Rangoon, had made determined efforts to advance down the Irrawaddy as quickly as possible in the faint hopes of beating Messervy. Before the advance, 33 Corps had already been busily engaged in clearing the Irrawaddy front. By 20 April the town of Chauk was taken after heavy losses had been inflicted on the Japanese. In the rear, fighting continued in actions against pockets of resistance and, in particular, at Kykukse where some soldiers of 15 Army stubbornly held on until 18 March.

Following the capture of Chauk, the way was open to the oilfields at Yenangyaung but, as was becoming customary, the Japanese continued to resist in bitterly contested but usually disconnected rearguard actions, with no chance of winning anything but time, at the cost of ever-mounting casualties. Undoubtedly 33 Corps had the less spectacular role but by pushing down the Irrawaddy they not only protected 4 Corps' flank but eventually cut off the remainder of 28 Army in the Arakan – minus the units that had already been moved through Sakurai's forethought. By now the Japanese were thoroughly confused by the speed, strength, and direction of the thrusts being made by 7 and 20 Divisions, while the armoured regiments in support had a field day, brushing aside pockets of resistance while pressing on as fast as they could. Prome was entered on 2 May by the armoured cars of 11 Light Cavalry (Prince Albert Victor's Own) – known throughout 14 Army as PAVO – while on the same day patrols from the 3 Carabiniers were at Inma. There were so many Japanese behind the leading armoured patrols that a halt had to be made in order to mop them up. The INA continued to show no stomach for the fight: earlier, on the outskirts of Madwe, the turncoat Indians were rushing to surrender at a time when the Japanese fought it out or were pulling back to hold another part of the town.

But by now logistical problems were bedevilling Stopford's move towards Rangoon. After he had seized Prome, a further cut in his air supply allowance of 4,500 tons was made; only about a tenth could be delivered at Prome immediately, the remainder had to come from Chittagong, and to complicate matters even more, this could not be delivered south of Magee. This meant that no more than a single brigade could continue towards Rangoon and even that would mean making severe economies elsewhere. The advance of 33 Corps could be treated as a diversion only, to assist 4 Corps and Operation Dracula. The advance was eventually resumed, and on 15 May Tarrawaddy was taken. A few hours later on the same day, a PAVO patrol met some Shermans, at Milestone 60 from Rangoon: they belonged to 1 Lancers, who had landed as part of 15 Corps' amphibious operation. Stopford needed to go no farther. Nevertheless, 33 Corps had played a major part in cutting off the remainder of 28 Army, still west of the Irra-waddy.

When 32 Brigade linked up with 71 Brigade of 26 Indian Division, the overland line of communications to Rangoon was firmly established. Although the rains did not help matters, remnants of the Japanese force, who had been resisting to the west of the Irrawaddy, made frantic efforts to escape, leaving behind much valuable equipment in order to make good speed. They were hampered and harassed from the air by the RAF and on the ground by the BNA who were now, officially, on the side of the British. Few of its members, from Aung San to the youngest recruits, seemed to have any inhibitions or doubts about turning against their old comrades in the Japanese army, now in the throes of defeat.

In spite of the fact that 4 and 33 Corps had been racing each other to Rangoon, striving also to get there before the first monsoon rains, there had always been the possibility that 15 Corps, as part of Dracula, would descend on Rangoon and seize the city before 14 Army could do so. Slim had thus taken out an insurance against unexpected delays or abnormally early rains but in view of 4 Corps' spectacular advance, there had been every expectation that Dracula might not be necessary. In the event it was mounted and beat Extended Capital by a very short head. Captured documents show that the Japanese anticipated that an amphibious operation against Rangoon could not be mounted any later than 12 April because they were convinced that the British would be deterred by an earlier than usual monsoon. This appreciation prompted Kimura to denude the city of defenders after 12 April, dispatching them in an attempt to hold up 4 Corps' drive. At 14 Army HQ, conflicting reports were received about the situation within Rangoon itself: rumours and unconfirmed stories abounded, painting a confused picture which changed from day to day. It seemed as if the garrison included about 5,000 members of the INA, whose morale and fighting efficiency had deteriorated badly after Imphal. Within the city precincts, Allied intelligence estimated that there were also some 9,000 Burmese army volunteers. These had been collaborating with the Japanese since the early days, but now were vacillating, preferring to sit on the fence or, if agents' reports were to be believed, had taken up arms against their old patrons. It was difficult to assess what might happen in such a fluid situation: equally, it was vital that the city and port should be taken quickly in order to avoid bloodshed, particularly as the volatile Burmese might have to be forcibly restrained from exacting revenge against their own countrymen, the quislings and collaborators. They might also punish the dejected Indians, who had been hoodwinked by Bose into betraying their 'salt', turning to treachery instead of obeying the officers they had sworn to obey.

All reports confirmed that the river, which ran from the city to the sea for a distance of about 25 miles, had been heavily mined so that it was estimated four days would be needed to sweep the waters clear. There were coastal defence guns at the mouth on the west bank and at Elephant Point. Some small towns along the river bank lay between the sea and the city and these, too, had been prepared by the Japanese for defence. These facts indicated to the planners that the main assault against the city could not begin until the channels had been swept clear of mines and the pockets of defenders, lying between the sea and Rangoon itself, had been eliminated. Accordingly, the amphibious operation began on 27 April when two naval forces set out from Trincomalee to give long-range protection to the convoys during their long voyage to the mouth of the Rangoon River. They were also prepared to intercept enemy warships attempting to escape by sea to the east. The naval force contained the battleships *Queen Elizabeth* and *Richelieu*, as well as a cruiser and five destroyers. The Task Force, under the command of Vice-Admiral Walker, sailed to the Nicobar Islands, then the Andamans, bombarding airfields and attacking coastal batteries as well as enemy shipping with air strikes and gunfire. No opposition was encountered at sea. Meanwhile another smaller force of destroyers patrolled the Gulf of Martaban during this period; thus protection at sea was complete and absolute.

The first blows against Rangoon began with an airborne attack on Elephant Point carried out by a composite Gurkha parachute battalion. The men, all volunteers, had been training for three years, waiting for such a chance. This was the only time paratroops were used in their traditional role in the Burma campaign. The Gurkhas dropped in the area of Tawkiai on the west bank of the river, landing successfully on 1 May. There they encountered some 30 Japanese who had either been left behind to observe or who had been forgotten by their superiors. The little band fought to the death, and only one wounded man survived. It was not one-sided in terms of casualties, because the Gurkhas lost more than the enemy did. But the majority of the Gurkha casualties were caused by American aircraft which hit the paratroopers harder than the Japanese did: an ill-aimed stick of bombs tragically brought death and understandable bitterness at the time. As the Gurkhas battled with the Japanese, minesweepers began clearing the mouth of the river. So far all had gone according to plan. Next day 36 and 71 Brigades, both from 26 Indian Division, landed east and west of the river, ready to probe towards the city, as well as linking up with the paratroopers. While the preliminaries were being enacted, 12 British and American bomber squadrons from the Strategic Airforce were on standby to deal with any untoward emergency. But there was no cry for help – nor were the other troops designated required to carry out their projected role.

The third brigade from 26 Division and the whole of 2 British Division stood by, instead of being called on to play a decisive part in clearing the city, as had been originally anticipated.

During the night of 1/2 May an Allied pilot reported seeing 'Japs gone' and 'Extract digit' painted on the roof of a building, later identified as the Rangoon jail where British prisoners-of-war were known to be in custody. Although this signal was in line with rumours that the Japanese were evacuating the city, and notwithstanding an unusual knowledge of RAF slang, Leese decided not to abandon Dracula in case the message was a ruse. The two brigades of 26 Division duly landed, while an air bombardment was carried out along both banks of the river in the early morning, before the troops made an unopposed landing. The local civilians were quick to state that the Japanese had left five days earlier. Meanwhile Wing-Commander Saunders (commanding 110 Squadron RAF), carried out a low-level reconnaissance during the afternoon of 2 May, and after deciding to accept the RAF messages as firm evidence that all was well, landed on the Mingaladon airfield. The cratered runway, badly damaged by Allied bombing, dented his Mosquito as he landed so that it was impossible for him to take off again. Accompanied by his navigator, Saunders made his way to the jail where he found more than 1,000 jubilant Allied prisoners-of-war, whose guards had disappeared during the night 29 April. In typical Japanese fashion, a message had been pinned to the main gate which declared: 'To the whole captured persons of Rangoon Jail. According to the Nippon Military Order, we hereby give you liberty to leave this place at your will. Regarding other materials kept in the compound, we give you permission to consume them as far as necessity is concerned. We hope that we shall have the opportunity to meet you again on the battlefield somewhere. We shall continue our war effort in order to get the emancipation of all Asiatic races'. Saunders made his way to the docks and after commandeering a sampan, sailed down the river eventually to reach Joint Force HQ, where he reported on the situation as he had found it.

Rangoon, which had been in enemy hands for three years and two months, was thus occupied without any fighting, two days before the surrender of Germany. Strangely enough, in 1942 the Japanese also had taken the city without a shot being fired. When the Indian and British entered the built-up areas, the people in their thousands welcomed the Allied soldiers with a joy they made no attempt to restrain. The city itself was in a sorry state because many of the essential services had broken down through neglect and sheer inefficiency, while the deliberate destruction of the electricity supply system by the Japanese, before they had evacuated the area, added chaos to confusion. The enthusiasm shown by the inhabitants was inevitably tinged with relief because their homes had been spared the horrors of bombing and house-to-house fighting. HQ 26 Division was established at Government House with one of the first priorities being to gather together the Allied prisoners-of-war and fly them back to India, where they were to begin a period of rehabilitation which, for some unfortunate individuals, was to last not weeks but months, and even years.

The launching of Dracula resulted in the reoccupation of Rangoon on 3 May which, as it transpired, was about seven or eight days earlier than it could have been effected overland by 4 Corps. Dracula enabled the urgently required port to be opened much earlier than it would have been, had the reoccupation been left to 14 Army. From an administrative point of view the saving of three weeks, especially as the monsoon started earlier than usual, justified the decision to undertake the operation. For the planners, Christison with his naval and air colleagues, Martin and the Earl of Bandon, it had been a magnificent achievement. And for 15 Corps it was a stirring climax to the heartbreaking operations they had undergone in the Arakan, invariably in appalling conditions, inevitably overshadowed by the more spectacular victories achieved by the other corps on the central front.

Slim held his disappointment in check. Typically, his comment was that if they could not get to Rangoon first, then the next best thing was for someone from 221 Group RAF (the gallant Saunders) to have pipped everyone else – including the Dracula forces! In fact, Slim recognized that his troops would have been in sore straits while operating in the Rangoon area if the port had not been in operation. Work on clearing the docks began immediately, while the sweeping of the river continued without a break. When, by 10 May, the river was fully open for ocean-going vessels, many berths in the dock were ready to receive ships. Top priority was then given to clearing the exits from the docks, which had been badly blocked by Allied bombing. Instead of 2 Division landing as a follow-up force – as had been planned – the convoys brought in administrative units. On 19 May the first convoy sailed in, so that Rangoon was functioning once again. It was a timely occurrence because with the monsoon in full spate, the ground forces would have had to rely on the long uncertain land link back to India, or on the airforces for their supplies. Now the bulk of their needs could come into the port by sea.

Kimura had been set an impossible task by Imperial General Headquarters, especially when he had already been ordered to transfer one division and most of his air strength back to Indochina. His soldiers had fought courageously against overwhelming odds to hold central Burma but, in retrospect, it seems clear that his superiors should have ordered a general withdrawal from Burma – after the monsoon rains had ended in 1944 – rather than attempting to hold an enemy who had such overwhelming air superiority, many more men with readily available reinforcements, and powerful armoured forces which, in close co-operation with other arms, cut their way across Burma, severing the Japanese armies as they did so. And to help the Allies as their strength grew, the attitude of the Burmese changed – their friendliness and willingness to co-operate was in marked contrast to their hostile behaviour during the dark days of 1942.

There was still work to be done in Southern Burma and elsewhere. The Japanese, even though dejected and defeated, were still psychologically incapable of surrendering at a time when the Pacific War was closing in on their homeland from all sides.

One of the greatest architects of Slim's triumph has not yet been mentioned by name – Air Vice-Marshal Vincent – whose 221 Group RAF played such a big part in the victory. In Slim's words: 'He discharged his responsibilities with unsurpassed thoroughness. Vincent and his men piled up our debt to them until we could never repay it and 221 Group RAF had as big a share in our victory as any army formation. We were proud to serve them, but I could not help thinking that sometimes the army recognized their achievements more readily than some of the higher Airforce headquarters'.

The airmen had been cast as leading actors in Burma rather than in a major supporting role. It took a little time for military commentators to recognize the fact. General Fuller did not hesitate, making a firm declaration: 'The campaign in Burma scattered those verbal clouds in which the meaning of air power had been obscured by so-called experts of 1914-18 and brought it into the sunshine of the essentials of war'.

During the early campaign the Japanese pilots ruled the skies over Burma, as they had done elsewhere in South East Asia, and as a result had hunted and harried the British and Chinese columns as they fell back towards India. Nevertheless, in spite of overwhelming superiority they were not able to bring the Allied retreat to a standstill. The movement continued towards the west and safety. Such a picture was to pertain even after June 1944 when the Allies had gained absolute supremacy in the skies over the greater part of Burma. Even after the Japanese soldiers had been rebuffed at Imphal, broken after Meiktila, their commanders were able to retain a measure of cohesion and a degree of flexibility in retreat, using the canopy of the jungle, or accepting with gratitude the inclement weather which grounded the Allied planes – or at the worst, using the hours of darkness for essential movement. Air power on its own did not win battles in World War II – as the Anglo-American generals were to discover at Cassino. Years later, the United States relearnt the lesson when the Viet Cong guerrillas could not be destroyed by bombing even when used to maximum effect – short of employing nuclear devices.

In 1942 the Japanese used their superiority in the air to facilitate the advance of their own soldiers as well as impeding the retreat of the British and Chinese units. To such close offensive support, the Allies added a new dimension involving techniques of air supply which had never been used before in warfare. Such methods enabled 14 Army and NCAC to 'shake loose from the tincan of mechanical transport tied to their tail'. Transport by aircraft was used to move Chinese troops across the Hump to Ledo, to switch divisions from the Arakan to Imphal, to evacuate the seriously wounded, thereby not only saving thousands of lives but enabling countless casualties to receive medical aid and return to fight once more. The capability of moving troops by air revolutionized tactics, simplifying the problems that faced ground commanders, by allowing them to think big and act boldly. Such a view was not confined to the British alone because General Marshall commented: 'The re-entry in Burma was the most ambitious campaign yet waged on the end of an airborne supply line'. From a slender start, the tiny, modest acorn of air transport and supply grew into the giant oak tree that buffeted Kimura and Burma Area Army into submission.

It was not surprising, therefore, that Slim paid such a generous tribute to the airmen before describing the last act in the struggle for Burma.

CHAPTER 9

The end of a long road

The problems of victory are more agreeable than those of defeat, but they are no less difficult – Winston Churchill

Viewed against the major defeats suffered elsewhere in the Pacific, the loss of Rangoon and the impending elimination of Kimura's forces were comparatively minor setbacks to Japanese hopes of salvaging something from the war. The defeat of Germany meant that the full resources of the Anglo-Americans could now be concentrated against Japan. Moreover, after the Americans captured Iwo Jima, from the end of March onwards B29s had begun attacking the Japanese homeland and did so with ease, escorted by fighters. Prime Minister Koiso, who had taken over in August 1944 after Tojo had been replaced, was confronted with the grim prospect of an ever-increasing wave of incendiary bomb attacks being made against major Japanese cities, knowing that there were no defences capable of stopping the bombers. General Koiso and his colleagues also appreciated that nothing could be done to check the onward surge of American victories in the Pacific which, week by week, were coming closer to the homeland.

And when Russia began to make troop dispositions in the Far East prior to entering the war against Japan, it meant that targets on the islands could be reached from Russian bases as well as from various points in the Pacific. No longer was China indispensable to the Allies, and Chiang Kai-shek, with his suspicious nature and devious ambitions, ceased to play a significant part at Allied conferences. The spurious prestige granted him by President Roosevelt dwindled rapidly. The Kuomintang regime had become most unpopular in China and when peace came, the communists emerged with a high reputation as more and more of the population began to turn against Chiang and his autocratic regime.

Although the Americans had been mistaken about China, elsewhere in the Pacific they were riding high: the United States was first and its European partners nowhere. Unlike the campaign in Europe, the top commanders were all Americans and if the invasion of Japan had taken place, then only a small token force of Commonwealth troops would have participated. It could be argued that by allowing herself to become embroiled in the reconquest of Burma, possibly for the wrong reasons, Britain lost the chance of having a major say in formulating plans for postwar Asia. Moreover, the United States made it quite clear that old-style European imperialism had no future and her powerful support would be given to emerging nations that were seeking to throw off colonial shackles.

Meanwhile, waves of bombers had begun to exact a ghastly toll in Japan. By the end of June, half of Tokyo and several provincial cities had been destroyed, and millions of people were homeless. The destruction in Tokyo was far greater than it had been in Hamburg, for example, because the flimsy structure of most houses meant that clusters of incendiary bombs spread devastation with horrifying speed. Compliant, obedient civilians – underfed, homeless, and terrified – began to turn against their military rulers. Even for a people who had suffered calamities from earthquakes with stoicism over the years, the experiences in the summer of 1945 were far more harrowing. After Koiso fell, an 80-year-old admiral, Baron Suzuki Kantaro, took over the premiership. His avowed aim was to bring peace, but unfortunately for his country, he moved too slowly to be able to save Japan from an ordeal that grew as the weeks passed. Life had been paralysed in most major cities, yet Suzuki still hesitated, fervently hoping that the Russians could be persuaded to act as mediators. On 26 July 1945 the Allies issued a final ultimatum to Japan to surrender but no definite answer was received. When it came, Suzuki's reply was ambiguous and the fateful decision was made to drop the atom bomb on Hiroshima on 6 August 1945. President Truman called it 'the greatest thing in history' but it was to take the whole world some time before the implications and terrible aspects of the disaster, the horror of the radiation, and the indescribable suffering of the survivors, were even partially understood. Nevertheless the loss of life in the atomic phase, which was magnified by the harrowing effects of the radiation, was still less than that caused by the succession of B29 raids, constantly pulverizing Japanese cities and ports from March of that year.

In the end, the Japanese Emperor emerged from obscurity and ceased to be a spectator of events. At the time of the crisis, Hirohito quietly, firmly, but with dignity, made his presence felt until the Prime Minister succeeded in getting agreement that the Emperor should be asked to decide what had to be done. His decision, an historic one, was announced: 'The unendurable must be endured' and that announcement terminated the war. On hearing his message over the radio, the Japanese people were reported to have shed tears of shame, relief and, not surprisingly, of disbelief. Within days, they had to change from being a nation at war to becoming welcoming hosts as the American occupiers arrived in their land, bringing with them a foreign culture that has since left a permanent mark on Japanese society.

The all-conquering army of Nippon trampled over many lands in 1942. In late summer of 1945 the remnants of those once proud and efficient armies faced death, starvation or, in the end, surrender, even though they stood defiantly at bay. So it was in Burma after Rangoon had fallen. The British had broken Kimura's hopes when the dash for Rangoon had torn the Burma Area Army assunder, to leave it scattered in four separate groups. Divided as they were, it was obvious that the Japanese were going to fight on because at that time their government had not given any indication of the final capitulation. In the Irrawaddy valley, the surviving units of 28 Army were slowly moving eastwards, hoping to cross the road between Meiktila and Rangoon before striking for the Sittang. Near Meiktila in the Shan Hills, 56 Division gathered together and shepherded stragglers from other formations and with its own units, attempted to move southwards. East of the Sittang River were the shattered remnants of 33 Army, estimated at about 25,000 men, while in the south towards Moulmein another hotch-potch of about the same strength stood defiantly waiting for another Allied onslaught.

Militarily the task that faced 14 Army appeared to be an easy one, but four factors complicated operations, imposing a heavy strain on those who remained in Burma to carry out the final elimination of Kimura's men. For a start, several Allied divisions had been withdrawn, or were earmarked for the projected amphibious landing on the west coast of Malaya, code name Zipper. Quite rightly the clearing and mopping up of Burma took second place in the minds of the Combined Chiefs-of-Staff. They assumed that Zipper would not only have to be launched but that the Japanese in Malaya would resist the landing with their customary tenacity. The second factor, an old enemy, was the monsoon. After Rangoon had been retaken, the rains grew in intensity, adding to the problems of maintenance and resupply by air and land. The American Air Transport squadrons were withdrawn while the RAF ones that remained were curtailed in number – to prepare themselves, after enjoying a few days of well-earned rest, for the launching of Zipper.

Another problem was psychological. British officers and soldiers once the war in Europe was over, were understandably eager to return to the United Kingdom – especially as thousands of them had spent four or five years in continuous service in the Far East without any home leave. Repatriation schemes began, but inevitably there were anomalies and genuine grievances as certain individuals suffered. At the same time, it was the senior ranks, the key men in units, who gained earlier repatriation deservedly earned by their long service overseas. Their departure invariably within the space of a few weeks, reduced the battle worthiness of units. With so much turbulence at unit level, it was not easy to keep maximum pressure on the Japanese forces left in Burma.

And finally, the army found itself being responsible for a large part of the country, containing 13 million inhabitants, who looked to them for food, administrative services, and the enforcement of law and order. In 1942 the Japanese realized that anarchy quickly prevailed when local government had broken down: now history was being repeated. Although the army was in a position to enforce discipline, the urgent need was for civil servants and local government officials to deal with the myriad of contentious grievances that arose. Most of the experienced officials had either accompanied the Japanese voluntarily or had been forcibly removed by them. Intermingled with this problem was the one already mentioned, the unpalatable but undeniable presence of the Japanese-raised Burmese National Army under Aung San. Although he had genuinely become disillusioned with old Japanese friends, his past unsavoury reputation could not be forgotten. Fortunately, Aung San and Slim had mutual respect for one another and in the short term a *modus vivendi* was established following a long frank discussion between the two men. Slim later commented: 'I was impressed with Aung San. He was not the ambitious unscrupulous leader I had expected. I judged him to be a genuine patriot and a well balanced realist and the greatest impression he made on me was one of honesty ... I could do business with Aung San'.

And he did – to great effect because it certainly hastened the downfall of the Japanese. Mountbatten ratified the agreement and the upshot was that the Burmese irregulars reported for duty to operate alongside British and Indian formations. Until the end of the war, they worked well in conjunction with the army, bringing back vital information as well as helping to track down and ambush the scattered groups of Japanese remaining at large within their country.

After Rangoon had fallen the reality of the situation was officially recognized when a considerable reorganization of the higher service commanders in South East Asia was effected. Slim was chosen to succeed General Sir Oliver Leese as Allied Land Force Commander, with his old 14 Army Headquarters becoming responsible for Zipper, under Lieutenant-General Sir Miles Dempsey who moved from Europe to succeed Slim. Meanwhile in Burma, Stopford was promoted to command 12 Army, which was left with HQ 4 Corps, three Indian divisions, 82 West African Division and 22 East African Brigade, augmented by 255 Indian Tank Brigade to provide the hitting power. Slim then went on leave to England, his first visit home for seven years, and it was while he was away that the last battle in the campaign, 'The Battle of the Breakout', was fought. In his book, Slim makes no mention whatever about an episode which Ronald Lewin covers under the heading, 'A little local disturbance' (*Slim: the Standard Bearer*). It is not intended to repeat an account of that episode because Lewin has already done so in detail, thereby providing a fascinating insight into the different temperaments of Leese and Slim.

Quite clearly, Slim was under the firm impression between 7 and 23 May that he had been sacked by Leese, a distressing blow for a commander who had just achieved final victory in Burma after months of stress and strain. Sacking was never intended by Leese but by mismanagement and a sad misunderstanding, the unfortunate affair left a sour taste in the mouths of those who were in the know or directly concerned. In the end, prompt action by Mountbatten, who had firm support from Alanbrooke, ensured that justice was done: Bill Slim became Commander-in-Chief of the Land Forces in South East Asia and promoted to full general on 1 July. For Leese, who undoubtedly had bungled an unhappy episode, there was nothing except a return to the United Kingdom, to be replaced by the man he had almost sacked – whether by design or ill-conceived good intentions is open to argument.

It was Stopford, therefore, who had to deal with the Japanese who remained in Burma. For the majority there was the stark choice of dying of exposure in the monsoon or from disease and starvation, or of trying to break out from the hills, and crossing to the east in an attempt to join up with the remainder of Kimura's forces. By this time 28 Army under Sakurai was an army only in name: its soldiers were in a bad way, attempting to live off the Burmese, with a few mules and pack animals for transport, and supported by a handful of light guns, with no armour whatever. Their plight was virtually hopeless and this fact was hammered home to them when Allied aircraft dropped hundreds of leaflets in the area, promising fair treatment after surrender, and pointing out that their cause was a forlorn one. Not one man responded – there was not a single surrender. Instead, Sakurai gathered his gallant stricken army together and prepared to make a dash for it.

Unfortunately for Sakurai, a copy of his operational plan for the breakout was captured by a patrol from 4 Corps so that it was learnt that he had split the army into five groups, and from bases between Tongoo and Myaunglebin, a front of about 150 miles, intended to dispatch a series of parties in an attempt to evade British patrols and ambushes. Forewarned, 17 Division – which was in that particular sector – was reinforced with units from other divisions in the Corps. Aung San's irregulars were sent out into the foothills of the Tegu Yomas. It soon became apparent that the attempt to escape could not be delayed any longer. The monsoon was at its very height and had flooded the whole countryside; patrols frequently moved in water up to their waists and in some instances Gurkha troops could not be used because of their short stature.

Towards the end of June, as a distraction, 33 Army began a spirited attempt to draw off British reserves by launching a counter-attack, particularly in the Nyaungkashe area, but whenever conditions permitted, 221 Group RAF bombed and straffed them mercilessly. A crossing over the Sittang to the west bank was made by 33 Army, which hoped to draw off the ambushes awaiting their comrades in 28 Army. Lieutenant-General Tuker, who was temporarily commanding 4 Corps while Messervy was on leave, was not to be misled or distracted by 33 Army's strategies: moreover, the captured order had already given him warning that the main breakout would begin on or about 20 July. While 20 Divison held up 33 Army, 17 Division remained on the alert, waiting for Sakurai to make the first move.

By now the ground had become so flooded that in many areas the only possible way to move was along well defined tracks or by boat and raft along navigable *chaungs*. Ambushes were ready, and adjustments to battalion positions finalized, with tanks and guns standing by to give support. The first engagement began in the early hours of 19 July and thereafter a series of parties continued to try to cross the road but meeting with little success. Sakurai may not have realized that a copy of the operation order had been captured, or possibly he did not have time or the radio communications to change it, but he and his officers persisted with the original plan to the letter, following the same routes in spite of disaster. The result was slaughter – his soldiers had no chance whatever. And, in the last grim hours, the local villagers, police, and Aung San's irregulars joined in, killing without mercy to swell the ever mounting casualty list. It is not necessary to give details of the dozens of actions that took place until 4 August: suffice to say, an appalling retribution was exacted and even when some groups managed to cross the road and escape the gauntlet, they

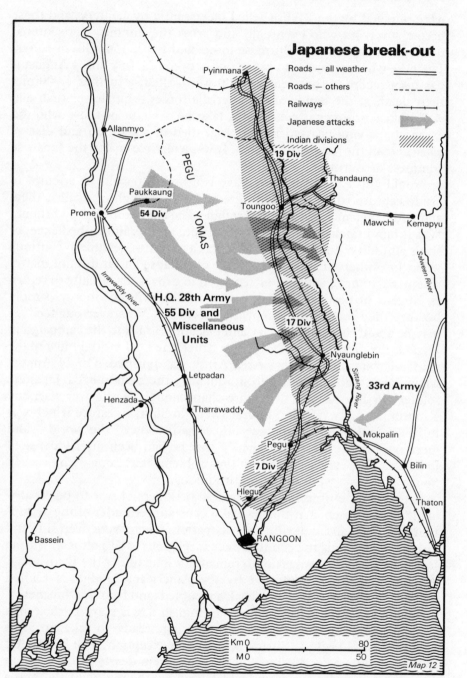

Japanese break-out

Roads — all weather	
Roads — others	
Railways	
Japanese attacks	
Indian divisions	

Pyinmana

Allanmyo

PEGU

19 Div

Thandaung

Paukkaung

Prome

54 Div

YOMAS

Toungoo

Mawchi Kemapyu

Salween River

Irrawaddy River

H.Q. 28th Army
55 Div and
Miscellaneous
Units

17 Div

Nyaunglebin

Sittang River

33rd Army

Letpadan

Henzada

Tharrawaddy

Mokpalin

Pegu

Bilin

7 Div

Hlegu

Thaton

Bassein

RANGOON

Km 0 ———————— 80
M 0 ———————— 50

Map 12

were pursued by the RAF, shelled incesssantly by artillery, and those heroic survivors who eventually did cross the Sittang, were hunted down one by one by the Burmese forces and Force 136. Out of 16,000 Japanese who attempted to break out between 21 July and 4 August it has been recorded that nearly 7,000 were killed; a further 4,000 met their death at the hands of the guerrilla forces – but fewer than 800 were taken prisoner. Such figures take no account of those who did escape or having crossed the Sittang, died of starvation and disease elsewhere in the jungles of Burma. It was a terrible end to the Japanese conquest of Burma.

Would any European army have continued to fight or attempt to evade capture when the odds were so heavily weighted against them and with no chance of coming through? The answer must be a firm no. Was it blind fatalism, magnificent patriotism, ingrained obedience, or sheer stupidity? In Western eyes it was a pointless gesture to continue when Japan herself was on the verge of collapse and it did not matter whether Kimura's soldiers surrendered in droves, eventually to return as citizens of post-war Japan, or were killed without mercy, simply because they refused to accept the inevitable. Whatever our feelings may be about this extraodinary and macabre climax to the campaign in Burma, the destruction of 28 Army struck the final mortal blow to the spirit of resistance. Burma Area Army was finished. On 14 August when Japan surrendered unconditionally, the demoralized Japanese soldiers in Burma had had more than enough of the war. General Kimura handed over his Samurai sword to Slim, a gesture which was full of meaning for a Japanese officer as it showed the world – and more important, his own soldiers – that he had been utterly defeated in battle. The war was over. But the problems that came with peace in South East Asia were to be multitudinous.

It took a long time for the Japanese prisoners of war to be repatriated. Their presence in Burma was a constant reminder of the disruption they had caused during the occupation. There were deep rifts and visions throughout the country: racial, religious, and political. Burma had been freed but it was not to remain for long under the British flag. An imperial army supported by the Americans, and to a limited extent, the Chinese, had won back a troubled land from the Japanese.

The lines, 'By English bones, the English flag is stayed', took on a new meaning. Asian peoples were stirring, ready to take up arms against their old rulers. Burma was to be an exception. The British left without a fight after a campaign that cost them dearly in lives and in financial and material aid, and which stripped them of their status as a leader with a voice in South East Asia. The future of that part of the world lay with the United States. The Americans emerged as victors even though their British Allies had managed to win the final battle for Burma – a military triumph that was to have a hollow ring about it as events continued to unfold in postwar Asia.

CHAPTER 10

Judgement

Posterity is as likely to be wrong as anybody else—
Haywood Brown

In 1942 within the space of four months the Allies lost Burma: subsequently, three-and-a-half years were to elapse before the British could claim, once more, that the Japanese no longer ruled their old colony. Eight more months were to pass before the state of emergency in Burma officially ended, the proclamation to that effect being made by the Governor, Sir Reginald Dorman-Smith, in April 1946. The disruption caused by the Japanese, which began with the invasion during early 1942, radically changed life within the country, while the unexpected and startling defeat of their British rulers caused the Burmese to view the army of Nippon with fear and respect – but without any affection.

After VJ Day the British tried to put the colonial clock back but it proved impossible to do so. Nothing was the same for there were deep divisions within the Burmese population; the hill tribes, who had staunchly defied the Japanese, refused to accept edicts issued by Burmans, especially the collaborators who had gained power during the occupation of the country. In their eyes, Aung San was a traitor, even after Britain had granted him respectability, although with grave misgivings. Not surprisingly, many areas remained troubled and unsettled; Burma enjoyed little peace during post-war British rule. The Governor was constantly aware that a situation could arise similar to the one that confronted British troops in Greece after the German Occupation had ended. The effects of Japan's Co-Prosperity Scheme were felt long after the surrender of Burma Area Army during August 1945. Violence and intrigue continued with Aung San in power, a leader who was not without powerful enemies seeking to overthrow his régime. Aung San's tenure in office was not to last for long, because in 1947 he and other leading members of the Burmese cabinet were assassinated.

At first by deliberate intent, and then inadvertently, Japan kindled nationalist causes in several countries in South East Asia. When the soldiers of Nippon were riding on the crest of victory from one land to the next, ambitious politicians and greedy collaborators abounded, ready to offer their services in order to gain power both for themselves and the parties they led. Thus it was in Burma and the revolutionary parties, notably the Thakins, were ready to seek aid and do anything calculated to bring about an end to British rule. In the first campaign the British suffered a drubbing at the hands of the Japanese army and although Burma Corps was embarrassed by the newly raised Independence Army, the rout automatically gained momentum as British, Indian, and Chinese soldiers attempted to reach India before the Japanese did. The reason for the military defeat has already been examined, and it is not intended to go over the same ground again. Retreat became a certainty after the Sittang Bridge was destroyed. Some may claim that the order to blow was given prematurely; others, like the commander on the spot, Major-General Jackie Smythe, will affirm that further delay was impossible. Radio communications at that time were inefficient and unsuitable for the fluid operations in progress so that even Japanese accounts of that episode have not been able to throw any real light on the timing of the order to blow the bridge. The location of units and sub-units on both banks of the river cannot be established with accuracy. Smythe's dilemma was a cruel one, especially as the decision that he took changed 17 Division from a reasonably well organized, cohesive formation into a truncated hotch-potch of survivors from various units. But who can say what the outcome might have been if Smythe had delayed the order, if the bridge had been captured intact by the leading Japanese troops?

The British accepted with reluctance the offer of the Generalissimo to send Chinese troops to assist in the defence of Burma, but only after the invasion by the two Japanese divisions had made excellent progress – before being reinforced by another two divisions after the fall of Singapore. Chiang Kai-shek took considerable umbrage at Wavell's original refusal to accept help from his troops – a reluctance that was based on suspicions about Chinese designs on Upper Burma as well as on fears that Burma Army could not stretch its limited supply and maintenance facilities to cover the extra burden imposed on them by the Chinese troops. If the Chinese divisions had been pre-positioned in Burma before the invasion, the pattern of the first campaign might have taken a different course; but, in the end, the outcome would have been defeat. A degree of rapport and a measure of co-operation might have been established before the withdrawal began; as it transpired, the Chinese arrived too late, complaining that the British did not treat them as equal partners, while the British considered the Chinese to be thoroughly unreliable. When the Chinese lost Toungoo, it was a major disaster that led to the swift disintegration of their sector. The bravery of the individual Chinese soldier could not hide grave deficiencies in equipment, crass inefficiency at high levels of command, and something that was to become increasingly obvious, the deviousness of the Generalissimo himself. His interventions were often made at the most unfortunate moment, while to make matters worse, he changed his mind with bewildering ease. Nevertheless, one thing that Chiang did achieve by sending troops into Burma was to arouse American interest in the theatre which eventually led to their armed intervention by the side of the British and Chinese.

It was to be a little time before American combat troops arrived in India. The numbers that came were comparatively few, even at the height of the Burma campaign. At their head was the man whom Slim described as 'The most colourful character in South East Asia' – General Joseph Stilwell. Stilwell was often viewed with antipathy, and even with fear, while his supporters regarded him with affection and served his cause with loyalty. For more than 18 months Vinegar Joe made his presence felt, whether it was by stirring the Chinese into some sort of activity, or goading the reluctant British partners, whom he disliked, or occasionally falling out with his own countrymen. But, Stilwell had been appointed by Roosevelt to carry out American policy in South East Asia; and as Commander CBI he was the servant of the President and was there to put the American Government's wishes into operation to the best of his ability. Stilwell's numerous disagreements with superiors, contemporaries, and subordinates did not help matters, but these were relatively insignificant when viewed against the deep rifts that existed between American and British policies in the Far East.

As 1942 dawned, Britain was still very much an Asian power, but within 100 days, most of her empire in the East had been trampled on and subjugated by the Japanese – with the notable exception of India. Thereafter, until the dropping of the atomic bomb on Hiroshima, British statesmen sought to regain their lost colonial possessions and while doing so engaged in an endless series of political dialogues with the Americans. There was to be an ironical twist to the story because, after Britain had granted independence to India in 1947, she then disposed of her eastern empire voluntarily – and some would affirm, with indecent haste. Britain changed from being a world power into a small island nation, an evolution which has not been effected without a severe disruption to the morale of her people. The opposite was true as far as America was concerned. Although isolationist by inclination, with an army no larger than Sweden's at the time of the Pearl Harbor attack, the United States thereafter developed with amazing speed, growing in self-confidence as her immense wealth was translated into military power, her tiny navy into a vast armada of warships, and her puny airforce into the largest the world had ever seen. The balance between British and American voices in formulating strategy did not change overnight, but having agreed that Nazi Germany had to be defeated first, the British did not have sufficient reserves in Asia to make a major contribution there – and could spare nothing for the Pacific campaigns. As a consequence, that theatre became the sole preserve and responsibility of the United States, so that the reconquest of Burma increasingly depended on what resources America was prepared to allot for a campaign which she did not rate very highly.

The primary aim of the Americans was to keep China in the war. Chiang had been grappling with Japanese invaders since 1937 and had calculated if he could hold out, then, sooner or later, Japan would come into direct collision with the United States or one of the European colonial powers. After Pearl Harbor, the Generalissimo's unannounced aim was to retire in stages from the active arena and leave the war to his Anglo-American partners. His long-suffering people had done their share, it was now the turn of his Allies who, once victory had been achieved, would find it difficult to deny him the right to a seat at the peace talks. He began a calculated game of bluff and blackmail, knowing that the US believed that Chinese territory was indispensable for bases from where they would be able to strike at the Japanese homeland. The island-hopping strategy in the Pacific had yet to be vindicated; for Roosevelt and his military advisers, China presented the route along which their armies might have to march, and where fresh airfields would need to be constructed so that long-range bombers could strike at the industrial heart of Japan.

There was a road from Burma into China until the Japanese swept through the country right up to India and China. In order to keep China in the war, the Americans tried to circumvent the Japanese occupation army by organizing an airlift over the enormous mountain barrier of the Himalayas. From airfields in India aid was flown into China, steps were taken to resolve her grave financial difficulties, and US army officers were seconded to the Chinese to help train hurriedly enlisted Chinese troops. The Allies, however, intended such aid for the whole of China. Britain, for example, gave 50 million pounds, a tenth of what the Americans were to subscribe, money that was supposed to assist anyone in the country who was prepared to take on the Japanese. Chiang Kai-shek had other ideas; in the long term, he feared that the party of revolution, the communists, would emerge from the war on equal terms with the Kuomintang government. Officially the Kuomintang and the communists under Mao were allies, pledged to fight Japan together, so that Anglo-American assistance should have been divided proportionately between them. With an eye to the future, the Generalissimo was prepared to accept the blackest of disasters phlegmatically. Stilwell had few illusions about the Generalissimo nor was he beguiled by the charm of Madam Chiang. But many months were to elapse before he succeeded in persuading his political masters in Washington to view the Nationalist government in Chungking with caution and realism. Roosevelt did not begin to get tough with the Generalissimo until the last few months of 1944. On the other hand, the British took a far more sober view about Chiang's value as an ally. He had upset the government of India during a visit to that country in 1942 when, without any real knowledge of Indian politics, he had offered himself as a mediator between the Viceroy and Gandhi, and other Congress leaders – for this he was not forgiven by British statesmen in London and New Delhi.

The Generalissimo's real aim in threatening to make peace was to make the Americans even more apprehensive in the hope that they would redouble their efforts on his behalf. In this game of bluff, he was helped by President Roosevelt who firmly believed that Britain and the other colonial powers had no further role to play in the Far East, and the vacuum that resulted after their final departure would have to be filled by China, fully supported by the United States. Stilwell, while admiring the Chinese peasants as soldiers, was convinced that the Generalissimo was playing a confidence trick on the Americans and accused the American advisers in Chungking of fawning on the Soong dynasty. As a result, Joseph Stilwell had an impossible task in trying to serve his two masters, Roosevelt and Chiang; matters worsened as his duties multiplied when he became Deputy to Mountbatten in 1943. At a time when the Chinese were reluctant to do much real fighting, Stilwell was doing his best to hustle them into trying to produce an army that would get him into Upper Burma in advance of the British. In spite of his fine qualitites – and he had many – Stilwell was certainly the wrong man at the wrong time, holding too many key appointments. His acute dislike of the British and their empire never wavered, and with the notable exceptions of Mountbatten and Slim, there were few senior British commanders who had much time for Vinegar Joe – and vice versa.

Generalissimo Chiang and Stilwell both cast shadows over the Burma campaign. The shadows united at one particular point and that was the Burma Road. Here the two men had a joint aim – to reopen land links between India and China. While the British talked about recapturing Mandalay or drew up ambitious plans to seize Akyab from the sea, or even Rangoon itself, the Americans concentrated on help-ing China, firstly by the ever-increasing supply missions over the Hump, and secondly by constructing a road through Upper Burma into the Yunnan province. Although the British held most of the senior command appointments in Delhi and South East Asia, the Americans had two trump cards; they 'owned' the bulk of the giant transport aircraft and could exercise a powerful veto on the use of amphibious landing craft, or indeed other resources, by refusing to allow those to be used on adventures they considered to be strategi-cally unsound. During much of the time under review top priority was given to the projected Overlord landings in Normandy and to the Pacific War. When Overlord was postponed, landing craft were switched to the Mediterranean, thus ruling out any seaborne assault aimed at retaking Rangoon, and eventually Singapore. In the main, American involvement was confined to Upper Burma.

The Chiefs-of-Staff, issuing directives from afar, wondered why ambitious offensives were not mounted during 1943 against numeri-cally inferior enemy forces. In reality, that year was to be needed for consolidation, including the establishment of a network of communi-cations and supply arteries in eastern India, transforming the region from a 19th-century backwater into a wartime base from which a major offensive could be launched. Time was needed but Wavell was goaded into premature action, by Winston Churchill. The Prime Minister had stated that he was not interested in 'very nice and useful nibbling minor operations': stirred by 'action soon' telegrams, the unfortunate Commander-in-Chief mounted the first offensive into the Arakan in the hope of winning an easy victory, thereby improving the morale of British and Indian soldiers. His military objective was a limited one but unwise and premature publicity led everyone, including Chur-chill, into anticipating a major victory without too much difficulty. False hopes died when a small but courageous holding force resisted in a campaign that was, for Wavell, a blind-alley because he had nothing to gain and much to lose. Indifferent generalship by Irwin only served to highlight the fiasco. But the most important result was that the flimsy structure of British and American harmony received another blow – with the Americans retracting what little trust they had in their partners' prowess as jungle fighters.

Britain and America also found little in common in their approach to the internal affairs of India. The Americans did not understand the complexities of Indian politics. They looked at the situation in simple black-and-white terms, comparing the struggle for freedom with their own War of Independence. Their sympathies were strongly on the Indian side. Nevertheless, they had deep misgivings caused by the fear that an independent India might secede from the war at a crucial moment, thus depriving them of a base from which they could supply their ally, China. India, huge sub-continent though it was, had few real pretensions to be classified as a strong military base from which organized counter-offensives could be mounted against the Japanese in Burma, and elsewhere. India was politically unstable, certainly until the Congress leaders were incarcerated for the duration of the war. And the primitive nature of road, rail, and river communications both within Assam and across the boundary into Burma, was another severe handicap delaying projected plans for a quick return to that country. Although the Americans had expected something far more sophisticated – and blamed the British for not developing India during their lengthy tenure as colonial rulers – their skilled engineers, using the most modern equipment, played a notable part in constructing airfields, in revitalizing old and creaking railways, and in laying a new road from Ledo through forbidding terrain at a most remarkable speed. The energy of the Americans plus their capacity to improvise when faced with unexpected problems, was seen to good advantage – even if the British may have been a trifle reluctant to give sufficient credit to them both at the time and after the war was over. Their example encouraged and shamed the Indian government into taking similar measures with far more vigour than had been displayed hitherto. Away from the South East Asian theatre, few realized or understood the problems posed by vast distances, the nature of the country, or the restrictions imposed on operations for about five months of every year by the monsoon, when even movement became hazardous. Fighting by modern armies in a jungle-type environment had never been seen before on such a scale: each army tackled the problems involved in their own particular manner.

The ease with which the Japanese won the first campaign in Burma had psychological undertones because they continued to underestimate their opponents thereafter – until it was too late. The astonishing success of the two divisions as they swept across Burma in 1942 was reinforced by British incompetence in the Arakan a year later. The Japanese High Command treated their enemies with disdain until their confidence was dented by the Chindits in 1943, and totally upset by disasters around Imphal in 1944. Bold, ruthless leadership reaped rewards when the enemy was weak, disorganized, and dispirited. Later, when the balance-of-power had changed, when British and

Indian soldiers had been trained to dig in and resist even when surrounded, and were supported in a generous fashion by their airforces, patriotism and blind courage were not enough to win battles. The Japanese soldiers changed but little; they fought to the bitter end and rarely surrendered even when death stared them in the face. They were let down by many of their senior commanders whose inflexible tactics, ill-conceived arrangements for administration, and unquestioning optimism became a dangerous mixture. Mutaguchi was a prime example, although in his defence we must remember his accusation that Kawabe's over-cautious approach at the height of the offensive ruined any possible chance of victory in his U-Go operation. What might or might not have happened if Dimapur had been snatched from British hands can be debated at length. Mutaguchi's overall direction of the battle around Imphal was reasonable and can be defended up to the time when 15 Army's original thrust had been blunted and when monsoon rains began to fall. Then his obstinate refusal to make a tactical withdrawal or admit defeat passed the sentence of death on thousands of his men, and very nearly destroyed 15 Army for all time. The monsoon alone saved the survivors who stumbled back towards the Chindwin, broken in spirit and weary in body.

At a lower level the Japanese had vigorous commanders whose determination and dash won dividends on the field of battle. Tanahashi was such a leader and there were several others. Given independent missions with clear guidelines, such men achieved much and were a constant thorn in the flesh of their adversaries. Fortunes changed when they had to work together, when a division had to co-operate with other formations, then weaknesses came to light. Archaic radio communications undoubtedly contributed to a sad lack of co-ordination as was seen in the closing stages of Honda's counter-offensive against Meiktila. Commanders rarely lacked resolution or courage but frequently showed themselves unable to react to an unexpected, unplanned situation. Honda was an exception, especially during the closing stages of the campaign. Kimura, as Commander Burma Area Army after the U-Go offensive had collapsed, showed that he did not lack imagination. He had a more flexible approach than the majority of his contemporaries.

'Kimura was to prove himself a commander with a much higher degree of realism and moral courage. An artilleryman regarded with some justification as one of the most brilliant officers of the Japanese Army.' (*Defeat into Victory*).

But Kimura was transferred to command Burma Area Army at too late a stage in the campaign; all he could do was to keep shuffling the pack to try and delay the inevitable.

Although the Japanese learnt little after their brilliant success in 1942, the British had to start from scratch, to study and devise jungle warfare tactics and techniques, before they could contemplate anything more ambitious than a diversionary raid into Burma. After initially underrating their enemy, the pendulum then swung in a violent curve until they granted the Japanese soldier superhuman powers, seemingly invincible in battle. It was at such a time that the pugnacious Stilwell and the erratic inspiration of Wingate kept spirits alive. In the background, Wavell, Auchinleck, Giffard, and others, laid solid foundations for a change in fortune, by establishing schools of instruction specializing in jungle warfare for officers and NCOs, and co-operating with the other services in evolving doctrines of joint warfare. All this was to take time and early reverses did not help interservice co-operation or, at a higher level, Anglo-American harmony. Nevertheless, solid foundations were laid, so that it was a considerable shock to the Japanese army when, first in the Arakan, and then on the Imphal Plain, British and Indian soldiers stood firm to repulse their attacks.

The remarkable transformation brought about by Stilwell and his team of American instructors with the Chinese divisions, based on Indian soil, must not be forgotten, either. Many had scoffed at the idea of Chinese soldiers going into action without a stiffening of 'foreigners' to steady them after contact had been made with the enemy. On this score the British, during their first Arakan adventure, were no better placed to boast either, being routed by a small force of enemy. After leaving Ledo, Stilwell found that his two divisions had a similar reluctance to close with the Japanese 18 Division. He tackled the problem by driving his subordinate commanders hard while, at the same time, he ensured that they had overall superiority in numbers at the point of contact. One early success led to another – and Chinese morale improved dramatically thereafter.

'By the end of 1944, jungle warfare became respectable in training manuals'. (Official History).

The exploits of Wingate and his Chindits have been examined in some detail already. His part in evolving new concepts of making war, in fashioning unconventional guerrilla tactics for use in the jungle, should not be underestimated. In 1945, when 14 Army was racing towards Rangoon from Meiktila, close co-operation between army and airforce was at a most impressive level, functioning with efficiency based on joint doctrines and experiences gained during training, thereafter tested on active service against the foe. One of these was

Operation Loincloth, the Chindit raids of 1943, when, for the first time in Burma, comparatively large bodies of troops were completely dependent on supplies received from the air. Mistakes were made, including one or two costly miscalculations, but Wingate was a man who was prepared to learn, to adjust to new situations, a commander whose fertile imagination continually sought alternative solutions. As a result, Operation Thursday saw those new ideas being put into practice, combined with some used before which had been brushed up during tough, imaginative exercises in India. But it cannot be denied that Special Force, as well as the other irregular forces operating in Burma, constituted an expensive way of waging war, and of testing new techniques under operational conditions. In *Defeat into Victory* Slim stated, with firmness, that the number of irregular units and formations in a theatre of war should be kept to a minimum. To support his argument there is the record of 36 British Division which, under the overall command of General Dan Sultan, achieved admirable results: their exploits tended to reinforce the argument that an 'ordinary' division, with its own organic arms and heavy weapons, was better equipped to cope with a long stint in action than were the lightly armed Chindits. Special Force had been trained and armed to carry out a short mission – into the jungle for about two months at the sharp end, then out for rest and re-equipping, before returning for a further brief bout of operational duty.

Much that was highly commendable was achieved by 36 British Division which was admirably suited for the role given it by Sultan. However, the way its soldiers lived, moved, and operated in the jungle was derived from lessons passed on to senior ranks from Chindit instructors. The irregulars paved the way; the conventional formation followed to reinforce early successes. Three major benefits to the Allied cause came from Wingate's men. The value of the Chindits was first felt in 1943 when, with morale low and the Japanese appearing to be unbeatable, British and Gurkha soldiers penetrated behind the Chindwin, to kick the antheap into feverish activity. They gained a moral victory but not a military one. The second benefit has been mentioned in the previous paragraph; the spin-off in testing and evaluating doctrines of jungle warfare which were developed for subsequent use by the whole army during later stages of the campaign. And the third, of crucial importance for Britain, was the fact that the US Chiefs-of-Staff were considerably impressed by Wingate at the Quebec Conference. As a result, and for the first time, they accepted, in principle, the necessity of some form of land operations in Central Burma. And, to such an end, committed No 1 Air Commando under

Colonel Philip Cochrane to assist the Chindits, first by helping the RAF to gain air supremacy, and then supporting the raiding columns in all phases of operations. The Air Commandos were to be the fore-runners of an ever-increasing American participation in the campaign with the emphasis being on the giant cargo transport aircraft which eventually outnumbered the RAF equivalent. The Chiefs-of-Staff had given reluctant approval to projected operations aimed at recapturing Mandalay and Rangoon, even though they harboured doubts as to whether the capture of those cities would contribute much towards the opening of the Burma Road into China. Wingate's eloquence at Quebec was instrumental in bringing US combat troops to Burma even if their representatives were to be one regiment – Merrill's Marauders – and later in the campaign, Mars Task Force. With troops on the ground and airmen in considerable numbers, the Burma cam-paign could no longer be ignored in Washington, even if it remained low on the priority list, of minor significance when compared with major US offensives being launched at various points of the Pacific.

American airmen, and a handful of GIs, came and played a vital part in Burma. It was fortunate for Anglo-American harmony that Admiral Mountbatten was selected to be Supreme Commander South East Asia. Mountbatten had the strength as well as the patience to with-stand a wide variety of pressures from the three governments in Washington, London, and Chungking. He had the tact and diplomacy to make concessions at the appropriate moment, provided he was convinced that the overall strategy would not be jeopardized: he was prepared to 'bend' the rules if necessary. Moreover, Mountbatten had the ability to harness difficult personalities such as Stilwell and Win-gate, to work within the Allied framework and was able to resolve several complex inter-Allied disagreements, thus enabling the three service commanders below him to concentrate on carrying out their allotted tasks. Mountbatten had a most difficult role to play and after he had settled into the appointment, his stature as a leader continued to grow. Adroit diplomacy in counsel was coupled with an ability to keep in close touch with operations, encouraging but not interfering, and intervening only when absolutely necessary. His presence and authority, as Supremo, enabled Slim to concentrate on 14 Army's battles, fully confident that he would be supported to the hilt at every stage. Even in 1943 when affairs were unsettled and confidence was still deficient, Slim wrote after Mountbatten had taken up his post as Supreme Commander: 'We began to feel that we belonged to an efficient show, or what was going to be one, and that feeling spread'.

After Mountbatten's arrival late in 1943, the complexities of administration rose to a peak not imagined in earlier campaigns. The gradual withdrawal of the Japanese airforce to other theatres – which accelerated its eventual subjugation by the US Airforce and the RAF – had a marked effect on the way Allied soldiers lived and fought throughout the rest of the campaign. The difficult country, with a dire lack of sophisticated communications, prohibited the use of road transport while enhancing the value of supplies from cargo-carrying aircraft. Much ingenuity was displayed to discover new methods: 'With us, necessity was truly the mother of invention. We lacked so much in equipment and supplies that if we were not to give up offensive operations altogether we had either to manage without or improvise for ourselves'. (*Defeat into Victory*)

This they certainly did. As a result, not only were fresh methods of supply and general administration introduced but, in addition, new tactics were devised to meet the strange conditions of fighting without established landlinks to bases in the rear. It is of interest that many of the methods used in Burma were to prove of inestimable value when, in the years between 1947 and 1967, the British Army had to operate against guerrillas in the jungles of Malaya and later, during the confrontation with Indonesia in Borneo. Modifications were made, inevitably, but the principles remained unchanged: air supply, the construction of roads, bridges and airstrips, techniques to enable men to cross rivers swollen by monsoon rains; medicines and drugs that allowed soldiers to fight in the most insalubrious of areas without being striken down by malaria and other tropical diseases; lightweight equipment so that rations, ammunition, and other necessities could be carried on the individual soldier's back without his being overburdened by the sheer weight of his load – the list is long and it only serves to highlight the long term value of the administrative measures taken by the Anglo-American commanders in Burma. In complete contrast, the Japanese generals tended to downgrade logistics to an inferior place in their plans, to leave their soldiers to rough it, comparatively unprotected against disease, exposed to the elements, and ill-supported by administrative services.

The collapse of the U-Go offensive only served to emphasize the inability of the Japanese High Command to resolve administrative problems. When squadrons of their airforce were withdrawn later in the year, the infantry soldiers had to rely on their own weapons, on their expertise at concealment and camouflage, backed up by a stubborn refusal to admit defeat, all to be enhanced by unswerving loyalty to the Emperor back in Tokyo. It was an honour to die for him: the numbers who perished unnecessarily for Emperor Hirohito increased in tragic fashion as the campaign drew to its climax.

The mighty part played by the Allied airforces has been covered in the previous chapter. Re-entry into Burma was achieved, and the campaign waged, at the end of a most effective airborne supply line. General Marshall wrote: 'Only by supply was the Burma campaign at all possible'. The USAAF, together with 221 and 224 Groups RAF, rendered magnificent support, even when the monsoon raged and hazardous terrain became even more dangerous under appalling climatic conditions. From late 1944 onwards the Japanese soldiers rarely saw any friendly aircraft and had to fight in a straitjacket imposed on them by American, British, and Indian pilots.

Combined with impressive air superiority was the imaginative use of armour which often appeared in the most unlikely places and invariably at a time when the arrival of tanks had a considerable impact on the morale of both sides. Tanks and armoured cars displayed their hitting power when 15 Army emerged from the jungles onto the Imphal Plain; defenders of the Admin Box during the Ha-Go offensive found the tanks' armament invaluable during their last-ditch stand; tiny bridgeheads on the east bank of the Irrawaddy were exploited after tanks arrived to strengthen perimeters; famous British and Indian cavalry regiments won further renown during the sweep towards Meiktila and, later, in the struggle to hold the city against Honda's counter-thrust. Their finest hours of glory came during the dash towards Rangoon. After the arid purple plain of Central Burma had been reached, armour came into its own, striking at the Japanese who were unable to hit back, unable to deal with the armoured cars and tanks which played havoc with bewildered infantry and unprotected administrative units behind the forward areas. Isolated acts of 'kamikaze' desperation won respect and bought time but could not halt the tide that was swamping Burma Area Army wherever it stood at bay.

Courage alone kept Kimura's soldiers fighting during 1945 but although we must admire such devotion to duty, in retrospect it seemed a pointless and futile gesture by the Japanese High Command to continue the struggle. After the summer of 1944, the High Command was no longer able to reinforce Burma Area Army and although a more flexible defensive policy was adopted, the rump of their forces was left to combat numerically superior ground forces, virtually unsupported from the air, with an administrative machine in tatters. A complete withdrawal from Burma would have saved thousands of lives without radically changing the outcome of the war in South East Asia. Without doubt, the Japanese by their obstinate refusal to admit defeat, prolonged the campaign until VJ Day, sentencing men to fight without hope of avoiding either death or the ignominy of becoming prisoners of war.

Nevertheless, it would be the height of injustice to blame the Japanese alone for protracting the struggle when, for months past, deep differences in American, British and Chinese policies rarely remained resolved for long – and often overshadowed the military battles fought between 1942 and the end of the war. As far as the American Chiefs-of-Staff were concerned, the road link from Ledo through Burma into China was all that really mattered – indeed, as soon as the first major convoy passed along the road, they lost interest in Mountbatten's campaign. In contrast, the British took a much more realistic view of the road, maintaining that it could be of little value until Rangoon had been captured, and stressing that its eventual capacity as a main supply route would continue to be negligible. Events were to support such an appreciation because the trickle of vehicles that eventually trundled down the road did little to help China's cause. Against this, American Transport Command operations over the Hump enabled fresh Chinese divisions to be raised and equipped and thus could claim much of the credit in keeping Chiang on the verge of active belligerency – if not always as an active ally.

After Myitkyina had been captured and the Hump missions to China were working at full tempo, there were no longer overriding military reasons for a town-by-town reconquest of Burma, although if a defensive posture had been adopted, the morale of 14 Army would have plummetted after their string of victories around Imphal. There is a well known Russian story about the man who grappled with a wild bear. So hypnotized was he by the struggle that he was loath to let go even when his friend intervened – he continued to battle. In the context of the war in Burma it can be asked if the British or Japanese, for that matter, did much good by remaining locked in such a lengthy struggle? In the end, there was to be an especial irony for Britain because she poured so much into the reconquest, in terms of men, machines, and money, to wage such a bitter 3½-year campaign, only to give Burma independence without being forced to do so soon after the war was over. It was to be the prelude to an unseemly scuttle from Asia.

The forces of nationalism had been unleashed by Japan in her bid for power, and these played an important part in her subsequent defeat – and an even bigger part in the post-war years when the political face of South East Asia changed in a dramatic fashion. The role of the BNA, switching sides when a British victory became a

certainty, has been described. Aung San achieved far more than did
his INA counterpart, Subhas Chundra Bose. The latter could claim
little of note while alive but in death he became a folk hero in India,
and more especially in Bengal, where his melodramatic exploits have
been exaggerated so that Bose has become a legend. The INA proved
to be useless in battle and were more of a handicap than an asset to the
Japanese. It disgraced itself in action; its largest losses were from
desertion while the numbers lost in combat were comparatively few.

Bose's idea of corrupting the Indian army failed dismally. The
Allies achieved countless wonders in air operations, in engineering and
administration, but perhaps the most remarkable achievement
belonged to the British officers of the Indian army. Only the oath of
loyalty to the King-Emperor overseas, and deep regimental pride, kept
the vastly expanded wartime Indian army firmly on the side of Britain.
For this, the main credit must go to Field Marshal Sir Claude Auchinleck, and the officers at all levels of command – in particular, at
regimental and company commander level where the ties of mutual
trust, of tradition for fair treatment, were able to withstand strong
external pressures and a steady stream of virulent Congress propaganda within India. The Indian Army with its cadre of British officers,
supported by a capable band of young Indian officers, withstood the
strain of political undercurrents in a most steadfast manner. Nowa-
days, a certain element in our society tends to denigrate the achievements of those who served the British Raj, in one capacity or another.
Perhaps they should ponder awhile over the fact that the two million-
strong Indian Army fought with such dedication and loyalty against the
Germans and Japanese under a mere handful of British officers, many
of whom had joined only for the duration of the war?

As one who served in the Gurkha Brigade, the author asks to be
excused by adding that the tiny country of Nepal – having no official
ties with Great Britain – sent nearly a quarter of a million volunteers to
fight by the side of British and Indian soldiers. It was fitting, therefore, that the man who played the biggest part in the victory, General
Slim, was himself an officer of the Gurkha Brigade.

Bill Slim, 14 Army, 'The Forgotten Army', and the Burma campaign have become synonymous in the annals of World War II. It
would be most inappropriate to end this account without a final tribute
to the man who led an army from despair and disaster to final victory,
and whose account of those momentous years remains a classic, a
model of such excellence that few generals are likely to attain such a
standard. And military historians cannot substitute diligent research
for three-and-a-half years spent as a corps or army commander at the

very centre of activities – truly the architect of victory. Slim was a generous man, a modest one, who had a deep understanding of strategy at the highest level, but remained a human person with a fund of anecdotes and stories about the officers and men who fought under his command. *Defeat into Victory* is a moving story of endurance told with skill by a great leader of soldiers. It is safe to claim that no book will ever be written about the Burma campaign without recourse to much background information, and appropriate quotations, from *Defeat into Victory*.

Certainly this book is no exception and if the thoughts and judgements of Bill Slim are reflected throughout the story, then that must be the measure of the man. To have been in continuous command of a corps or army in action for so long speaks volumes for his robustness, his skill as a tactician, and an outstanding record as one of the greatest commanders of World War II. Under Slim 14 Army did not reconquer Burma nor win the battles that changed the course of the campaign unaided – but without their contribution the history of postwar India and Burma would have been startlingly different. The war in Burma was a soldier's war and what better way to end than quoting the last paragraph of *Defeat into Victory*: 'To the soldiers of many races who in the comradeship of the 14 Army did go on, and the airmen who flew with them and fought over them, belongs the true glory of achievement. It was they who turned Defeat into Victory'.

Bibliography

All five volumes of the *War Against Japan* series in the British Official History have been frequently consulted, as well as relevant volumes in the *Grand Strategy* series. And, as has been mentioned in the text, *Defeat into Victory* has been one of the solid pillars of this book.

The following books were also helpful:

Abyankar, M. G. *Myth Exploded*. India: Bombay Press, 1965.

Allied Land Forces, South East Asia (Operational Record of Eleventh Army Group and ALFSEA Nov 1943–Aug 1945) 1950.

Barker, A. J. *The March on Delhi*. UK: Faber, 1966.

Belden, J. *Retreat with Stilwell* UK: Cassell, 1943/US: Knopf, 1943.

Bond, B. *Chief-of-Staff: the Diaries of Lieutenant-General Sir Henry Pownall* Vol 2 UK: Leo Cooper, 1974/US: Shoe String, 1974.

Calvert, M. *Prisoners of Hope*. UK: Cape, 1952/US: Clarke Irwin, 1952.

Fighting Mad. UK: Jarrolds, 1964/US: Nelson, Foster & Scott, 1964.

Campbell, A. *The Siege: A Story from Kohima*. UK: Allen, 1956/US: Macmillan, 1956.

Churchill, W. S. *The Second World War*. UK: Cassell, 1948–54/US: Houghton, 1948–53.

Davis, P. *A Child at Arms*. UK: Hutchinson, 1970.

Dorn, F. *Walkout: with Stilwell in Burma*. US: Pyramid, 1971.

Eldridge, F. *Wrath in Burma*. US: Doubleday, 1946.

Evans, G. *Slim as Military Commander*. UK: Batsford, 1969/US: Van Nostrand-Reinhold, 1969.

Evans, G. & Anthony Brett-James *Imphal: a Flower on Lofty Heights*. UK: Macmillan, 1962.

Fergusson, B. E. *Beyond the Chindwin*. UK: Collins, 1945.

The Wild Green Earth. UK: Collins, 1946.

Ho, Yung-Chi. *The Big Circle*. US: Exposition, 1948.

Karaka, D. F. *With the Fourteenth Army*. UK: D. Crisp, 1945.

Lewin, R. *Slim: the Standard Bearer*. UK: Leo Cooper, 1976/US: Shoe String, 1976.

Mackenzie, C. *Eastern Epic*. UK: Chatto, 1951/US: Clarke Irwin, 1951.

Masters, J. *The Road Past Mandalay*. UK: Michael Joseph, 1961/US: Harper, 1961.

Mosley, L. *Gideon Goes to War*. UK: Barker, 1955/US: Scribner, 1956.

Owen, F. *The Campaign in Burma*. UK: HMSO, 1946.

Romanus, C. F. & Sunderland, R. *Stilwell's Mission to China*. US: Department of the Army, 1953.

Smith, E. D. *Britain's Brigade of Gurkhas*. UK: Leo Cooper, 1973.

Smythe, J. G. *Before the Dawn*. UK: Cassell, 1957.
The Valiant. UK: Mowbray, 1970.

Stilwell, J. W. *The Stilwell Papers*. UK: Macdonald, 1949/US: Sloane, 1948.

Sykes, C. *Orde Wingate*. UK: Collins, 1959/US: World Publishing Co. 1959.

Thorne, B. K. *The Hump: the Great Military Airlift of World War II*. US: Lippincott, 1965.

Tulloch, D. *Wingate in Peace and War*. UK: Macdonald, 1972/US: Futura, 1976.

Vincent, S. F. *Flying Fever*. UK: Jarrolds, 1975.

Wint, G. & Calvocoressi, P. *Total War: the Story of World War II*. UK: Penguin, 1972/US: Ballantine, 1973.

War Monthly. Various articles published 1975/76.

Index

By Joanna Smith